ISA GENZKEN

October Files

ISA GENZKEN

edited by Lisa Lee

essays and interviews by Isa Genzken, Birgit Pelzer, Benjamin H. D. Buchloh, Isabelle Graw, Diedrich Diederichsen, Pamela M. Lee, Wolfgang Tillmans, Lisa Lee, Lawrence Weiner, Juliane Rebentisch, Yve-Alain Bois, Josef Strau, and Hal Foster

OCTOBER FILES 17

The MIT Press
Cambridge, Massachusetts
London, England

This book was set in Bembo and Stone sans by the MIT Press.

Library of Congress Cataloging-in-Publication Data is available.

ISBN:Isa Genzken / edited by Lisa Lee.
    pages cm.— (October files)
ISBN 978-0-262-02841-7 (hardcover : alk. paper)—ISBN 978-0-262-52711-8 (pbk. : alk. paper)
1. Genzken, Isa, 1948 — Criticism and interpretation. I. Lee, Lisa, 1978- editor.
N6888.G459I83 2015
709.2—dc23

                    2014019595

149353208

Contents

OCTOBER Files addresses individual bodies of work of the postwar period that meet two criteria: they have altered our understanding of art in significant ways, and they have prompted a critical literature that is serious, sophisticated, and sustained. Each book thus traces not only the development of an important oeuvre but also the construction of the critical discourse inspired by it. This discourse is theoretical by its very nature, which is not to say that it imposes theory abstractly or arbitrarily. Rather, it draws out the specific ways in which significant art is theoretical in its own right, on its own terms and with its own implications. To this end we feature essays, many first published in *OCTOBER* magazine, that elaborate different methods of criticism in order to elucidate different aspects of the art in question. The essays are often in dialogue with one another as they do so, but they are also as sensitive as the art to political context and historical change. These "files," then, are intended as primers in signal practices of art and criticism alike, and they are offered in resistance to the amnesiac and antitheoretical tendencies of our time.

The Editors of *OCTOBER*

Acknowledgments

Isa Genzken's "Two Exercises, 1973" was first published in German in *Interfunktionen* 11 (1974); the English translation is reprinted from Alex Farquharson et al., *Isa Genzken* (London: Phaidon, 2006). "Axiomatics Subject to Withdrawal" by Birgit Pelzer appeared in German as "Axiomatik auf Widerruf" in *Isa Genzken: Skulpturen, Zeichnungen, Fotografien / Horst Schuler: Bilder* (Krefeld: Museum Haus Lange, 1979). It appears here in English for the first time. "Isa Genzken: The Fragment as Model" by Benjamin H. D. Buchloh was originally published in *Isa Genzken: Jeder braucht mindestens ein Fenster* (Cologne: Verlag der Buchhandlung Walther König, 1992). Buchloh's "Isa Genzken: Fuck the Bauhaus. Architecture, Design, and Photography in Reverse" appeared in *Isa Genzken: Early Works* (Cologne: Galerie Buchholz, 2014). Genzken's "Sketches for a Feature Film" initially appeared in German as "Skizzen für einen Spielfilm" in *Isa Genzken* (Bremen: Kunsthalle Bremen, 1993). We publish the first English translation of this text. "Free to Be Dependent: Concessions in the Work of Isa Genzken" by Isabelle Graw was published in Sabine Breitwieser, ed., *Isa Genzken: MetLife* (Vienna: EA-Generali Foundation, 1996). Diedrich Diederichsen's "Subjects at the End of the Flagpole" is reprinted from *Isa Genzken: Sie sind mein Glück* (Braunschweig: Kunstverein Braunschweig, 2000). "The Skyscraper at Ear Level" by Pamela M. Lee appeared in *Parkett* 69 (2003). Buchloh's "All Things Being Equal" was first published in *Artforum International* 44 (November 2005). Wolfgang Tillman's interview with Genzken first appeared in *Camera Austria* 81

(2003). Diedrich Diederichsen's conversation with Isa Genzken is reprinted from *Isa Genzken* (London: Phaidon, 2006). Lisa Lee's "Make Life Beautiful! The Diabolic in the Work of Isa Genzken (A Tour Through Berlin, Paris, and New York)" was originally published in *October* 122 (Fall 2007). Lawrence Weiner's "Isa Genzken Again" appeared in *Isa Genzken* (Cologne: Verlag der Buchhandlung Walther König, 2010). "The Dialectic of Beauty: On the Work of Isa Genzken" by Juliane Rebentisch was published in *Isa Genzken: Oil* (Cologne: DuMont, 2007). "The Bum and the Architect" by Yve-Alain Bois is reprinted from *Isa Genzken: Open, Sesame!* (London: König Books, 2007). Josef Strau's "Isa Genzken: Sculpture as Narrative Urbanism" is an altered version of a text that originally appeared with the title "I'm trying to write a text about Isa Genzken in New York!" in *Isa Genzken* (Stockholm: Jarla Partilager, 2009). "Fantastic Destruction" by Hal Foster appeared as an exhibition review in *Artforum International* 52 (February 2014).

The editor would like to thank Daniel Buchholz, Christopher Müller, Katharina Forero, the contributing authors, and Isa Genzken.

Two Exercises, 1973[1]

Isa Genzken

A large, empty, white-painted room with a black floor was available. The exercises were carried out by Isa Genzken over seven days from 30 July to 4 August 1973.

Day 1, exercise A

Lying on my stomach with my chin on my hands so that I had the widest possible view.

When I tried to concentrate on the exercise I felt a sense of resistance and fear, so I had to break off and start again.

For the short periods (two to three minutes) when I forgot my fears and my body calmed down, I felt that I was getting heavier and lighter at the same time. The first impression was that the perspective of the room was getting lost; the line of the floor along the two side walls became a single horizontal with the end wall.

The colors of the floor and walls got mixed up; the black of the floor became a transparent gray and the horizontal seemed like a bright, glowing strip. I always broke the exercise off at this point because I was afraid of losing consciousness.

Day 1, exercise B

Even though I felt I was concentrating a lot better after the first exercise, I had a lot of trouble with exercise B. Even my attempt to lose sight of the ceiling, which I had fixed on at first, by changing my focus, did not work out.

The exercise took a lot out of me. I stood up immediately, needing to move and look at something so that I could relate to my usual reality again. After quite some time I felt sick.

Day 2, exercise A

The horizontal turned up as it had on the first day and at the same time I had the impression that the floor was undulating in a way that seemed to relate to my breathing.

The floor changed more and more into a mobile mass that slowly rose and that I started to sink into (associations with lava). Toward the end the floor started to get more transparent and I had a sense of layers.

Day 2, exercise B

This time I had the floor in view on both sides. The contrasts between floor and wall slowly blurred. The floor took on a misty gray color. I had the impression that the floor as a whole was rising minimally.

Day 3, exercise A

I was not in a position to concentrate on the exercise; I felt distracted by every noise.

Every attempt was immediately broken off again.

Day 3, exercise B

When doing this exercise I fell asleep very quickly while lying on my back, but woke up at the precise moment the exercise was due to end.

Day 4, exercise A

I started the exercise immediately after drinking a glass of champagne so that I wouldn't fall asleep again, but immediately this very badly affected my ability to concentrate. This again made me aggressive and I didn't get any further with exercise A.

Day 4, exercise B

I pulled myself together to the extent that I found out something else: I felt very strongly that the floor was concentrating itself in my body along the line of my spine from both sides at the same time, and was rising with me.

Day 5, exercise A

For the first time I was able to concentrate on this exercise for its duration without interruption. It started with the same phenomena as on the previous days. The floor was rising so much now that I sank into it completely. I didn't have a sense of physical resistance any longer. I felt I was floating in high, mobile layers of gray, each of a different density. They were quite distinct from each other, but blended and changed constantly. The impression of their three-dimensional quality was extraordinarily strong. I perceived myself to be part of what I was looking at.

Day 5, exercise B

Here too I was able to concentrate throughout. The sensation of the previous day recurred more intensely this time. The floor did not rise evenly with me, but rather with the rhythm of my breathing.

Day 6, exercise A

Day 6, exercise B

Contrary to my expectations, I had no results from either of the exercises today.

Day 7, exercise A

I had no difficulty starting the exercise. The same sensations I had on day 5 got more intense after I had sunk into the floor, to the extent that my ego merged into this three-dimensional space.

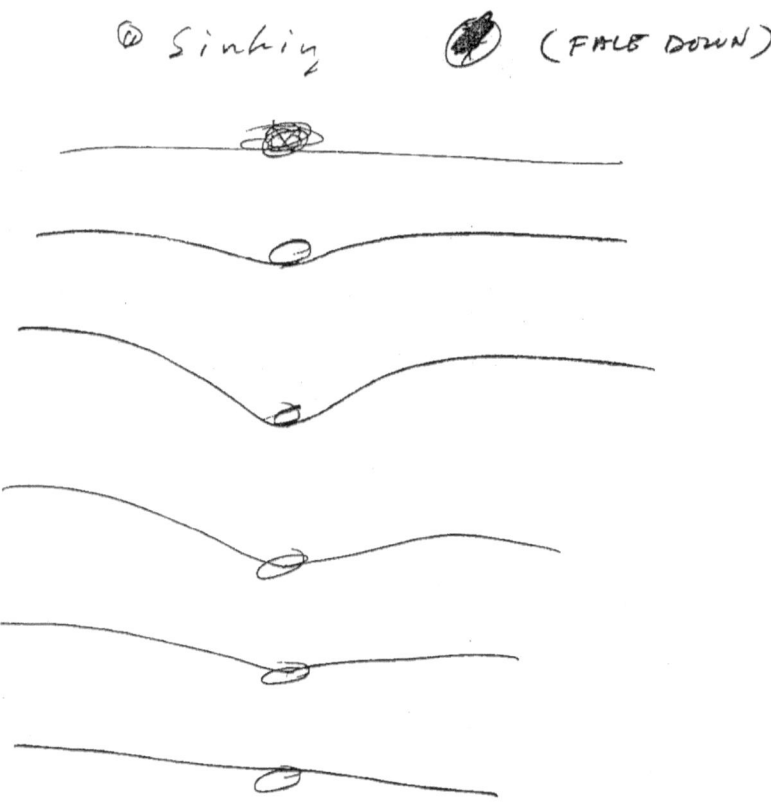

Sketches for Bruce Nauman's "Instructions for a Mental Exercise."
Originally published in *Interfunktionen,* no. 11 (1974).

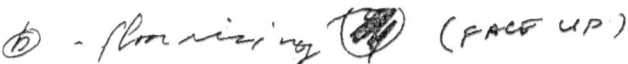 (FACE UP)

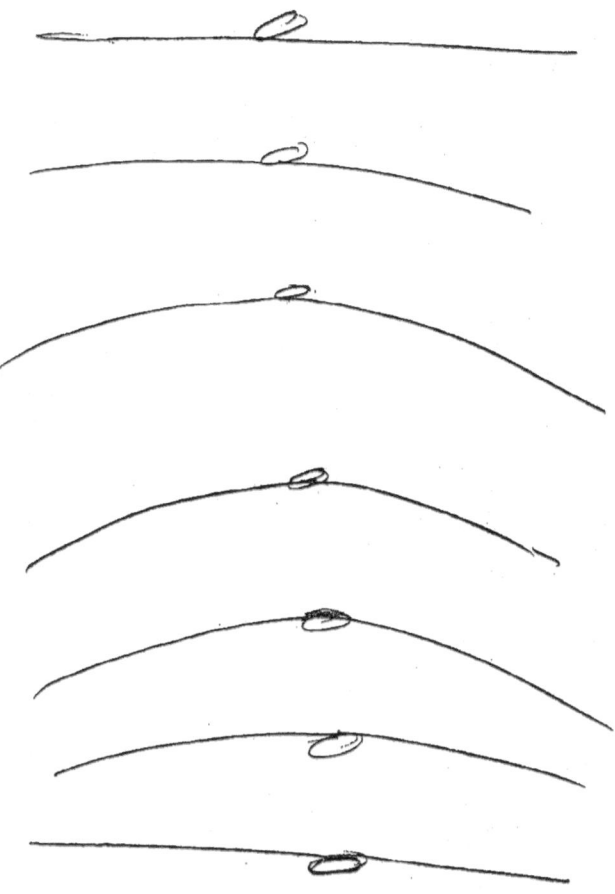

Day 7, exercise B

With this exercise I felt after a short time that I was part of the floor, or that the floor was going through me. I felt concentrated into two dimensions with the floor and distinctly raised higher.

After the exercises I needed about half an hour in each case to collect myself, and then felt very good.

Translated by Michael Robinson.

Notes

1. These notes record Genzken's sensations while carrying out Bruce Nauman's "Instructions for a Mental Exercise" at Galerie Konrad Fischer. Nauman's instructions and Genzken's notes were initially published in *Interfunktionen,* no. 11 (1974), pp. 122–124; Nauman's instructions are reprinted in his *Please Pay Attention Please: Bruce Nauman's Words*, Janet Kraynek, ed. (Cambridge, Mass.: MIT Press, 2005), pp. 76–77. [Editor's note.]

Axiomatics Subject to Withdrawal

Birgit Pelzer

At first sight these Ellipsoids by Isa Genzken are just beautiful—a statement that, according to the criteria of contemporary art criticism, already creates an obstruction of sorts.

But on closer examination a sense of discomfiture sets in. The viewer is at a loss—are these drawings, paintings, or sculptures? The most striking feature of these works seems to be their capacity to achieve the greatest possible ambiguity despite the greatest possible, almost mechanical, precision of their construction.

Painted on all sides, including those that are not immediately visible; with just one point of contact with the floor; long, yet so narrow that they occupy space but, as it were, through omission: these Ellipsoids convey such a sense of speed that they appear to be both present and absent.

Although these three-dimensional bodies (as forms that perfectly comply with specific geometric principles of conic sections) rely on what appear to be the simplest facts of spatial perception, their clarity and stringency generate a zone of uncertainty. This paradoxical outcome could be described as a crisis of perception.

After all, what is the viewer to make of a body that is so elongated as to simultaneously appear to be a volume, a plane, and a line? In other words, its volume suggests a more definite plane, while the plane (since it is so much longer than it is wide) suggests a more definite line, which in turn raises the confusing question as to whether this process can in any case be described as perception at all.

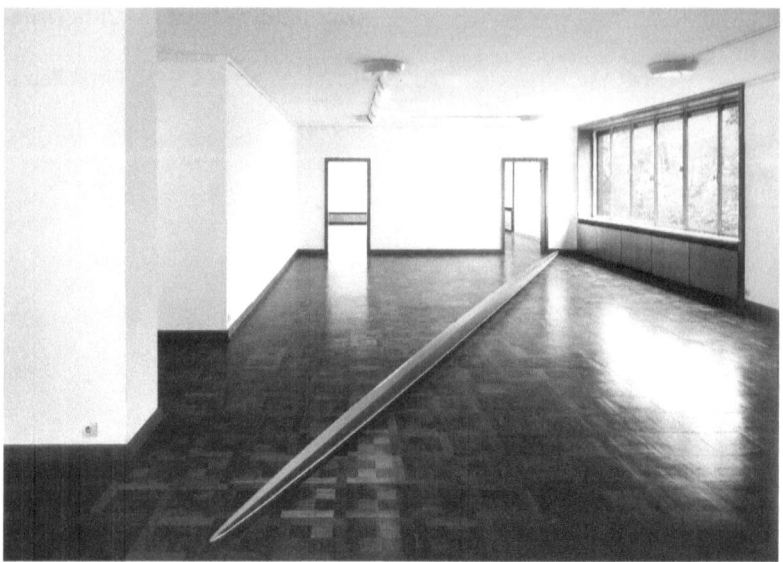

Rot-graues offenes Ellipsoid (Red-Gray Open Ellipsoid), 1978. Installation view, Museum Haus Lange, Krefeld 1979. Lacquered wood. 1180 × 18 × 26 cm.

To sum up, the Ellipsoids are extremely complex forms (despite their apparent simplicity) in which the tension between curved and straight lines produces a gliding identity that involves such contradictory motifs as the spatialization of a plane and its plastic reduction. At the same time it also becomes apparent that, among other things, there is no clear dividing line between empirical media such as wood and air.

In these elongated bodies one fundamental distinction becomes blurred, that is to say, the distinction between dimensions. If a curve can become a plane and, just as imperceptibly, this plane can become a volume—in other words, if the laws that apply to one dimension appear to be maintained in another dimension—how is the viewer to distinguish between one-, two-, or three-dimensionality?

It is as though Genzken were endeavoring to make the most precise model of zones of indeterminacy and of minimal distinguishability at the same time as she holds back from any exhaustive disjunction. The fractious confluence of affinity and lability, the fluctuation between over- and under-determination, between probability and legality, and the use of high-definition and blurred vision are all constantly hovering at the point below which it is possible to make out distinctions and boundaries in spatial seeing. And in the process it becomes evident, if not obvious, that in fact the usual circumstances of visual perception might best be described as inconsistent.

However, the use of an elliptical form does make some things clearer. As we know, an ellipse could be said to be half-way between a straight line and a circle, each of which represents a degenerated extreme form of ellipse. In the case of a circle the two focal points are congruent; in the case of a straight line, they have been relocated in infinity. The elliptical form thus proves to be the form within which the principle of duality is perfectly fulfilled, but also the principle of eccentricity.[1]

In an ellipse a curve loops back on itself yet has two ends. It is deceptive yet not deceptive when, within its course, a seemingly constant line manifests a direction of movement at every point. In other words, it is also a function of time at every position. Or to put it differently: it shows that nothing is more porous than a continuum and nothing is harder to discern than its innate inconstancy.

In their weightless density these Ellipsoids thus demonstrate most decisively the real course of movement, that is to say, as a phase in a vectorial space. At the same time, and by means of a completely different notion of space, they counter the limits of the architectural cube, defined by the planes in which they themselves are located. Or rather, they do not so much counter it as compromise it by de-activating such familiar aspects of central perspective as stasis, angle of inclination, and coordinates, which otherwise serve as means of orientation. Unlike the finite space in which they are lying—lying freely (i.e., as Isa Genzken has pointed out, without taking account of the space's straight lines and right-angles), only touching the floor at one point, almost hovering, almost like flying objects—their most striking feature is their referential nature. As flying objects they point to the open space as an always excluded third term (as it happens spatial problems are regarded as solved if this space has in fact been excluded), although we know that it is actually impossible to inscribe any straight lines into the Earth's surface, only arcs, and that it would therefore be as presumptuous as ever to believe that we had found an answer to the old epistemological question as to the true nature of experiential space. It is as though a situation is created by means of these objects (methodically, i.e., without invoking other factors) wherein the lack of refinement of our sensory organs, which barely allow us to feel the curvature of the surface on which we live, is

at least partially compensated for; as though, in a defined space, the negligible discrepancies—negligible because they are never more significant
than the inevitable inaccuracies that arise from the imperfection of the
measuring instruments—regain their proper status as differentiators by
dint of an increasing level of calculation, i.e., computerized technical
precision. These otherwise so strictly economical objects in fact convey
a sense of a concentration of the totality of movements within space, a
totality that leads a figure into itself or disassociates it from itself. This
also explains in part the sense of speed and the extreme tension and
energy of these objects, despite their sparing elegance.

The logical and, in my view, most interesting development thus
arises from the transition from the first full Ellipsoids to the open objects
and the two- or three-part objects, in which that same disassociation of
movement is made visible. At the same time, Genzken progressively
abandons the three primary colors in favor of in-between colors that
clearly accentuate the changing structures, albeit with an element of
determined evasiveness. A process ensues here that deliberately sets itself
apart from all minimal art. The referential nature of the objects already
points in that direction.

These general characteristics of the works are reinforced by a systematic non-identity of form. In these hollow or multipart objects,
which are seemingly intended to fundamentally embody the possibility
of constructing a geometric entity, there is—contrary to expectation and
by virtue of their differing lengths and diameters and the irregular distribution of their mass—a constant relativization of the congruence of the
form with itself. Evidence is thereby generated and retracted in the same
breath, through the ensuing demand that it should be accepted as evidence. A concrete axiom is constructed yet its coherence undermined.
Logic is neither clouded nor contradicted; it is deferred with the help of
and on behalf of its own means.

Each of these objects maintains its own secret excesses and disclaim-
ers, in that, by dismantling its inner structure, it lays bare the entirety of
its organizational laws and, by means of this same intervention, displaces
them through transformation. One momentarily has a sense of how
much caprice there is in a concept such as that of precision and how
much guile there is in a rationale that rapidly deteriorates. Because no
figure has exactly the qualities that we would by definition ascribe to it,
the asymptotic adjustment of object and law is constantly drawn into the

realms of the inadmissible. Adjustment, of the most acute kind, is only present here in the provisional fact of a method of approximation. These works thus provide a glimpse of the contradiction that is inherent in the notion of measurability as such—that is to say, if measuring involves the determination of the conjunction of two marks but also relies on Archimedes's axiom that any line can be outdistanced by shorter lines laid end-to-end. But how, in this reversal of dimensions, does the whole behave toward the parts? And what is the meaning of notions such as "the same," "bigger," "smaller"?

The type of transformative variation practiced in these works (by means of partial self-negation, projection, hollowing-out, mirroring, etc.) thus only apparently poses the topological question as to the properties of a spatial body that remain invariable despite random distortions. It is as though Genzken had devised an upside-down system designed to discover the number of parameters that can still apply in a particular process of transformation—in other words, to discover the level of

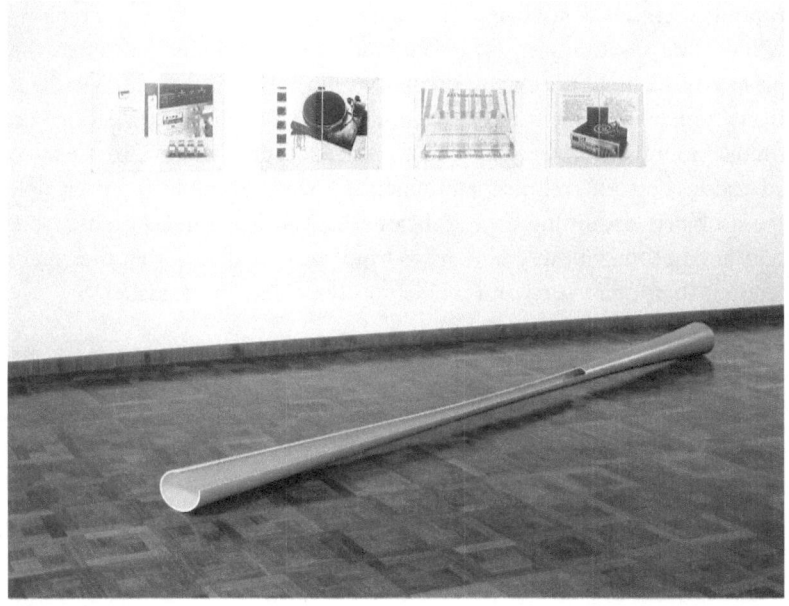

Grau-grünes Hyperbolo 'Jülich' (Gray-Green Hyperbolo "Jülich"), 1979 (on the floor) and Hi-Fi series, 1979 (on the wall). Installation view, Museum Haus Lange, Krefeld 1979. Lacquered wood; three gelatin silver prints and one chromogenic color print, each in two parts. 480 × 20 × 25 cm; each 92 × 64 cm.

freedom she can enjoy. This leads to an inner discourse that is homogenous with the form. In turn this inner discourse generates an active doubling of the object and its latent dynamics, which in effect negates it as a self-contained reference.

There is a blurring of the alternatives of consequence and sequence, of local and global, logic and time, system and history—and even familiar thought processes such as dialectics and causality. Causality is no longer worthy of the name when it is no longer irreversible, when the effect is in turn influenced by the effect of its own effect. In addition, in view of the multiplicity and complexity of the ways in which mediation is realized here, the term dialectics is not applicable either. If anything, an understanding experiments with multiple access points and connections, an understanding that—more flexible than a metaphor and far in advance of its meaning—is not reflected in any model as in its normative or symbolic index.

Finally, the remarkable thing about these Ellipsoids is that they reveal the rivalry that is inherent in their technical exactitude by interrupting themselves at their most exact point. That is to say, precisely where the technology enters into a kind of unquestioned harmony, the process of naturalization that emerges within it becomes fixed as such. It is not unmasked, but stopped by means of a delaying intervention. (A similar approach is seen in Genzken's photographic series based on advertisements for technical equipment.) Instead of stabilizing their use, these objects demonstrate its arbitrariness. And it seems to me that the relevance of their beauty also arises from the fact that, for all their perfection, their perfectness and their smoothness stay undecidable.

Translated by Fiona Elliott.

Notes

1. In an ellipse, which is not discussed by Euclid in his *Elements*, two straight lines always determine one point. The sum of the distances from any such point to the ellipse's two focal points is constant.

Isa Genzken: The Fragment as Model

Benjamin H. D. Buchloh

From Modernist Autonomy to the Culture Industry

A number of historical references could trace Isa Genzken's work in the immediate context of the early 1970s in West Germany, particularly that of the Düsseldorf Academy of Fine Arts where she resumed a second phase of studies after having completed her studies at the West Berlin Academy in 1971.

The first contextual condition could be considered as one concerning the *historical formations of artistic identities*. Soon after she had joined the Düsseldorf Academy, Gerhard Richter became Genzken's teacher. Richter was part of a generation of German artists (with Blinky Palermo and Sigmar Polke) who since the early 1960s had attempted to define West German artistic identity in terms of an international reception of contemporary aesthetic positions. Rather than trying to rediscover cultural references of the pre-Fascist German past in the paintings of Lovis Corinth or in German Expressionism (as practiced at that time by Georg Baselitz, for example) within which one could establish a dubious national and cultural continuity, Richter seems to have insisted that artistic practice had to be radically *modernist* in its distanciation from the legacies of Nazi-Fascism, yet it would have to be regionally specific and acknowledge the problematic conditions of the utopian principles of modernism in their German postwar resurrection. Furthermore this identity had to be internationalist (and *internationalist* at that time meant for this group to look primarily to New York School artists rather than to European artists of the postwar moment).

Genzken shared with Richter the conviction—particularly emphatic among postwar German artists if one compares them for example with their French and Italian counterparts—that aesthetic experience had to be reconstructed as autonomous. Within this relative autonomy, artistic practice could still operate as an exemplary communication, one which by definition would resist all forms of fetishization and reification within advanced consumer culture. Genzken's subsequent interest in Theodor W. Adorno's *Aesthetic Theory*—a text which she considered as of the mid-1970s to be among the foundations of her theoretical insights into the current conditions of artistic practice—would only confirm this aspiration.

In this particular constellation, however, the concept of aesthetic autonomy, which had previously appeared guaranteed, faced conflict: on the one hand there was the desire to construct a cultural identity that emphasized regional specificity, yet one that positioned itself distinctly outside of contaminated German history. On the other hand one aligned oneself with internationalism which was determined primarily by the American model of international-style consumer culture. And finally one wanted to establish a range of both institutional and discursive sites where this relative autonomy could be first of all credibly located and articulated. Yet the difficulty consisted precisely in anchoring the bourgeois capacity to experience the aesthetic as the disinterested and as the sublime in a social realm which was increasingly controlled and instrumentalized, continuously subjected to the most massive and organized campaigns at restructuring public experience according to the parameters of the culture industry.

From "Homeless Abstraction" to the Corporate Lobby

The second of these contextual conditions could then be identified as one of *artistic reception history*: the almost cultic veneration of American postwar abstraction which seemed to embody the newly conquered aesthetic field of autonomy was an essential element of the Düsseldorf situation at that time, evident in Genzken's emphatic appreciation of the work of Barnett Newman and Ellsworth Kelly. Their denial of any affiliation with both the legacies of the politics of surrealism, as much as with the discredited legacies of abstract art and its largely socialist utopian aspirations, was particularly attractive to the German artists of that moment. What went unrecognized, of course, was the fact that the price that had been paid by these American artists in order to achieve the sublime appearance was a rigorous and systematic subjection to a process of depoliticization along the parameters of cold war liberalist ideologies and that the decision of European artists to follow suit inevitably entailed a similar process of retroactive and contemporary depoliticization of artistic practices. This particular history of 1960s abstraction that Clement Greenberg had once identified as "homeless abstraction" was mediated in the Düsseldorf context through the local figure of Blinky Palermo, who had established new parameters for non-representational relief sculpture, seemingly emancipating it from the discredited traditions of European non-representational painting of the immediate prewar (e.g., Abstraction-Création) and postwar periods (e.g., Tachism and Informel).

Since the developments that had led to the postcubist relief design in Newman's work as early as 1950 (for example, *The Wild*) were for the most part unknown to German audiences, the reiteration of these formats in the work of Palermo exerted a tremendous influence on the young generation of students. Like Palermo, Genzken would learn of the legacy of 1950s and 1960s American painting primarily through exhibitions such as *Art of the Real* (1968–69), through her encounters with the work of Kelly and Newman at the Stedelijk Museum in Amsterdam, and—in the same manner that the American artists had learned from the European magazines in the 1940s and 1950s—through the study of color reproductions in American magazines.

Newman of course had insisted that the dimensions of his paintings were such that the viewer would be engulfed entirely by the monochrome expanse and that the viewer's field of vision would thereby be expanded beyond the traditional limitations of the pictorial boundaries into a phenomenological dimension where the painterly surface would envelop the body. Newman's chromatic bliss resulting from the extreme reduction to the monochrome or bi-chromatic order seemed to guarantee such a sublime experience of liberation from the partial or the instrumentalized, the particularized and the fragmented experience in what was otherwise a rigorously structured and functional experience of space.

The absence of either institution or audience to credibly support such an autonomous experience of the sublime aesthetic necessitated the ever-increasing sizes of the paintings in search for an actual, if not social space where their claims could be credibly asserted. One could venture as far as saying that it was precisely the ever-increasing emphasis on scale, size, and dimension in Kelly's, Morris Louis's, and Newman's work from the late 1950s that reveals the deeply felt loss of an *actually given social space*, either as an architectural framework to correspond to the claims for autonomy in the spaces of the paintings themselves or in the sense of an audience with which these communicative structures could be enacted. The vastness and the grandeur of the canvases has its corresponding element in the danger of a vacuity that Michael Fried already observed courageously in the early 1960s when he once referred to Newman's paintings as resembling "handball courts" when unsuccessful as pictorial objects.

It is precisely this dialectic of grandeur and vacuity, however, that distinguishes the work of these artists from that of the previous generations which had still perceived abstraction as the beginning of a universal world language. It is precisely this understanding which generates a potential transition from painting to architecture at every moment of its pictorial definition: yet it remains equally conscious that this transition in fact can never be achieved. Already in 1951 Kelly seems to have known all too well that if *Colors for a Large Wall* had actually have been executed for a publically accessible architectural space it would only have ended up in the utter banality that demarcates every moment of experience in that space, and that only painting in its continuous insistence and refusal of the transition into the architectural dimension would hold out against the complete and final falsification of the legacies of abstraction.

Or to put it differently: to recognize that if painting would actually achieve its promised transition into architecture it would at the very best become the decoration for the corporate lobby space. This is the condition that generates the dialectic between relief, abstraction, and architecture in the work of these American artists of the 1960s, and it is precisely this dialectic which Isa Genzken's work has incorporated from the beginning into her large-scale sculptural work of the mid-1970s as an inescapable condition of contemporary sculpture.

From Painterly Space to Phenomenological Space

Yet at the same time the ultimate restriction to the pictorial format in Kelly, Newman, and Palermo, their resistance against *actual* architectural dimensions and their social implications, seemed to hold out against yet another inevitable consequence: to recognize that the transition which leads from the pictorial to the phenomenological concept of space will lead inevitably to the institutional and discursive definition of socially constructed space. That transition to the architectural dimension, however, (for example, in El Lissitzky's work) was conceived from the very beginning of the challenges to the traditional two-dimensional categories in terms of a qualitatively and quantitatively increased viewer participation, precisely not in terms of a generalized experience of the abstract sublime. Especially after her encounter with the work of El Lissitzky it seems that Genzken recognized that the expansion of chromatic fields and the extreme attenuation of the spatiotemporal continuum in the linear design of Newman's and Kelly's paintings suffered from the fact that the aesthetic "space" outlined in these fields and gestures lacked the elementary definition of space as social and discursive in order to recognize it as a real departure from pictorial to phenomenological space.

Genzken's discovery of El Lissitzky's work, specifically the project of the *Proun Room* from 1923, made her recognize the extent to which a systematic exploration of the transition from pictorial to sculptural, from sculptural to architectural space had already been articulated. More concretely speaking, Genzken recognized in the *Proun Room* the very same procedures that she admired in Newman's and Palermo's work, such as the extreme attenuation of the linear painterly or sculptural relief figure, the demarcation of the field of vision with large monochromatic surfaces, and the continuous reflection of the difference/similarity between the canvas support and the wall support and their eventual integration in the direct application on the architectural support surface (after all it had been in Lissitzky's *Proun Room* that one had really encountered the first definition of the type of "wall painting" that would become so prominent in the late 1960s work of Sol LeWitt and Palermo).

The last of the formative influences to be discussed in Genzken's development would be the encounter with minimalist sculpture. Here it seemed that the emphasis on the inextricable triadic unit between spectator, sculptural object, and architectural container was reconfigured in a manner that seemed to have understood at least the implications of the Lissitzky of the *Proun Room* period. Minimalist sculpture furthermore made evident its opposition to the conception of a purely pictorial abstract sublime, both in its literal incorporation of phenomenological thought into the conception of sculptural and spatial constructs as much as in its emphasis on the industrially produced, i.e., collectively and historically overdetermined forms of spatial experience: it is by these means that minimalism distanced itself manifestly from the debts to its precursors Kelly and Newman.

Yet in the constitution of a phenomenological subject minimalism still remained attached to the notion of an emancipatory and purified spatial experience that sculpture would provide as a utopian counter-construction for this neutral phenomenological subject—a subject which in minimal sculpture (much less so than in phenomenological thought itself) was of course neither bound by the parameters of gender nor class, ethnicity nor political determination.

What neither Kelly and Newman nor minimal sculpture could address, however, was precisely the question why the abstract sublime utopian function as much as the pure and neutral phenomenological subject produced utopian spaces that were not only uncannily devoid of subjectivity (the utopian function being after all precisely to constitute or reconfigure the particularized and falsely socialized subject in terms of an emancipatory constitution in parameters of self-determination), but worse yet, as it would become evident soon thereafter, that the abstract sublime and the minimalist aesthetic would merge almost without resistance with those architectural coding systems whose strategies and avowed goals were precisely the uninhibited display of control and power in the corporate spaces of the administered world.

One of the most difficult tasks postwar sculptural production faced was to recognize the degree to which every attempt at reconstructing a utopian space with chromatic or sculptural means alone would inevitably lead to this cul-de-sac of corporate decor. Another one was to recognize that the claim for simultaneous collective reception as a mode of constructing the social experience in the utopian spaces of sculptural architecture were no longer to be envisaged, but that they had to be reconceived in ways that would acknowledge the already advanced forms of individuation and subject constitution that the differentiation of social institutions had established in the postwar period. In other words, one of the most difficult tasks to be faced by the postwar artists was to recognize not only the extreme importance of the practices of the constructivist and the de Stijl models of shifting from sculpture to architecture but more importantly to recognize precisely the profound inapplicability of these models: that the degree of necessary discontinuity was higher than the potential of reconstructing continuity. We can say now with historical hindsight that for the most part neither the first nor the second aspect of avant-garde reception was consciously achieved by the neo-avant-garde artists in either Europe or the United States in the 1960s.

Genzken's sculptures of the late 1970s radicalize this particular condition, which distinguishes them from both Kelly's and Newman's painterly work, and transcend the limitations of phenomenological neutrality inherited from minimalist sculpture. On the one hand she literally inverts Newman's pictorial strategies of enveloping the spectator within the color field by fusing color exclusively within the spatial and formal definition of her sculptural objects. Yet these elements of the abstract sublime appear no longer in the hieratic position of a vertical plane but are defined by Genzken as pure stereometric objects, discrete and separate from the body of the spectator. Yet they invite, partially due to their position as horizontal floor objects, partially due to their morphology as exact stereometric bodies, partially due to their complex interplay between surface and volume, exterior and interior volume, an extremely precise degree of phenomenological identification. One could almost say that Genzken literalizes the relationship of Newman's *zip* structure to its surrounding pictorial field by transferring it to a mathematically exact sculpture: what is linear division in Newman's plane becomes physical edge in Genzken's volume, what is monochromatic expansive field in Newman's painting becomes a compressed, attenuated sculptural body in actual space. What had been, after all, a rectangular plane on a flat architectural surface becomes in Genzken's sculptural objects a continuous enactment of the actual curvature of space and of the physiological processes generating the perception of that space.

The oppositions constructed in Genzken's work of the second half of the 1970s revolve around yet another axis, an axis that is typically embodied in the contradiction between minimalist sculpture and arte povera sculpture of the mid- to late 1960s. Genzken's work emphasizes the techno-scientific paradigm underlying most of modernist sculpture in the constructivist tradition and identifies with that tradition. Yet at the same time she exaggerates the logic of that paradigm to its utmost extreme where the most precise and exactly calculated delineation of contour, volume, and space generates paradoxically the most organic appearance.

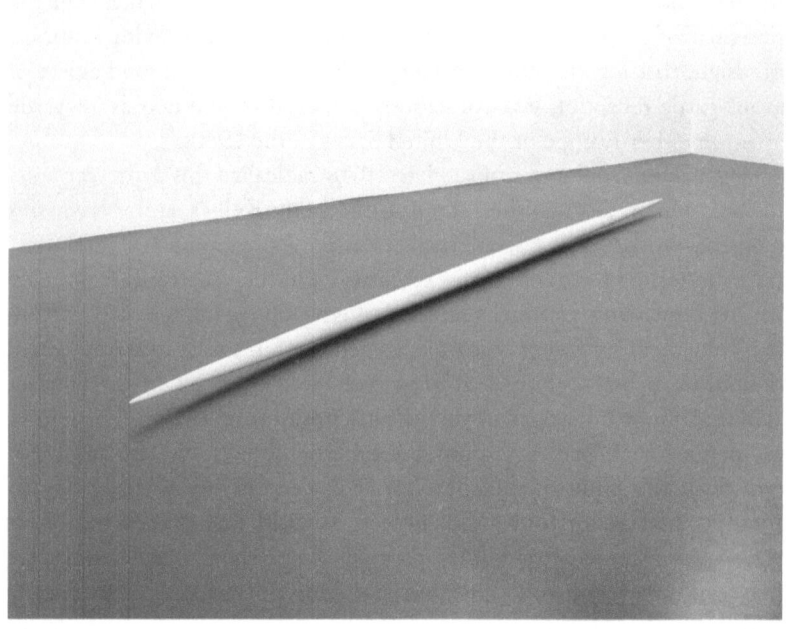

Gelbes Ellipsoid (Yellow Ellipsoid), 1976. Lacquered wood. 486 × 9 × 9 cm.

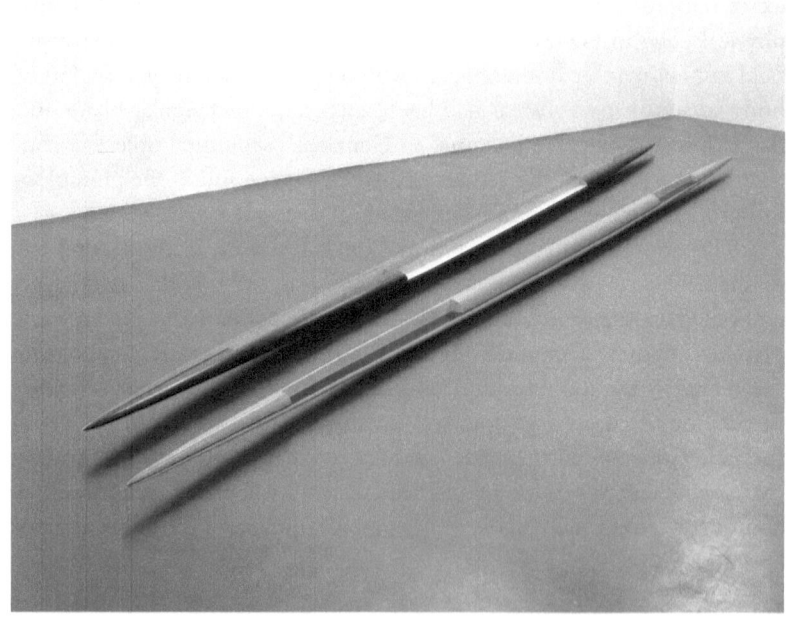

Rot-gelb-schwarzes Doppelellipsoid 'Zwilling' (Red-Yellow-Black Double Ellipsoid "Twin"), 1982. Lacquered wood in two parts. 13 × 20.5 × 600 cm; 11 × 14 × 602 cm.

The Other Tradition of Sculpture

Ever since the matrix of anthropomorphic representation was abandoned in modernist sculpture, sculptors from Constantin Brancusi to Richard Serra have attempted to find other given forms as sculptural paradigms. In Brancusi's work the catalog of alternate models is almost systematically rehearsed and in its paradoxical discontinuity it establishes an exact record of the conflicting results of the search for new matrices: from the African sacred object to the Rumanian peasant architecture, from the anthropomorphic metonymy to the detail of a machine, from the image of a "natural" and randomly chosen, yet formally perfect object such as the biomorphic pebble to the fundamental concepts of stereometry—all could function either side by side or in developmental sequences as the great alternatives to the anthropomorphic paradigm.

Very rarely, however, did this paradigmatic shift allow for the initiation of a radically alternate approach to both fundamental conceptions of space as well as the concepts within which the body, the procedures, and the materials of the sculptural object itself were reconfigured: even in Brancusi's most antithetical redefinitions of sculptural paradigms—on the one hand the bodily metonymy (such as *Princess X*, 1916, for example) or, on the other, those works approximating architectural structure or the utilitarian object (such as *The Benches* or *The Arch*, 1917)—the underlying *foundational* conception of space and matter is never abandoned: sculpture "masters" the definition of the voluminous object as much as it designs and controls the expansion of space.

Yet in the immediate postwar history a radically different approach had emerged in the work of a number of artists, one that Yve-Alain Bois has associated in his brilliant essay on Lucio Fontana with Georges Bataille's notion of the *informe*.[1] This approach clearly alters these underlying conceptions of the spatial and the volumetric more radically than almost all of the previous paradigm shifts in twentieth-century sculpture. Suddenly the seemingly ontological certainty that all sculptural objects are either circumscribed or solid, but definitely volumetric, and that sculptural space is architecturally bound and defined in the terms of Euclidian geometry is challenged if not outright abandoned. Artists such as Louise Bourgeois, Jean Dubuffet, Lucio Fontana, and Leonardo Leoncillo introduce since the late 1940s a morphology and a spatial design into twentieth-century sculpture which operates in distinct opposition to *all* sculptural principles that had governed modernism. They now oppose the concept of the formed volumetric body with that of the randomly arranged, accidentally determined flow of material and mass (culminating in the late 1960s in work such as Richard Serra's *Splashing*), and they oppose those concepts of space which were ultimately based on conquest and mastery, on order, design, and domination, with a notion of spatial experience that seems derived from withdrawal and interiority, incorporation and inclusion rather than expansion.

Fontana's space of radical negativity seems to take into account the conditions of a postwar experience where any and all aspirations toward a conception of public social space as a sphere of communicative action have already been buried, where any ambition toward the restitution of the conditions of simultaneous collective reception—and be it only the one of the abstract sublime—with the means of artistic practice is perceived as always already irretrievably lost. It is in this way that one could begin to understand the differences between the structural and monochromatic definition in Fontana's paintings of the late 1940s and those of Barnett Newman's paintings which operate with almost identical strategies to exactly opposite ends at the very same historical moment. What makes Genzken's sculptural work so enigmatic is of course the fact that she seems to have internalized both models (that of an aspiration to the abstract sublime in Newman and that of a radical denial of metaphysical aspirations in Fontana) and fused them into a rather contradictory structure.

This conversion of sculpture is first of all enacted within the materials—specifically plaster and clay acquire a sudden prominence after having been relegated by modernist sculpture almost entirely to the margins as being too close to modeling and to traditional crafts. Now these materials are reintroduced because of their capacities to negate structural boundaries and to deny definitive form. It is not their higher malleability or the promise of increased manual control that makes them attractive as materials, and certainly least of all is it a return to the originary craft procedures of sculpture. In fact it is the opposite: the relative loss of control that fluid materials and casting processes can set free, the randomness and undecidability, the aleatory qualities of their definition, their relative escape from artistic interference qualifies them for the new sculpture and its negation of a traditional mastery of space and voluminous form.

Spatial concepts are equally inverted, regarding both the placement of sculpture in architectural space and its internal spatial definitions: this would be most evident in Fontana's work such as *Ceramica Spaziale* from 1948 or more explicitly in his series of *Concetto Spaziale / Natura* which he begins in the late 1950s. Their irregular spherical shapes, their baseless floor-bound condition as much as the dialectic of interior and exterior space convey to the viewer the sense of a contracted and compressed rather than expanded space, a contraction that seems to remove spatial experience into the immanence of the sculpture rather than radiate outward into architectural space: spatial experience in sculpture here enacts the destruction of social space, the absence of communicative action, and the dismantling of the public sphere. The sense of spatiality is relegated in these works to the recesses of the body of the deprived individual, a sense of involuntary internalization emanates from these tragic-comical sculptural figures, pierced and perforated on the ground.

Ten years later a similar evacuation of the essential concepts of sculpture occurs in the American context within the work of Carl Andre. His elimination of both the anthropomorphic model and its sculptural and spatial correlatives equally generate a sense of both profound loss and liberation. Defining sculpture as a "place" and comparing it to the radicality of a "road that runs along the earth" (Andre) his work (and Serra's radical response to it in *Splashing*, 1968) continues the development of an *informe* definition of sculptural structure and space. Yet the spaces which emerge from his metal floor pieces still anticipate—unlike Fontana—a residual external exchange of spatial interaction as social communication.

Inevitably the question emerges in retrospect whether this radical negation of traditional concepts of space, in its decentering effects, could also be perceived as a critique of the connotations of gender inherent in traditional spatial and sculptural constructs. Fontana and Andre would appear to be the worst of all possible candidates for such an inversion.

Especially Fontana, since all of his gestures seem to be charged with the most traditional heterosexist energy and his work seems to adhere to the most traditional model of artistic activity as sublimatory and substitutive. Paradoxically, however, Fontana's gestures of piercing and slicing as the driving forces of painterly/sculptural gestures contribute all the more—almost like a manifest travesty—to a recognition of the fatal and finite condition of traditionally male-gendered concepts of sculpture and space.

It is of course not accidental that while his work was met (at least in Europe) with a slowly growing recognition, the work of Louise Bourgeois in its programmatic development of a feminist sculptural morphology and the inherent threats to traditional sculpture would be excluded for this very reason from reception until recently.[2]

Genzken's open husk shapes run along the floor and are simultaneously suspended within space (as exact stereometric ellipsoids they only touch their support surface ideally at one singular tangential point). They seem to perform a synthesis of Fontana's *Concetto Spaziale / Natura* from 1959 and Carl Andre's radical redefinition of sculpture as *place* where the traditional verticality of sculpture is challenged as much in its anthropomorphic foundations as in its spatial domination. And yet they are less paralytic than Fontana's chthonic monuments to inertia and silence; at the same time, as a model of possible interaction within the public sphere, Genzken's floor sculptures are less heroic (and less naive) than Andre's neo-constructivist aspirations for communicative action within the sculptural environment.

The Gender of Sculpture from Hesse to Darboven

Nowhere is the socially imposed construction of gender roles more grotesquely evident than in the traditional categories of painting and sculpture and the manner that they have sustained and enforced sexual stereotyping in cultural production: painting and sculpture (as opposed to photography and writing for example) were—and continue to be—considered essentially male practices.

Even after doubts had emerged in the late 1960s concerning the credibility of these procedures of production in general, and doubts which addressed in particular the false identifications of artistic categories with unconsciously gendered role behavior, the domains of painting and sculpture remained all the more associated with the performance of virile tasks. This was most evident in the fact that even when male artists abandoned certain production procedures and materials in the late 1960s and replaced them with operations within language or within the discursive and institutional frameworks of art (such as Lawrence Weiner or Michael Asher) the response by their minimalist and postminimalist sculptural colleagues (Andre and Serra, for example) was patriarchal and polemical: their argument was that the work of these artists—whatever interest it might have as poetry or as critical intervention—had certainly nothing in common with sculpture as a quasi-ontological category.

This argument was of course applied all the more to the work of women producing three-dimensional objects or conceptual work: one only has to remember how long it took art audiences in Europe and the United States to as much as even look at the work of Louise Bourgeois, for example. Or, subsequently, the work of Eva Hesse, as of the mid-1960s, and that of Hanne Darboven, as of the late 1960s, seemed acceptable to their male peers only under the condition that their work appeared to have circumvented the conflict inherent in the paradoxical proposition of "female sculpture."

Hesse's and Darboven's work had to generate different categories altogether ("eccentric abstraction" for example was one of the epithets with which Hesse's was identified early on). Hesse's objects with their morphology of the hollow, the *informe*, and the void, their translucent and fragile texture (the flaccid and the malleable), and their scattered or serial structure were clearly bypassing traditional concepts of weight, mass, and structure as much as spatial and volumetric design still operative in minimalism.

Hanne Darboven's work shifted these traditional boundaries of sculpture altogether by transforming solid and material masses into principles of quantification, the spatiotemporal dimension of sculpture into sequential writing, and the supposedly sculptural activity of drawing-in-space into the highly regularized activities of notation and record keeping. Darboven's strategies both literalized the traditional sculptural epistemes of quantity and mass, space and design, and expanded these traditional definitions and the forms of perception encoded in them while simultaneously dismantling these unconsciously gendered parameters of sculpture altogether.

The reconstitution of traditional forms and production procedures of figurative painting and sculpture in the mid-1970s reconstructed these socially guaranteed forms of sexual stereotyping as much as it reinstituted the most traditional artistic categories (painting, sculpture), ultimately reorganizing the distribution forms along the axis of private property. Underlying the reenforcement of sexual role behavior was the affirmation of a traditional model of artistic sublimation, one which seemingly could be more successfully and credibly performed by male "procreators" and "progenitors": its latent argument equated artistic production with substitution and mastery, investing definition and perception of space with sexual metaphors as it invested procedures and materials (i.e., "the virgin canvas," "commanding space") with unconscious gender identity.

Genzken decided in the mid-1970s to develop her work within the field of traditional *sculpture* rather than with the means of conceptual practices or the means of photography, for example—tools for which her education and her admiration and knowledge of the work of the conceptual artists had perfectly prepared her. As much as the work of Eva Hesse and Hanne Darboven would have influenced Genzken in the early to mid-1970s she seems to have opposed one instruction their work seemed to hold: that a woman cannot engage within the traditional territory dominated by male sculptors. Hence the prejudicial anger and confusion in the early responses to Genzken's work by the governing male figures of the German art world of the late 1970s accusing the work of its explicitly gendered structure and morphology. Bringing out the vilest pseudo-Freudian arguments to defend their own threatened gender identity, these figures suggested that her work originated typically in female hysteria, inevitably generating unacceptable hypertrophic forms.

Genzken's decision to position herself deliberately within the most difficult and resistant of the male-dominated practices and materials from the start, was clearly motivated by the protofeminist recognition that it is within the artistic categories themselves as much as within social and institutional practices with which they are enforced that patriarchal domination is exercised. In the same manner that artists continuously seek to confront themselves with the past, to confront the extreme difficulty of artistic tradition as both a site of cultural memory and as a site of control and domination, or to the same extent that artistic practices inevitably inscribe themselves within the seemingly insurmountable rule of ideology in the present, it seems that Genzken's choice to confront the male-dominated and the most sexist domain of visual production was a necessary condition for her sculptural project as an emancipatory and critical one in spite of its apparently traditionalist concerns and means.

What is astonishing is the degree of internal logic with which Genzken integrates since the mid-1970s the various components of the European and the American discourses on sculpture. If extreme attenuation for example is an issue that the work clearly observes in its encounters with the transcriptions of extreme attenuation of spatiotemporal relationships in Hanne Darboven's work, then it is the transfer and reinscription of that phenomenon onto the sculptural volume itself that occurs in Genzken's floor sculptures of the mid-1970s. But in Genzken's work the same rigor as in Darboven's transcripts is applied, yet shifted onto the level of techno-scientific organization. Genzken's early deployment of the computer and the architectural plotter to design the extremely elongated spatial and voluminous configurations of her sculptural work corresponds to and extends both the rigorous reduction of Darboven's work to the actually constitutive elements of sculptural experience as much as it completes the cycle of minimalist promises to subject the design of the sculptural body to the same criteria and qualities of the more advanced forms of scientific and technical production as well as the production of functional and utilitarian voluminous objects in general. Yet this emphasis on the universally governing principles of techno-scientific order constitutes only one dimension in Genzken's floor sculptures, a dimension which is rigorously denied in the work's extreme organicity and concrete bodily references, qualities that derive clearly from Genzken's familiarity with Maurice Merleau-Ponty's *Phenomenology of Perception*.

Moreover one would have to recognize that already in the work of the 1970s Genzken problematizes the notion of a merely neutral and universally applicable phenomenology of the bodily experiences of sculptural objects and place, but that rather already at that point the body inscribed in Genzken's sculpture is the female body in opposition to the governing principles of the patriarchal body ruling the laws of sculpture.

The dichotomies of bodily inscription into the sculptural object are—as we have seen—in and of themselves a subject of sculptural reflection: Genzken inverts the parameters of her own work once again in 1985 when she abandons the complicated and carefully conceived technical production of large wooden sculptures altogether to begin—as it seems—an entirely different series. The change of matrices occurring around 1985 is first of all one of procedures and materials in that she begins to model and to cast and in that she seems to move away from the technical manufacturing process altogether. At the same time she abandons wood, computer design, and color in favor of monochrome plaster and cement sculptures that are modeled or cast in wooden molds that she constructs as though architectural units would have to be cast in concrete. A similar inversion occurs on the level of morphology: where the series of Ellipsoids and Hyperbolos are ultimately all based on an extremely differentiated and a systematically embodied spatial curvature, the new series of concrete sculptures is based on irregularly sided rectangular volumes or cubic shapes that have been either fragmented or left incomplete.

Whereas the techno-scientific model was clearly the underlying paradigm in Genzken's first series of wood sculptures from 1977 to 1984, the architectural fragment and the ruin determine her sculptural morphology in the second series beginning in 1985. And in the same manner that in the wood sculptures a tendency toward an ever-increasing calculated exactitude prohibited any association with the biomorphic tradition in twentieth-century sculpture (as in Jean Arp with whom the early wood sculptures could at first be mistakenly associated), so does a major shift within the second series prohibit any association with the legacy of Expressionist architecture (Hermann Finsterlin comes to mind when looking at Genzken's earliest plaster models) or the sculptural objects of Kurt Schwitters, with whom the first series of Genzken's plaster objects and models could equally be compared. Genzken's decision to abandon plaster as a material highly charged with both painterly qualities and subtle ranges of plasticity as much as with an entire history of sculptural conventions and to forego it for the crude and relatively unmanageable inertia of concrete proves once again her sense for the artistic necessity of absolute contemporaneity as much as for the highest possible resistance (of categories, of materials, of conventions) as a seemingly inescapable condition for that contemporaneity. The concrete of the second series does not allow for an infinite variation of textures and surface effects in the way that plaster would have suggested, neither does it allow for the seductive historical associations with architecture models. Moreover, the light-absorbing surface of plaster gave Genzken's early sculptures in the new series both a painterly as well as an expressionist appearance that was ultimately at odds with her approach, whereas the qualities of cast concrete (or the lack of qualities, rather) introduce the same radical technological anonymity into the work that had been previously provided by the computer and the plotter design. It is this voluntary subjection to a decreasing number of aesthetic options, the self-imposed limits of the format as well as of the material in the concrete sculptures, that generates their significance both as fragments and architectural models. It is precisely because they deny architectural vision and variation, richly modeled surface effects and painterly texture, that Genzken's concrete sculptures enable us to think about architecture at all (as much as about sculpture's definitive inability to ever again claim a transitory function between the two disciplines): in their reductive iteration they address both the actually existing conditions of architecture as much as those who actually exist in these conditions of architecture.

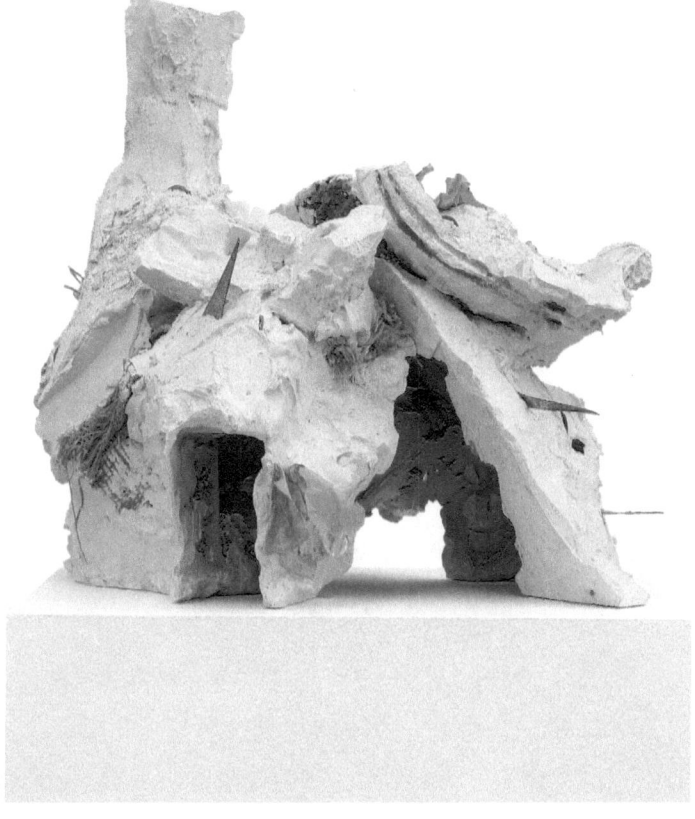

Müllberg (Pile of Rubbish), 1984. Plaster, metal, paper, and cloth. 42 × 42 × 47 cm.

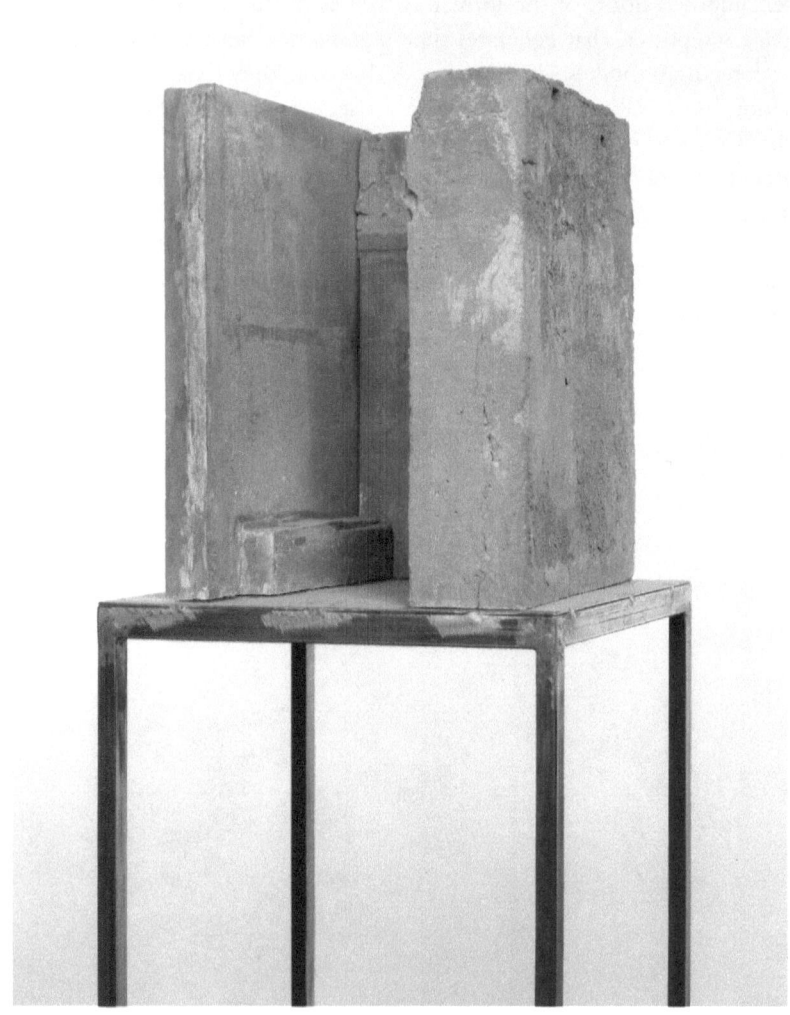

Kirche (Church), 1986. Concrete and steel. 198 × 50 × 60 cm.

Unlike the majority of her peers in Düsseldorf, the generation of new sculptors called the "model builders," Genzken's sculptural work never opens up to the comforts of play with the privileges of postmodern architecture, but rather insists on the recognition that a truly contemporary definition of sculpture depends ultimately on the most common denominator of existence in architectural space. The dual nature of Genzken's concrete sculptures as both a negative sculptural model of architectural space as much as a remnant and a ruinous particle of an architecture of the (recent) past, suspends these sculptural objects in a peculiarly temporal dimension. Neither melancholic or commemorative nor utopian and anticipatory, these models denounce any false reconciliation with the past or the future that the present practices of architecture seem to offer under the guises of postmodern privileges. In that respect the radicality of Genzken's sculptural models should not be underestimated since it is her work as sculpture that insists conspicuously and consistently on addressing the collective conditions of existing in architecture.

Notes

1. Yve-Alain Bois, "Fontana's Base Materialism," *Art in America* (April 1989), pp. 238–48, 279.

2. As late as 1986, in a major survey exhibition of twentieth-century sculpture (*Qu'est-ce que la sculpture moderne*, organized by Margit Rowell for the Musée National d'Art Moderne, Centre Georges Pompidou in Paris) the work of Louise Bourgeois is absent from both catalog and exhibition.

Isa Genzken: Fuck the Bauhaus
Architecture, Design, and Photography in Reverse

Benjamin H. D. Buchloh

"[A] Swiss architect, Max Bill, has undertaken to restructure the Bauhaus where Klee and Kandinsky taught. He wishes to make an academy without painting, without research into the imagination, fantasy, signs, symbols—all he wants is technical instruction. In the name of experimental artists I intend to create an International Movement for an Imaginist Bauhaus."

—Asger Jorn, Letter to Enrico Baj, December 1953

"Modern art is already not so, when the artist who makes it begins to understand it, when those who could understand it begin to not want to understand it, and when those that have understood it want an art that they can't yet understand."

—Max Jacob, *Art poétique,* 1922

To be equally attracted and repulsed by the legacies of modernist design and functionalist architecture that had also defined the utopian aspirations of many of the key painters and sculptors of the twentieth-century avant-gardes had been one of the paradoxical artistic positions of the post–World War II period. Asger Jorn for example, as is evident in his letter quoted in the epigraph above, formulated his project for an *Imaginiste / Imaginaire Bauhaus,* explictly in opposition to Max Bill's schemes to resuscitate the Bauhaus legacies for the reconstruction and design supplies of West German and European consumer culture in his new Bauhaus at Ulm in 1953.[1]

Photography's Architectural Archives

Another example of this artistic reorientation toward the state and status of architecture and design in the post–World War II period would be the melancholic archive of anonymous industrial architecture which Bernd and Hilla Becher had started to assemble in Düsseldorf since the late 1950s (programmatically turning their backs on French *Nouveau Réalisme,* the transformation of Duchamp's readymade into an apparent cult of fetishized objects, evident in Arman's accumulations of the outlived and Tinguely's machines of enacted obsolescence, both prominently present in Düsseldorf at that time). A third example would be the archives of vernacular architecture collected in Ed Ruscha's photographic books emerging in the early 1960s, equally reflecting on the avant-garde's lost architectural horizons (in Ruscha's case the desire to dislodge the spellbinding objects of consumer culture was triggered by the artist's encounter with Andy Warhol's exhibition of *32 Campbell Soup Cans* at the Ferus Gallery in Los Angeles in 1962).

In the early 1970s Isa Genzken would also discover Dan Graham's almost haphazardly collected photographs of banal architecture of the everyday in New Jersey and New York. Produced in the wake of Ruscha's books in the mid-1960s, they addressed the status of architecture and the conditions of the public sphere from yet another vantage point. Deskilling photography even more provocatively, Graham challenged minimalism's historical deficiencies concerning the analysis of public and architectural space where contemporary sculpture was supposedly to be situated and operative.

These fundamentally different, yet historically deeply connected photographic ventures of anomic architectural archives, were all equally formative for Genzken's astonishing early photographic book project *Berlin, 1973* (initially untitled). Genzken's book shares some of the crucial questions posed in these projects—neither explicitly formulated at the time by anybody but these artists themselves, nor posed in the literature ever since. First of all, there was the question whether the pre–World War II avant-gardes' aspirations to sublate artistic practices within public space could any longer resolve the historical limitations of easel painting and sculpture, readymade or artisanal. Given the demise of what had once been the bourgeois public sphere, and even more so, what had been the avant-gardes' hopes for the construction of a proletarian one, a second question emerged: To what extent were photographic projects alone able to query the current conditions of simultaneous collective experience and architectural space?

Trauma Photography

Genzken's book, rediscovered just now, presents seventy-eight photographs selected from a presumably much larger number of images that the artist took during the late 1960s and early 1970s in West Berlin. While these photographs clearly address the status of architecture and the disappearance of the public sphere in post–World War II West Berlin, Genzken also assembled them as almost sculptural objects, directing her critical attention specifically toward the particular photographic representations of architecture which she had encountered after her arrival at the Arts Academy in Düssseldorf in 1973.

The first and most striking feature of Genzken's book is its cumbersome size. Its proportions vastly exceed what at the time would have been considered an appropriate book format in the context of conceptual art—as in Ruscha's publications, for example, in which the shift from precious and authentically artisanal photographic prints to the medium and distribution form of a printed reproduction had implied a reduction of scale and size. Second, the size of Genzken's volume with its thirty-nine large—scale diptych pages is matched by a discomforting thickness of its display boards. Thus the book appears to be on the verge of becoming a material, if not a sculptural object itself. Suspending the images between the heavy boards of a classic photo album, the artisanal photographic print, and the mere reproduction, Genzken challenged the recently asserted neutrality of the conceptualist photographic image and its handy little booklets, as much as she opposed the conventions of the classic modernist photobook (even Bernd and Hilla Becher's *Anonyme Skulpturen* [Anonymous Sculptures], published in 1970, had combined both the format of the modern photobook of the 1920s, such as Albert Renger-Patzsch's *Die Welt ist Schön* [The World Is Beautiful], and Ruscha's standards of understatement).

Third, rather than producing a grand archive of melancholic images of architecture and urban settings of the kind that the Bechers were inspiring in the work of Thomas Struth and Thomas Ruff, Genzken—in a comparably forthright and unsentimental manner—focused on the worst aspects of ruination, destruction, and fragmentation in post–World War II West German architecture. Shown are the shards and derelict remnants of Berlin's self-destruction as well as the city's Brutalist and hastily inflicted attempts to present itself as a new concrete metropolis distanced from the horrors of the recent past.

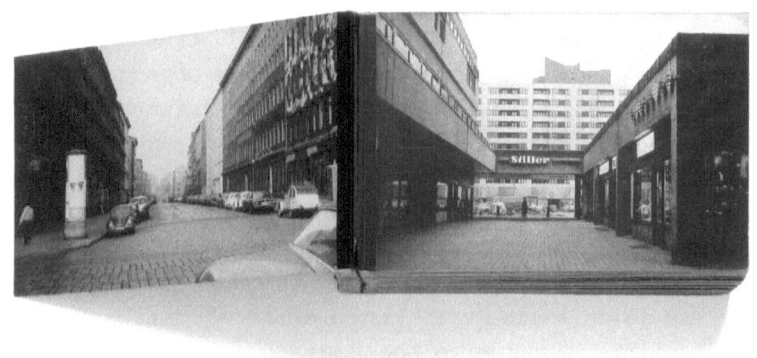

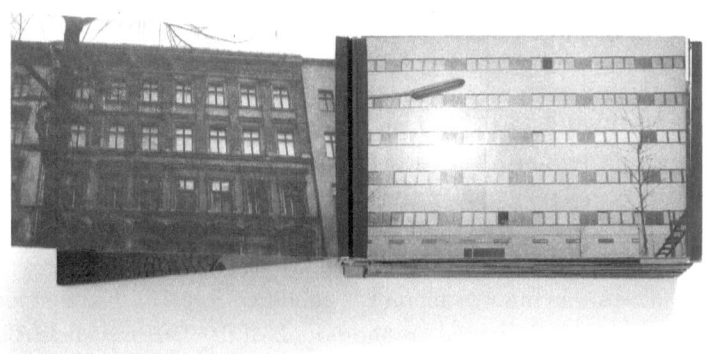

Berlin, 1973. Prototype of artist book. Seventy-eight gelatin silver prints mounted on cardboard, adhesive tape. 19.5 × 31 × 8.5 cm.

Lastly, a fourth strategy sets Genzken's photographic project apart from that of her Düsseldorf peers. Rather than resuscitating the well-tempered tonality of the highly differentiated gray scales of German Neue Sachlichkeit photography, she printed her photographs in stark black and white, in an aggressively crude high-contrast printing that emphasizes the ruinous state of many of the old buildings as much as the hauntingly alienated innovations of reconstruction architecture. Thus, rather than providing what could have been perceived as a melancholy reconciliation with the status quo, or an elegiac mourning of the past, Genzken's images register the actually governing conditions of architectural and social devastation of post–World War II West Germany and West Berlin as a manifestly traumatic present.

Commodity Photography

Genzken's Berlin images also recite and radicalize a number of photographic tropes from earlier moments in the twentieth century, evident in her frequent selection of shop windows and display cases, with their mute animation of the inanimate, the spatial inscription of the gaze within the glass display cases, and the confusion of inner and outer spaces, of architectural surfaces and the surfaces of mere optical reflection. Artists and photographers, from Atget to Lisette Model and Umbo, from Walker Evans to Gisèle Freund, had attempted again and again to come to terms with the fundamentally altered conditions of the subject's perception of self and other, the confines of both subject and object experience that the rapidly expanding encroachment of public space by architectures, designs, and objects of consumption had brought about. This peculiar paradox of a perpetually expanding public exhibition of the collectively fetishistic attraction to a new world of objects, whose previous provenance had been the presumably intimate sphere of the private subject, became one of the challenges for artists confronting the question of the subject's situatedness in public architectural spaces and pondering the possibilities of photographic representations.

Obsolescence

Owing to its status as a forlorn outpost surrounded by a regime of state socialism, lacking any significant economic infrastructure comparable to the rapidly advancing, modernized public and commercial spaces of West Germany, West Berlin long retained sites and designs of outlived forms of consumption. Genzken's obvious attraction to these signs of forgotten development and of the *retardataire* transformation of public spaces into sites of spectacular consumption, at times seems comparable to Sigmar Polke's drawings, similarly seductive travesties of German reconstruction culture. These drawings had equally mobilized archaic and impoverished forms promising at least the humorous, if not the liberating effects of obsolescence.

When Genzken's photographs of the derelict cityscapes of West Berlin invoke abandoned spaces (in particular the nightmarish playgrounds telling us all about the culture's love of children at that time), earlier forms of existence—beyond or beneath the totalizing control of the new regimes of consumption—appear as problematic and sentimental remnants. On the diptych's opposite pages, the artist almost always confronts mnemonic recollection with stark sights of innovations, i.e., conditions that have already erased the seemingly protective spaces of the capital of decrepitude.

Genzken's book *Berlin, 1973* ultimately is most engaged with the imminent transformation of object relations, in the subject's private and public spaces. The book gives us a full spectrum of photography's capacity to read architecture in reverse, so that rather than positing a horizon for simultaneous collective experience, it reminds us of the failure of these utopian aspirations. The book's diptychs alternate dialectically: they range from almost accidentally preserved locations of mnemonic intimacy to a violent erasure of the subject's bonds with the material urban world, from the involuntary resistance against the new object regimes in the display of the older ones to the reconstruction architecture as a symptom of collective disavowal. The new city will no longer even pretend to offer the subject a sense of being housed in socially communicative relations, or of constituting the subject in interactions with the materials, surfaces, and structures of architectural space.

Musical Photographs

A second set of early important photographs was taken by Genzken during one of her first trips to New York at the end of the 1970s. On that occasion the artist toured what was then still a rather romantically dilapidated Lower East Side. She visited the alternative music scene and rock clubs such as CBGB with Dan Graham. The artist's heretofore more traditional concerns for an autonomous plasticity of abstract sculpture were opened up in these photographs. First of all they articulate the artist's new willingness to accept what she previously might have perceived as irresolvable conflicts between her sculpture and her infatuation with mass media culture. Both image groups, the clubs and the shop windows of the Lower East Side and their displays of musical instruments, announce intersections that would increasingly define Genzken's oeuvre since the 1980s.

The musical instruments' perfect fusion of mechanomorphic and biomorphic sculptural forms seems to have caught Genzken's attention. Even if these objects were discovered only in an accidental, almost surrealist chance encounter, they corresponded to Genzken's increasing desire to integrate the conflicting high- and mass-cultural elements in her artistic project. In the frequency with which she selected industrially produced instruments (saxophones, tubas, trombones, hi-tech drumsets, and reams of electric guitars), the artist further pursued an opposition equally central to her sculptural practice: the tension between technological rationality and forms of somatic and sensuous pleasure. The attraction of these musical instruments as relatively easily accessible commodities is comparable to earlier sculptors' attraction to the tools and wonders of the industrial hardware store.

Genzken's penchant for these instruments seems to have also voiced her desire to animate sculpture itself. And even if that animation tended toward the potential of sound, it would still have to remain within the parameters of the muted sculptural object. It is precisely this suspended state of the object between function and sound on the one hand and sculptural self-reflexivity on the other hand that also would define the Hi-Fi series of 1979. No longer merely a more or less haphazard snapshot collection, it would be presented as a fully formalized work, as I will argue in the final part of this essay.

These parallels between Genzken's sculptural concepts and her photographic encounters with ready-made industrial objects are evident even more clearly in her images of the serial displays of electric guitars. Their bodies, cast from artificially tinted resins, featured perfectly calibrated volumes, digitally plotted curvatures, and sinuous shapes. The tight linearity of the instruments' strings appeared stretched like the sculptural avant-garde's former tension wires (e.g., in Tatlin's reliefs) above the guitar's neck and sound hole. These commercial guitars might have reminded Genzken of yet another opposition that is foundational to modernist sculpture (ever since Picasso's *Guitar* in 1912): how to reconcile a sculpture's volumes and its voids, how to reconcile bodily mass and spatial delineation, how to equalize latent interior and manifest exterior surfaces.

But Genzken likewise addressed a different, less formalist set of contradictions that had already defined Constantin Brancusi's sculptural visions of the late 1910s and 1920s: the extreme challenges posed by technological objects to the traditional process of artisanal sculptural manufacture. Surface perfection now had to match industrial standards of immaculate functional precision. The famous anecdote of Brancusi's visit to the *Salon de locomotion aérienne* in Paris in 1912 in the company of Marcel Duchamp and Fernand Léger had brought the conflict to the point: when confronted with a large airplane propeller, Duchamp rhetorically asked Brancusi whether any artist in the present moment would be capable of producing an object of comparable beauty. Brancusi knew all too well that sculpture from then on would have to compete with the technocratic and industrial delirium of the nascent Second Machine Age, its cars, airplanes, and steamboat propellers. Just as much as Duchamp would prove soon thereafter that these conflicts could not be resolved by mimetic assimilation alone, when he made the world of design, decoration, and the fashion fetish the matrix of the readymade.

Beyond these still rather formalist considerations it is equally obvious that the photographs of the club scenes testify just as much to Genzken's increasing fascination with Anglo-American music of the 1960s and 1970s (extended later to German groups like Kraftwerk and Einstürzende Neubauten). While indisputably a private passion, Genzken's embrace of musical phenomena ranging from subversive subcultures to mass cultural entertainment would also signal the emergence of one of the artist's many future challenges: how to sustain an artistic project developed along the lines of late-modernist sculptural abstraction, while simultaneously recognizing the irreversible permeation of all experiences by mass cultural and industrial forms.

The generation of German artists preceding Genzken, whether Joseph Beuys, the Bechers, or Hanne Darboven, had still followed T.W. Adorno's prescription that artistic practices had to remain autonomous and impervious to the products of American mass cultural industries. And that generation would remain deeply skeptical, if not outright phobic when the culture industries encroached on the sphere of artistic production. However, for Genzken and the post-pop generation in general, the infatuation with both American subcultures and mass-cultures seemed to provide a viable cure for a whole range of specifically German post–World War II ailments. First of all, the new forms of mass desublimation offered a new internationalist delusion. Even if it could not sustain the promises of the avant-gardist or the political internationalism of the 1920s, mass cultural internationalism would now at least promise various compensations: particularly for the loss of any viable local or national continuity of cultural production in the aftermath of Nazi Fascism and World War II. Furthermore, the exacerbated enchantment with American subculture undoubtedly also served as a treatment of the inability to experience pleasure resulting from the collectively ruling "inability to mourn" still defining Genzken's generation.

Yet at the same time and beyond these specifically West German features, a more general generational shift occurred among artists in the wake of pop art and Warhol. After all, in the same way that Graham's masters had been Dan Flavin, Donald Judd, and Sol LeWitt (all equally hostile to the domains of rock and roll and certainly to new wave and punk), for Genzken, one of the most salient historical references throughout the early and mid-1970s had been Ellsworth Kelly's abstraction; Blinky Palermo's work had been perhaps even more important, since it was local and powerfully present. When Genzken encountered Graham's surprising devotion to popular forms of collective desublimation, it suddenly seemed that a fusion of these conflicting dimensions was perfectly plausible. In fact, Graham been one of the first artists to resolve this historical schism in his aforementioned photographs of vernacular architecture from New Jersey and New York. Yet the age-old dialectics of avant-garde and mass culture were not just re-enacted as a generational opposition, or articulated merely at the iconographic level, as in the differences between pop art and minimalism. Graham's propositions became clearly more influential for Genzken precisely at the moment when citations of the subcultural forms of musical transgression and dissent were incorporated into his writings in *End Moments* (1968) and later resurfaced in works of his such as *Rock My Religion* (1982).

Subculture as Substitutional Public Sphere

What were the secret and manifest attractions for artists like Graham and Genzken to associate their initially purely sculptural, photographic, or textual practices explicitly with the public spheres of mass cultural music? Perhaps these strategies had been primarily motivated by the artists' spontaneous transgressive or plain hedonistic desires. To frame them retrospectively in terms of an art-historical analysis might be a preposterous undertaking. But a few explanatory comments could still illuminate the rather drastic chasm occurring in Genzken's oeuvre. Once she had taken the first steps, she increasingly fractured her once purely phenomenological sculpture with ever intensifying assemblage assaults. These traced mass cultural object production seismographically, and recorded the erosion of perception and cognition, of object relations and spatial conceptions, inflicted by the rule of totalitarian consumption in the present. Furthermore, the musical subcultures of the 1960s and 1970s offered Graham and Genzken contemporary variations of the initially august avant-garde promises of the 1920s, even if these were at present only accessible in seemingly degraded forms. The once radical promises of altered distribution forms had mutated into technologically mediated systems of mass distribution. The avant-garde's utopian aspirations toward architecture and public space, toward conditions of simultaneous collective reception were now experienced, as we might emphasize once more, in reverse: First of all, these systems relentlessly enforced the ultimate industrialization of experience itself, and rigorously eliminated whatever the subject's transgression and dissent had formerly opened up discursively or enacted phenomenologically. Second, musical subculture now offered various modes of spectacularized audience address. These differed fundamenatlly from the circumscribed audiences of high art connoisseurs and collectors, commercial galleries, and museum institutions, but also from the apparently incurable esoterics of neo-avant-garde concerts and performances. And lastly, and most importantly perhaps, club cultures and music scenes would provide an intense delusion of a newly won immediacy of communication. Offering the semblance of an actual and direct impact of artistic events, these situations promised once again to fulfill the very desire with which the radicality of avant-garde art had operated throughout the twentieth century, from dada to Cage.

The Matrix of Design

Those general reflections on Genzken's attraction to industrial music culture allow us to address a third and last group of photographic images produced by Genzken in 1979. The aforementioned Hi-Fi series originated once again in the artist's increasing fascination with the collective conditions of perception and listening, and her bewilderment (or was it despair?) at sculpture's problematically self-sufficient autonomy, sustaining its apparently eternal muteness.

Genzken's citational presentations of international advertisement campaigns (Anglo-American, Japanese, French, German) for what were then the technologically most advanced models of stereo equipment, trigger at least four major queries of reflection. The first begins with a historical detail, largely overlooked until now and therefore all the more astonishing: the fact that Genzken's re-photographed advertisements initiated a practice of appropriationist photography, certainly unique in Germany and Europe at that time. It is a citational strategy that would soon thereafter become one of the most widely claimed original operations of

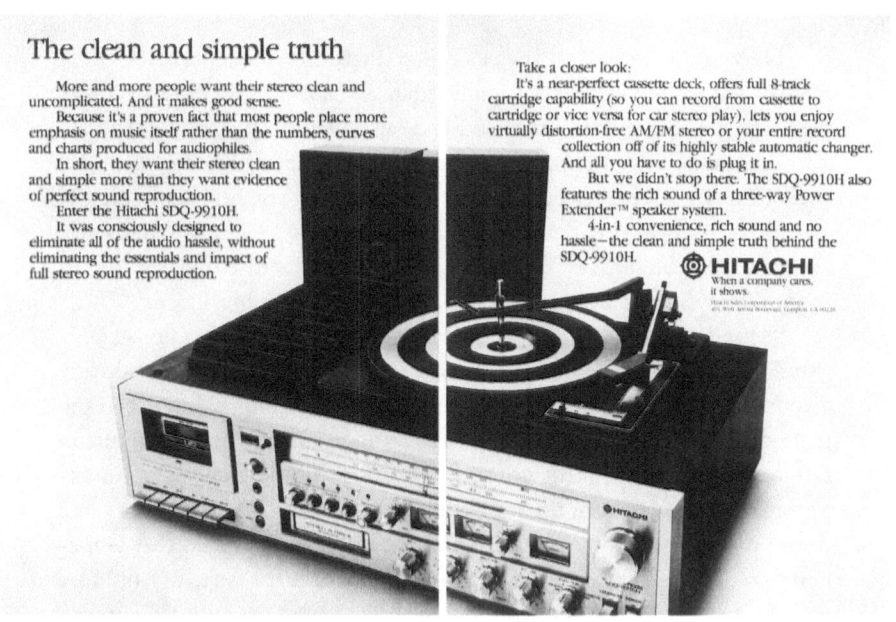

Hitachi, 1979. Gelatin silver print in two parts. 49.5 × 76.9 cm.

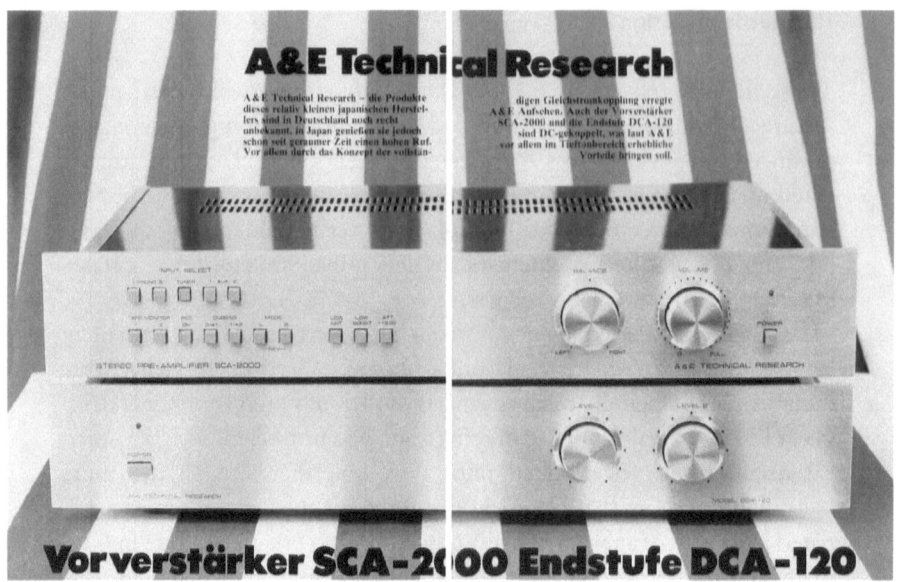

Technical Research, 1979. Chromogenic color print in two parts. 49.5 × 76.9 cm.

the New York artists of the so-called Pictures Generation; Richard Prince, for example, re-photographed his *Marlboro Men* only in 1980. Genzken was no less fascinated with these advanced forms of corporate photomontage than Brancusi had been with the airplane propeller. But unlike the artist's earlier enthusiastic cathexis on computer technologies and their immaculate design (for her Ellipsoids), Genzken does not embrace the standards of exquisite design and advertisement—the culture industry's most powerful armatures—without ambivalence.

Second, the objects and images of Genzken's citations (almost universally illegible works at the time of their inception) have already acquired a paradoxical datedness. With thirty years' hindsight, given the technological advances that digital technologies have brought about in the meantime, these motifs now trigger an air of obsolescence, an unexpected detachment from the compulsive ordering of desire that they had once powerfully enforced. And while we are not convinced that Genzken's re-photography of images had anticipated that effect, it would be equally wrong to surmise an almost futurist fascination with these technocratic apparitions of design and distribution.

Third, these works prove that yet another avant-garde promise of the emancipatory effects of photography and advertisement had been utterly delusional (a fusion that had been touted as innately progressive in the writings and works of László Moholy-Nagy and Herbert Bayer in the 1920s and 1930s, for example). In Genzken's appropriated images, as quintessential examples of corporate photomontage, the historical dialectics between emancipatory avant-garde production and mass cultural practices of object domination have been finally reversed. All that her artistic practice can now demonstrate is the extent to which design and photography in the service of advertisement and consumption have become unsurpassable matrices of power and control. Even though the dialogic and dialectical relationships with the photographic practices of what would soon be called the Düsseldorf School remain visible, nothing could be further from the melancholy aesthetics of the Bechers with which Genzken had still struggled in her photobook *Berlin, 1973*, discussed above.

And a fourth and final aspect, so far overlooked in the responses to Genzken's Hi-Fi series of 1979, is the careful selection of the languages in which these devices are presented: a Japanese and an English example are matched by a French and a German advertisement campaign. Thus the design of the most advanced technological equipment as much as the design of the advertisements themselves appear as articulations of a monolithic idiomatic and iconographic order. These images function within an international regime of globally operative marketing and design strategies which efface even the last residual differences between local, regional, and national cultures.

These citational photomontages of corporate culture are the turning point in the extraordinary reversal Genzken's work will perform in the shift from the "classical" works of her first phase of phenomenological abstraction to the second and third phase of the type of work that would increasingly overdetermine her production of the past twenty years. If Genzken's early abstraction had depended at least partially on the artist's visionary incorporation of advanced forms of computer design for her sculptural production, she had therein performed a last synthesis of seemingly irreconcilable principles: a fusion between the grand spiritual legacies of abstraction and the unfulfilled social promises of technological design. Consequentially, these earlier principles, which she had sustained in the first seven years of her work, appear here at the very point of transition. A transition which occurs precisely at the historical moment when the shift from a rationalist utopian and progressive modernity to an industrial confinement of design and consumption had become irreversible. Therefore none of the promises of abstraction could be maintained any longer: it would not abolish the hierarchies of class, fulfill the promises of a universal legibility, or alter the distribution form of the work of art. And even the more pragmatic promises of the Bauhaus, to provide an industrialized culture which would actually improve the collective perceptual and utilitarian conditions of everyday experience through the technological design of consumption, could no longer be sustained as credible. Genzken recognized that while these grand idioms of abstraction had still tried to reconcile technology and nature, collective regimes and self-constitution, material control and spiritual enactment, they had never reflected on the actual social transformations that had taken place in the aggressive desublimation of experience under the conditions of post–World War II mass consumption.

This was the historical schism that would eventually determine the specificity of Genzken's later oeuvre: to have started out with an early and very advanced accomplishment as a European sculptor whose Ellipsoids and increasingly complex stereometric mutations could easily be accepted within the international canon of a primarily phenomenologically ordained minimalist abstraction. But it is precisely within this post-utopian conception of the historical deficiencies and decline of abstraction, the phase when abstraction meets the demands of design for the first time in a totalizing manner, the moment at which all of its principles succumb fully to instrumentalization, to controlling and exploiting the subject, that abstraction confronted its greatest crisis in the post–World War II period. It was this realization that triggered the dramatic fissures and fractures in Genzken's work, the rapid reversal from the idealizing technological aspirations to the ruinous fragments and architectural shambles, the mere particles of devastation that will eventually demarcate the work of the 1980s, and finally leading to the type of work on which Genzken's recent reputation has been built.

Since then her sculpture appears to have been permeated by the chaos of semiotic refuse, the massive erosion that industrial and consumer culture now inflicts on the masses in ever-intensifying and ever-expanding cycles of violence. The schisms that erupt here in the sphere of plasticity are not at all the results of a fracture of the artist's subjectivity. Previously it might have taken two generations of artists for these changes to be articulated. But in this case they are registered within the oeuvre of a singular artist, and they result from Genzken's almost self-destructive desire for change and transformation. If there remains any need to illuminate the astonishing complexity of her oeuvre, this would be an occasion to recognize it.

Note

1. Jorn's actual official foundation of the movement, called IMIB (International Movement for an Imaginist Bauhaus), will however only take place two years later in Alba, with Giuseppe Pinot-Gallizio in 1955.

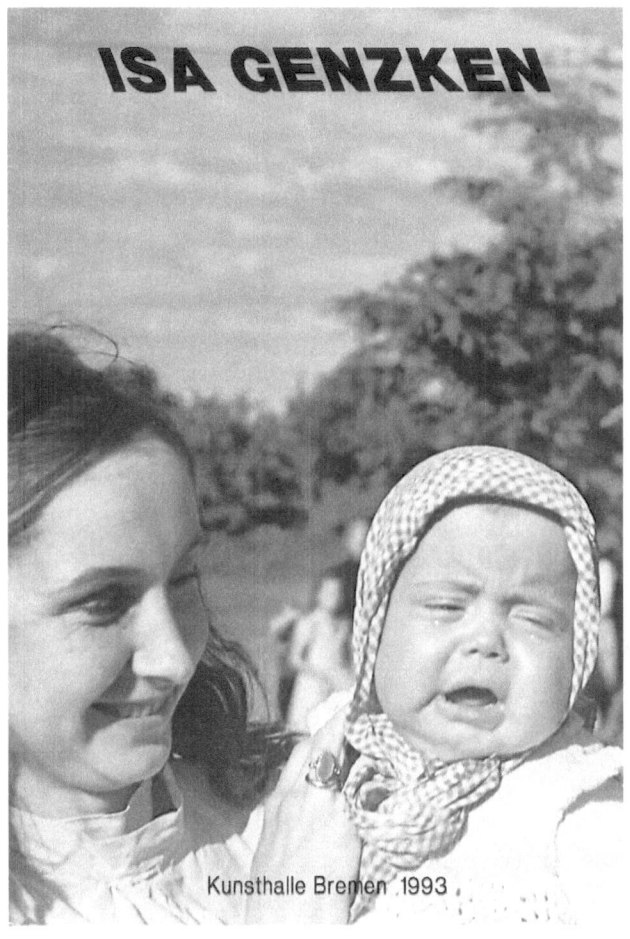

Cover of the catalog for Isa Genzken's exhibition at Kunsthalle Bremen, 1993.

I Bad Oldesloe, November 1948

27 November 1948: a cold, rainy afternoon in Bad Oldesloe, a small town on the North German Plain.

A man on a red bicycle, not much more than thirty, is peddling at top speed toward a large, red-brick building, the local hospital. Uwe Genzken, for that is his name, abandons his bike at the entrance, races up the steps and into the maternity wing, where he runs past a long line of beds until he comes to his wife.

She's beaming, "Look Uwe, it's a girl."

He smiles at the baby—a little hesitantly, awkwardly—and asks his wife, "What's her name?"

"I don't know yet," she replies, "maybe Petra. I was actually hoping for a boy."

Uwe bends down over the child and says, "Hanne-Rose, that's your name, like your mother."

II Bad Oldesloe, February 1949
an attic room

A sparsely furnished attic room with sloping walls and a round window; water is dripping from the leaky ceiling. Close under the window there's a laundry basket with a blue umbrella attached to it; it's there to protect the baby lying quietly in among brightly colored cushions. Suddenly someone unlocks the door and comes in; Uwe rushes toward the basket and picks up his child.

He clasps the baby with both hands and covers her with extravagant kisses. She starts to cry.

"Oh, sweetie, don't cry, Papa will make you some food."

With the baby on one arm, he prepares some porridge at the cooker, takes the pan from the hotplate and allows the food to cool a little.

He feeds the child with a little spoon. "There you are, eat up nicely, there you are, eat up nicely.... Mama will be back very soon, but now Papa has to go out again."

Swiftly he puts Isa back in the basket and leaves.

The room falls silent again.

III the same place, October 1949

The basket with the baby is still standing in the same place.

Her father has put a ladder up next to the basket and is using a hand-brush to dust the curtain rod. The dust drifts down onto the basket. Lenna, the child's godmother, is watching and cries out in indignation, "Uwe, the dirt is falling down onto the baby, can't you see?"

He smiles down from the ladder and goes on dusting.

He's in a good mood.

IV the same place, October 1949

The father and the godmother are sitting by Isa in her basket; she's playing happily with a ball.

Her mother, laden with shopping bags, comes into the room and greets the aunt, "Hi, how's it going?"

"Look, I've sewn a beautiful nightie for Isa," says the aunt and shows it proudly to the child's mother. Hanne looks at the nightie, picks up a pair of scissors lying on the table and cuts off both sleeves.

"Isa doesn't like sleeves."

She gives the nightie back to the godmother, who is gazing at her in stunned amazement.

V Hamburg, Sophienterrasse 15a, June 1950

A grand residence in a beautiful location, near the Alster, with a small, formal front garden, of the kind that so many old Hanseatic houses have. It's a bright, sunny day.

From inside the room with empty white walls, stucco ceiling, and parquet floor, there's a view out through the floor-to-ceiling windows to an untended, overgrown garden.

Inside the room there are a few garden chairs standing around and a large mattress on the floor. Despite the paltry furnishings the room creates the impression of luxurious yet bohemian spaciousness.

In one corner of the room there's a child's cot, separated and protected from the rest of the room by a cupboard.

Isa is lying in the bed, asleep. There's no one else there.

VI   the same place, June 1950

The door to the garden is open; the atmosphere is welcoming and summery.

The child's father is sitting in one of the chairs, poring over an anatomy book; all around him there are stacks of medical textbooks.

Hanne comes into the room, greets the studious father, looks around, and asks, "Where's the baby?"

"I put her in the garden, the sun's so lovely. I think she's sleeping."

Hanne goes into the garden to find her. A few seconds later she screams out loud, "She's dead. Get a doctor, now! Do something!"

In her mother's arms, the child's face has a blue tinge.

"What's happened?" her father cries in disbelief.

"Her pillow, on her face, couldn't breathe. No idea how long…," she stammers.

He takes the girl in his arms, lays her down on the table, gently strokes her, moves her arms to and fro, massages her little body. After a while Isa opens her eyes and blinks at her parents. They both sigh with relief.

VII   the same place, 1952

Isa has an unbelievably soothing dream.

She's flying. Very slowly she floats across huge, wide meadows filled with flowers in all colors. Cows and sheep are grazing in the meadow and they look up tenderly toward her.

Isa feels completely at ease and opens her eyes just a little. She hears the sound of the sea from far away, murmurings and other sounds, and she feels the gentleness of the air all around her.

VIII   the same place, 1954

In the garden. Uwe and Hanne are sitting facing each other in blue garden chairs. Dialogue:

H: Miracles like that just don't happen.

U: Of course there aren't miracles in medicine, but these days you can do a lot to minimize the effects of epilepsy.

He strokes her hair.

H: Although, I'd say my father worked miracles, real miracles!

U: He's a real man of the world, your father. Perhaps I'll go to sea soon and learn how to do that, too. I want to be a great doctor, if not a great orchestral conductor.

H: You're far too lazy to become anything great.

U: Be nice to me, please. I am terribly lazy, I know, but what can I do about it? Help me, please!

He looks at her pleadingly.

H: You just need devote yourself to whatever you're doing. You're far too much of an egoist! You've always got a bad conscience because all you do is chase your daily fix of pleasure. Sadly, that's how it is.

Uwe pulls a face.

U: Come on, stop it. You and your endless reproaches! I just love life.

Pause.

Best of all I'd like to get away from here, far away…Australia or America, emigrate somewhere really far away. We could go together.

H: Okay, why not? Let's think about it.

IX   the same place, June 1952

Night-time, the room is dark and quiet.

Suddenly the door is wrenched open, the light goes on, and all at once the room is flooded with light. Uwe and Hanne, the worse for drink, stagger into the garishly lit room.

Uwe makes straight for the record player, Maria Callas is heard at full volume. He goes behind the cupboard, draws himself up by Isa's bed and shouts with drunken fervor at the child, who is by now wide awake: "Listen! Just listen to that! That's the most famous singer in the world. Maria Callas. It's important for you. Listen! That music is coming from her guts. From her guts, not from here."

He points at his forehead.

"Piangete voi? Al dolce guidami." ("Are you weeping? Lead me back.")

X the same place, June 1953

Sunday Afternoon

Isa is sitting alone on the floor, wearing a pink-and-white dress and black patent-leather shoes. Lying on the floor around her are all kinds of drawing utensils, brushes, and paint boxes—a lot more than she needs at the moment.

She is drawing big faces and coloring them with watercolors. She's not bothered if the paint drips on her dress. She's humming and seems to be lost in concentration.

Suddenly she stands up; she lays all the painted sheets on the floor in a row. Carefully she steps back a little and looks at her pictures.

"I like this one a lot." She points to one with a big face, rolling its eyes upward. "This is me. That one's Papa and that's Mami. Papa is green, Mami's yellow. Papa's stupid, Mami's stupid, too!"

Then she starts clearing her things away, putting everything carefully under her bed. She sits down in one of the deck chairs very close to the window and looks out into the garden.

Very quietly she whispers, "I haven't had anything to eat yet today."

XI the same place, June 1954

A sunny afternoon.

The camera pans slowly along the fronts of the houses. It stops at 15a.

Isa, who has been standing in the open front doorway, steps outside. She walks daintily through the garden to the road.

Suddenly a voice from behind asks, "What's your name?"

She turns her head and finds herself gazing into a friendly-looking man's face.

"Would you like to star in a film?" he asks.

"Yes," she replies, shyly.

XII   Hamburg, June 1954

An elegant café on the shores of the Außenalster.

Hanne Genzken and a young man are sitting together, talking:

YM: …No, I'm not married, I pour all my energy into my films.

H: I can see that—you're a serious person. I'm not averse to your ideas. Do you believe in a light other than the future?

She smiles sideways at him.

YM: I believe in the light that is in film, that's my life. I would be very happy if you would allow your daughter to take part in my next project.

She looks down.

H: Yes, yes, of course, she can certainly do that.

XIII   Hamburg, September 1954—after the last day of shooting

A simple Italian restaurant.

A large crowd of people is sitting at a long table, eating, drinking, and talking. It's noisy.
        The woman sitting next to Isa says, "By the way, the dresses and soft toys we bought for you while we were filming, they all belong to you, now!"
        Isa sobs a little.

XIV   Hamburg, by the River Elbe, 1956

A Sunday walk in winter. Isa and her mother are clambering on big, white lumps of ice.

I: Mami, imagine there were horses here, real horses.

M: I've never seen any here. Come on, let's fight against the icy wind instead. That's healthy!

I: See, the ice looks like big wrecks, ruins. It's beautiful, but I'm cold.

M: Look at the seagulls, they're not cold. Just imagine you're a seagull.

XV   Düsseldorf, February 1978
Academy of Art, end-of-term party

Klaus Rinke has invited everyone to a huge Academy party. All the
teaching rooms are filled with multicolored, wild decorations. In the
corridors real, live creatures are running and flying around, making
noises and primal-forest sounds. You really can see elephants, apes,
giraffes, and birds. All the rooms and passages are overflowing with
people and animals. Isa has come with her friend Anne, who's from
Chicago. The two girls are speechless.

There's a bar on the second floor.
    Around it there's a group of artists who used to study together—
Thomas Schütte, Thomas Struth, and Gerhard Martini.
    Opposite this bar there's a champagne bar.
    Standing around over there are members of staff who used to teach
them—Gerhard Richter and other professors.

GR *calls out*: Hello, Ms. Genzken, long time no see! Nice to see you
again. How are you? Might I invite you and your friends for a glass of
champagne?

IG: Yes, absolutely.

After another few rounds of champagne:

GR: Ms. Genzken, I'd very much like to dance with you.

XVI   New York, in the Kiew, a Russian bar, December 1979[1]

Dan Graham and Isa are sitting together, talking:

DAN: You should go to Crazy Eddy, they have all the things very cheap
there. Tape recorders, cameras, and so on. If you want, I go with you.
    Also tonight there is a concert at the Pyramid Club. Kim and
Thursten are playing maybe very late, but you should definitely go
there. I know you will like it, you should take your camera with you.

ISA: Okay. I go. Are you coming too?

Dan, I have to tell you, your work has really changed a lot in the last time from video to architecture. The last two pavilions you did, I love them.

They have a psychedelic quality. They are a real surprise! The social aspect in it is very sublime to me. It's more romantic and has a family function in it.

DAN: Isa, you are very nice to me.

ISA: I know you long enough to know your needs.

DAN: Okay, let's go.

XVII –1–

Cologne, March 1988

Isa and Gerhard are sitting together in their kitchen over a glass of wine.

I: Gerhard, the question that bothers me most is, why you love me.

Gerhard smiles.

G: That's too complex, it's far too big a question, there's no way of answering that.

I: Yes, but it could be that there's some kind of an answer, even if it is that complicated.

G: But you also have to bear in mind that I've got flu at the moment.

I: It could be that you might just come up with something or other…

Gerhard gazes at her for a while.

I: Just one answer in the midst of all the confusion that one always feels.

Gerhard says in a very decisive voice: Because I need you!

I: That's nice, I'm pleased.

G: So it seems.

I: It's the same for me. Although sometimes I have the feeling that I might be mistaken, but I do have the feeling that we're a very special couple.

G: Well, you know history is full of special couples. We might be, but we can't know that yet, and I wouldn't be all that keen on the idea anyway, because it seems to me that that always involves some kind of tragedy, which makes me afraid, so in fact I'd rather we were not a special couple.

XVII –2–

I: Oh, I see, but for me it's very different, the way I think about it, it's exactly the opposite of tragedy, for me it's about the future and not Kleist and all that.

G: If anything, I'd say we were an especially odd couple.

I: Ideas come about that are sacred, that are of value, that's the reason why I love you.

XVIII Chicago, Mayfair Regent Hotel, June 1992

Isa is standing at the window, leaning out a little. She's fantasizing about her Chicago film.
    She is gazing out directly over Lake Michigan.
    The huge lake looks like the sea.
    Running along the edge of the water there is a wide, sandy, public beach.
    The people of Chicago can swim there and relax, right in the middle of the city.
    It's a wonderful sight.

XIX Cologne, Buchholz und Buchholz, antiquarian bookshop and small exhibition space, June 1993

Thinking about an exhibition project.
    Michael Hengsberg and Isa are sitting in the front shop, talking about their next exhibition in September 1993.

M: And you really want to go with that wallpaper idea?

I: It would work well in this small space, but I'm not quite sure yet.

She turns round and looks toward the back of the shop.

It would be good if we could free up the skylight, then the space would have natural light.

M: I don't think that's possible. The window's just recently been covered over with tarred roofing felt. It would be too expensive to remove it, and then the whole ceiling would start leaking again.

I: Too bad!

She ponders.

What about if I make two standard lamps?

M: What sort of standard lamps?

I: For instance, with a colored light that slowly moves and casts shadows and patterns on the walls.

M: That would completely alter the dimensions of the space. I like that idea.

I: Yes, exactly, you'd have a sense of the space, but no more than that.

M: It could have a time switch. Once a minute the normal light would go on, which would create a kind of nakedness for that moment. Suddenly the room is as it is.

I: Yes, that's a good idea. A bit like lightning, and perhaps some wallpaper, too. Everything a room needs.

XX   Bremen, Kunsthalle, Sunday, 18 July 1993, 11:30 a.m.

Opening of the Isa Genzken exhibition, *Jeder braucht mindestens ein Fenster* (Everyone Needs At Least One Window).

Isa is standing alone in the Kunsthalle's exhibition space. Her works are well presented. Little by little the first visitors arrive. She loves that North-German accent.

In the museum's main lecture room the opening speeches are starting.

The director of the museum stands at the lectern in front of the audience, welcoming the guests.

He says he is delighted that so many have come.

As he thanks the artist for realizing this exhibition he peers into the audience, trying to spot her.

But Isa has found a place near the back.

When he can't see her anywhere, he continues with his talk and gives a chronological account of the development of her work.

Translated by Fiona Elliott.

Notes

1. Section XVI appears in English in the original. [Editor's note.]

Free to Be Dependent: Concessions in the Work of Isa Genzken

Isabelle Graw

Torn This Way and That

At first sight, the work of Isa Genzken seems classical. This may stem from the very art-like look of the early objects in particular: streamlined configurations such as the so-called Ellipsoids, with the look of aerodynamic forms or canoes. They appear classical, partly because they stake their claim to autonomy through catalog illustrations that present them as isolated and self-sufficient objects.[1] We initially look in vain for any trace of the circumstances of the artist's life. At a second glance, however, this impression is impossible to maintain. Genzken's earlier and later works alike contain covert or overt references to the relationship between artistic and social concerns. This is not to say that she undertakes any analysis of society. The signs that stand for "society" exist on a metaphorical plane—as, for instance, in titles or in the mode of installation, in which social factors regularly leave telltale traces. In the earlier installations, for example, elongated wooden shapes were set on the floor, while the Hi-Fi series hung on the wall behind them: photographs of advertisements for record players, which served as clues to an external reference. Again, Genzken's works in concrete were often to be found close to a window, suggesting a connection with the outside world.

These references to the outside world were even more manifest in the titles: *Halle* (Hall) (1987) or *Tor* (Gate) (1987), as names for large blocks of concrete, gave these the status of architectural models with a reference to reality or a potential existence in reality. The same went for

Genzken's projects for public sculpture, in which she often anticipated the realization of the work by incorporating collaged photographs of herself (as in *Entwurf für eine Gartenskulptur* [Design for an Garden Sculpture], 1986) or of influential art world figures (Kasper König with his wife alongside *Model für einen Brunnen* [Model for a Fountain], 1987), just as if the projects had already been approved and executed. This is a device commonly used by architects to emphasize the feasibility of their projects.

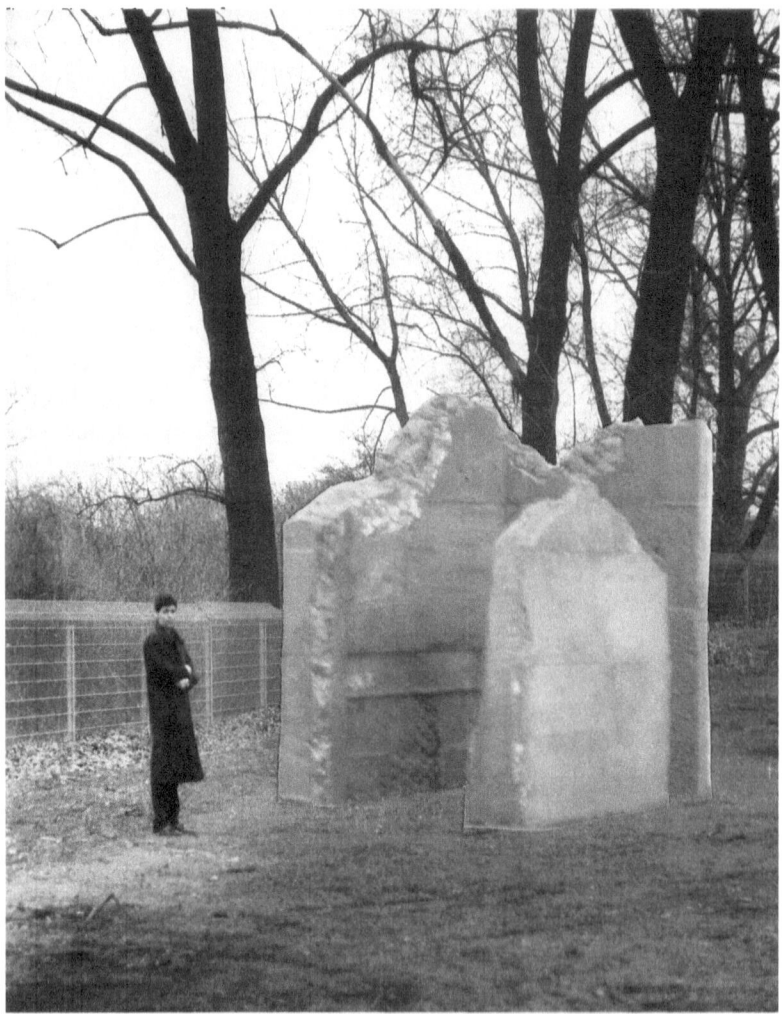

Untitled (Entwurf für eine Gartenskulptur) (Design for a Garden Sculpture), 1986. Collage, design for Projekt Stoffel, Cologne.

The fact that a work of art (or of architecture) aims for social recognition does not in itself mean that it lays claim to a social function. Which is why it must be emphasized that, despite their architectural allusions, Genzken's craggy plaster fragments and massive concrete walls signal their presence primarily as sculpture. This is indicated first of all by the presence of supports: the thin steel frames that serve as bases for the concrete sculptures. The artistic takes priority; why else, in her *Haus* (House) (1985), would areas of social function, such as rooms, be left out in favor of a ruin-like uncouthness of form?

Far more marked than Genzken's interest in urban realities is her impulse to create architectonic form. A study of architectural students has shown this bias to be typical of the males, who manifest a "form-centered approach." Women's designs, by contrast, are said to employ smaller spaces and display a utilitarian bias.[2]

So it seems that Genzken's works should be categorized under a mode of working traditionally identified as male. Of course, even the choice of art form—sculpture, a traditionally male preserve—in itself implies adaptive mimesis. Conformity in formal terms may well turn out to be a kind of admission ticket. This does not necessarily mean that the individual has to compromise either self or principles. On the contrary, the presence of adaptive reflexes goes to show that individual identities are inseparable from their environments.

To the same degree in which Genzken's works reflect definitions of sculptural quality, they also contain personal references. This is evident in a photograph of her work *Haus* (1985), in which Gerhard Richter—to whom Genzken was then married—can be seen apparently entering it. For every concession to artistic criteria (modeled, painted plaster) there is an acknowledgment of social factors. Thus, in the famous *Weltempfänger* (World Receiver), only the antenna affixed to the concrete block makes the association with "radio" inescapable.

Even so, where individual and social factors merge, they mostly do so on a metaphorical level. In this light, the ear images (1986) can be read as an instance of a personal distinguishing feature that coincides with a receiving point for social contacts—a double coding that also characterizes the catalog *Jeder braucht mindestens ein Fenster* (Everyone Needs At Least One Window) (1992). Photographs that look private (Genzken naked in a hip bath) are followed by strings of photographs of exhibition scenes. Not that the catalog abolishes the distinction between private life and art; but a distinction that was previously quite clear begins to shift.

How is this artistic evolution to be explained? It rests on decisions governed by social and artistic constraints. In order to understand works of art, it is necessary to reconstruct this interplay between a specific logic of production and other factors.

The Inclination Toward Autonomy

Isa Genzken was born at Bad Oldesloe, between Hamburg and Lübeck, in 1948. Her socialization process as an artist took place in the 1970s, a decade commonly associated with artistic experimentation, process art, conceptual art, and politicization. When Benjamin H. D. Buchloh now recalls, in his text on Genzken, that she was then concerned with salvaging the concept of autonomy, which is central to bourgeois art, this initially comes as a surprise.[3] Was she totally unaffected by all the contemporary arguments in favor of the equivalence of art and life? Or was she deliberately setting out to counter them? The numerous techniques that lend her work its aura of autonomy tend to point to the second alternative. Genzken regularly changed styles, providing a constant succession of surprises: horizontal works in wood were followed by plaster models, then works in concrete and later epoxy resin hoods.

When new phases come in, the effect on the viewer is often that of a fait accompli. This applies above all when—as in Genzken's case—the innovations can only be either described in formal terms or inferred from the internal evidence of the works themselves. The changes seem to be very obviously couched in terms of form and material: plaster replaced by concrete. With such an emphasis on formal criteria, who is going to dare to trace these works back to personal or historical factors? Indeed, the adherents of formalistic art history can point to the presence of all their criteria (one of which is innovation).

However, it remains an obvious fact that, when artists make apparently inexplicable changes of direction, they may perfectly well have social considerations in mind (one of which might be that of attracting attention). Pablo Picasso and Robert Morris are just two examples of artists who have used sudden U-turns to mobilize interest in their work. Genzken had every reason to expect the same result in her own case.

I remember, for instance, the adverse reaction of some people in the art world to her lamp paintings. Their criticism was, however, always expressed in the form of arbitrary judgments of taste, on the lines of "good" and "bad." These subjective opinions mostly derived from a judgment made on formalistic criteria. The preponderance of formal responses to Genzken's production must also, however, be seen as an answer to a body of work that went out of its way to emphasize its arbitrary nature. Only in relation to Genzken's own specific artistic context does this mode of operation on her part become comprehensible.

The dominant artists in the Cologne/Düsseldorf area have long been those whose work is largely devoid of personal or social references. One need only think of Imi Knoebel, Blinky Palermo, and Ulrich Rückriem. Gerhard Richter, too, under whom Genzken studied in Düsseldorf between 1973 and 1978, has stated in interviews that he does not want to see the world in a personal way and that he regards art with a message as stupid.[4] This is a view that Genzken probably shared. It is only recently, with his *Atlas* (1996), that Richter has begun to disclose personal sources: his new paintings are about "private happiness."

Genzken's situation has never been comparable—then or now—with that of such artists as Richter or Sigmar Polke. Unlike them, she *had* to minimize the "personal" factor as far as possible. Where Polke and Richter photographed each other in bed at the Hotel Diana (1967), Genzken steered clear of all such performance-linked activities. Polke's occasional use of his own figure (Polke as a palm tree, for example) has not affected the general assessment of his work. But if Genzken had put her own body on show in this way, she would have risked being reduced to the label "Woman."[5]

Is this why she was so laconic and aloof in the few interviews that she gave? She demonstrated a reserve that reminds us of the taciturnity of Palermo, whom she valued highly. By refusing to make a statement, Palermo sent out the message that his work was meant to speak for itself.[6] In Genzken's case, however, what enforced her silence was her social status as a woman artist. Immediate reactions to her work, in particular, must have confirmed her conviction that every additional word would be a word too many. Her sculptures were accused of being, "in their seemingly phallic hypertrophy, the typical product of female hysteria."[7] Hard though she tried to lend them a neutral, sculptural aura, the fact that she was a woman impinged on the metaphorical interpretations of her viewers. There was no sign of the disinterested pleasure that is the expected reaction to artworks designed to be autonomous. This made Genzken all the more determined to give away no personal information, and to keep her work free of allusions to "Woman."

To gain recognition as an artist, was it therefore necessary to deny any connection between art and gender? That depended on the circles you moved in. In the late 1970s there were, of course, some women artists who took up the slogan of the Women's Movement: "The personal is political." Ulrike Rosenbach, for instance, founded a feminist school in Cologne in 1976 and labeled her own works "feminist." For Genzken, this was not a possible option, because it would have taken her in the opposite direction from the canon that was her objective. In terms of a dominant, male logic, she would have been disqualified as a serious artist. Logically enough, therefore, Genzken adopted exclusively male mentors, Barnett Newman, El Lissitzky, Dan Graham[8]: names that art history associates with paradigmatic turning points. To gain admittance to such a pantheon, Genzken had to deliver work whose formal aspects carried conviction in terms of the artistic ideas that then enjoyed a hegemony.

Institutions such as Museum Haus Lange in Krefeld or Galerie Konrad Fischer in Düsseldorf would never have taken an interest in Genzken's work if she had presented herself as a feminist.[9] They promoted an avant-garde that did not express its advanced nature through explicitly political or personal content. Among the artists represented by Fischer were Carl Andre, Ulrich Ruckriem, and Daniel Buren (whose work can after all be interpreted in formal terms). It was no accident that the same gallery's women artists included Hanne Darboven—and Genzken herself. Both made artistic propositions to which the "Woman" identity did not seem relevant.

The manner of Genzken's self-presentation as an artist reveals that she was trying to disengage art from the social position defined by the word "Woman." There are, for example, photographs in which Genzken stands upright with arms folded, next to a reclining Ellipsoid (1981) but making no attempt to relate to it. In another photograph (1995) she holds out a Hyperbolo toward the viewer, as if claiming authorship of something completely detached from herself. Again, in *Meister Gerhard* (1983), she sits beside her work and at a little distance from it—as if to avert the psychological implications contained in the title. These attempts to counter the glib attempt to equate life with work are entirely understandable in the light of the traditional response to women artists. Now, as ever, there is a pronounced tendency to read their works as 1:1 copies of their lives.[10]

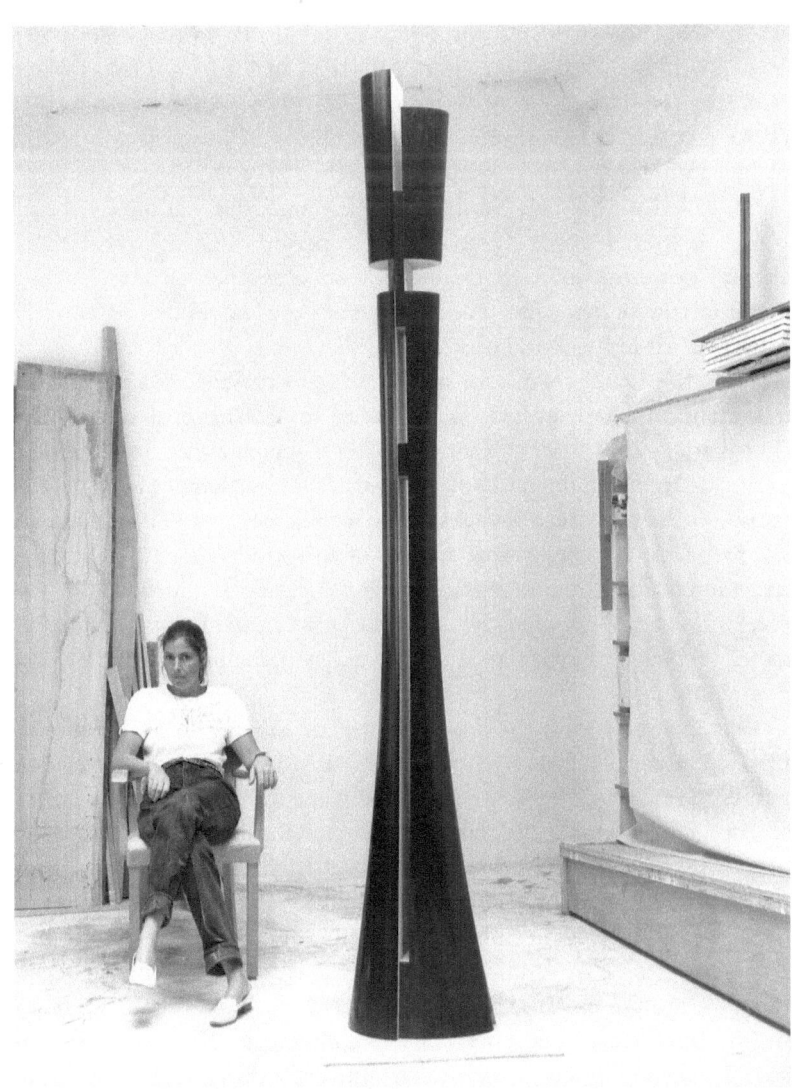

Meister Gerhard, 1983. Studio view with Isa Genzken, Düsseldorf, 1983. Lacquered wood.
292 × 48 × 32 cm.

In this context, it must be borne in mind that in the 1980s there existed exhibitions of women's art with titles like *Typisch Frau* (Typical Woman) (1981) and *Die andere Avantgarde* (The Other Avant-Garde) (1983). As soon as a woman identified herself as an artist, she was bound to be subsumed within a "female" aesthetic.[11] Genzken's reluctance to be identified as a "female" artist meant that her name was mostly absent from the women's art exhibitions of the period.[12] To my knowledge, she did not work in cooperation with other women artists. Genzken opted for the individualist model of the artist, a model that perennially reasserts itself in the world of art.

Did this strategy work for her? Genzken's presence at a number of important landmark events on the route to international recognition (Documenta 1981, 1992; Westkunst 1981) suggests that it did. However, this kind of individual advantage pales into insignificance by comparison with the concomitant structural disadvantages. The price that has to be paid for individual success of this kind is that it leaves the structures of the art business unchanged, because untouched. On the level of society as a whole, too, the split between the individual and the social, between the private and the political, helps to maintain the dichotomy that reinforces social inequalities.

Paradoxically enough, this very idea of clinging to an individual, private life—as practiced by Genzken—is now being advocated by some feminist theorists. They see the secluded space of "the private" as necessary for the unfolding of "autonomous individuality."[13] Certainly, the private sphere has aspects that are well worth protecting; to make them public would signify only control or punitive discipline. But that is not to deny that the private sphere is pervaded by social power relations. The very idea of an "autonomous subject" is itself problematic—even though situations can arise that make it necessary for women artists to go on the offensive in reclaiming or exemplifying it. Not every woman artist is able at any given time to assume a self-image that replaces the idea of the autonomous subject by the concept of social linkage.

Genzken herself was one of those artists who avoided naming their own sources in order to present themselves as self-confident and independent. In the catalog *Schlaglichter* (Highlights) (1979), when asked to name her artistic influences, she answered laconically, "All progressive artists." In this way she snatched back the power of definition: it was for her to say who was or was not a progressive artist. Her refusal to admit to influences was also prompted by the widespread assumption that, by definition, women artists are the recipients of influence. Regularly, the first question asked of any female producer of art is "What artists have influenced you?" The artists then often go to the opposite extreme and deny being influenced by anybody. This does not necessarily mean that they regard themselves as autonomous subjects.[14]

Do women artists, whose public statements are so often discussed in private terms (problems, dependencies; see for example the heavily biographical interpretations of the later work of Eva Hesse), have an interest in eliminating any linkage between private and public spheres? The only alternative model currently available is the display of personal experience—or so the work of the women artists currently successful in Germany would suggest. Either their art is labeled "female" and transposes private events into public ones (Rebecca Horn); or else it appears—at least as conventionally and superficially observed—to be totally gender-free, as with Hanne Darboven or Katharina Fritsch. Both approaches are tantamount to collusion with the public/private dichotomy that is basic to the structure of bourgeois societies.

Personal Politics

Over the last few years, Genzken's works have included numerous coded references to the private dimension of her life. This is not to say that they necessarily reveal the "truth" about it. What emerges in the catalog *Skizzen für einen Spielfilm* (Sketches for a Feature Film) (1993) is a fragmentary biographical construct. This includes, for example, an imaginary conversation with Gerhard Richter and a brief dialogue with Dan Graham. Genzken has high praise for Graham's pavilions; her interest in his work is also evident in her own *Spiegel* (Mirror) (1990) and *Camera* (1990).

Genzken's early fear of admitting to an influence has thus been replaced by a confident handling of that influence. It was Genzken who took the initiative in this demonstration of personal relationships. In summer 1996 she conducted an interview with Lawrence Weiner. Why is it that Genzken can now allow, indeed encourage, her name to be linked with those of other artists? One possible answer would be that the artists concerned are exclusively male artists of high status, whose willingness to become involved signifies that they respect Genzken's work.

This serves to consolidate Genzken's position as their artistic equal. Her status also results from the institutional recognition that she has gained from a succession of museum exhibitions in recent years.[15]

Nonetheless, there is no causal relationship between recognition and the courage to reveal oneself—in spite of the numerous celebrated artists whose late work is crammed with confessional and autobiographical material. In Genzken's *Skizzen für einen Spielfilm* (1993) there are childhood scenes depicting the neglect suffered by the child Isa. This information, which appears authentic, is the kind of thing Genzken would never have revealed earlier in her career. Can she now afford to cast back to her childhood because she feels secure and enjoys greater self-confidence? The opposite might equally well be the case: success might be the cue for major crises of content, and for an anxious scrutiny of childhood. The significant thing, in Genzken's case, is that the seemingly autobiographical sequences in her film scenario are accompanied by illustrations of exhibitions. The borderline between the "private life" construct and the image of the public world becomes fluid. To put it another way: content is present, but only as modified by form.

Genzken's methods of formalization filter her objects—whether the photograph shows her feet in a hospital bed or preparations for her Chicago film in a hotel room.[16] As soon as there is content, it exists only in terms of dependency on formal interests, and vice versa. For instance, if more people than before now appear in the exhibition photographs, this is partly because their presence attests to the successful handling of social situations. Earlier, Genzken clung to total artistic control, showing her works in occupation of an otherwise empty exhibition space. Now she can acknowledge the significance of the social, and can link it with her own formal principles.

If eyewitness reports are to be believed, Genzken herself has always led an active social life—though no one would have guessed it, to judge from her early catalogs. In her Düsseldorf days she was one of the regulars in the artists' bars and at Konrad Fischer openings. When you meet her today, she strikes you as a very sociable person who likes to get involved. Why could she not express this interest in social life earlier, in her work?

The answer is that the dominant definitions of relevant contemporary art have changed. Nowadays many artists of both sexes regard it as imperative to deal with social issues and to integrate them symbolically into art. Genzken's work, however, never claims to analyze or register a fact: it confines itself to a phenomenological representation of the social. By contrast with Thomas Struth's photographs of visitors to exhibitions, which are investigative in their approach, hers have more of a lapidary character. Almost casually, Genzken pulls out the most varied stops in her catalogs: you barely notice the transitions between private and public.

This seamless linkage of disparate realms once more reminds us of current social developments, in which the private is more and more exposed to public intrusion (bugging) or goes out and makes itself public (talk shows)—quite apart from the economic redefinition of public space, which is increasingly becoming privatized. In light of these contemporary changes, should we not draw a firm line between the private and the public, and stick to it? The danger here would be that this would make us into the accomplices of an untenable dichotomy. Ought we not to take the concept of autonomy seriously, at least in specific situations, now that the private sphere is under siege from the State? This might work, within limits. In the wake of the current fashion for art as a service industry, the value of the artist's personal space might well once more be on the agenda. And Genzken is certainly one of those women artists who lay claim to that space, or who give symbolic expression to it (in spatial sculptures). But, on the other hand, in arguing in favor of autonomy, even for strategic reasons, we risk falling prey to the illusion that the artistic is free of the personal or the political. Genzken's recent works, and the catalog in particular, emancipate themselves from this illusion. The fact is that—even if the abolition of the private/public dichotomy, which is hinted at here, were to form a part of current deregulatory trends within society—there is still no way back.

Notes

1. See for example the illustrations in *Isa Genzken*, exh. cat. (Munich: Galerie Fred Jahn, 1986).

2. Marianne Rodenstein, "Mehr als ein Dach über dem Kopf: Feministinnen wollen 'Raum greifen und Platz nehmen,'" in *Die sichtbare Frau: Die Aneignung der gesellschaftlichen Räume*, ed. Margrit Brückner and Birgit Meyer (Freiburg: Kore Verlag GmbH, 1994), pp. 234–269.

3. Benjamin H. D. Buchloh, "Isa Genzken: From Model to Fragment," in *Isa Genzken: Jeder braucht mindestens ein Fenster*, exh. cat. (Cologne: Verlag der Buchhandlung Walther König, 1992), pp. 135–141.

4. Gerhard Richter, *The Daily Practice of Painting: Writings and Interviews 1962–1993*, trans. David Britt (Cambridge, Mass.: The MIT Press, 1995).

5. Gisela Wülffing, "Die öffentliche Frau: Ein vertrautes oder fremdartiges Zauberwesen?," in *Die sichtbare Frau*, pp. 57–75.

6. Fred Jahn, ed., *Palermo: Die gesamte Graphik und alle Auflagenobjekte, 1966–75, Sammlung J. W. Froehlich* (Munich: Galerie Fred Jahn, 1983).

7. See note 3.

8. See note 3.

9. Genzken exhibited jointly with Horst Schuler at the Museum Haus Lange in Krefeld in 1979, and in 1976 she showed at the Galerie Konrad Fischer.

10. See such current biographies of women artists as Mary Ann Caws's *Women of Bloomsbury: Virginia, Vanessa, and Carrington* (New York: Routledge, 1990) or Josyane Savigneau's biography *Marguerite Yourcenar: Inventing a Life*, trans. Joan E. Howard (Chicago: University of Chicago Press, 1993).

11. See also the issue devoted to "Frauen/Kunst/Kulturgeschichte," *Ästhetik und Kommunikation*, no. 25 (September 1976).

12. With the exception of the exhibition "Kunst mit Eigen-Sinn," Museum Moderne Kunst, Vienna, 1985.

13. Seyla Benhabib, "Feministische Theorie und Hannah Arendts Begriff des öffentlichen Raumes," in *Die sichtbare Frau*, pp. 270–300.

14. The writer Ingeborg Bachmann had a standard answer to the question of what poet had influenced her: "None." See Ingeborg Bachmann, *Wir müssen wahre Sätze finden: Gespräche und Interviews*, ed. Christine Koschel and Inge von Weidenbaum (Munich: Piper, 1983).

15. Exhibitions at the Renaissance Society, Chicago (1992), at Portikus, Frankfurt (1992), and at the Palais des Beaux-Arts, Brussels (1993).

16. As in the catalog *Isa Genzken: Jeder braucht mindestens ein Fenster*, op. cit.

There is a connection between electronic dance music and skyscrapers. This is nothing new. There is a connection between modern, in particular minimalist, sculpture and psychedelia. Nothing new here either.[1] Neither connection features in the relevant official discourses of legitimation. Those who normally justify and advocate skylines or minimalist objects take no notice of them. They are nevertheless, I'm convinced, present in the minds of all concerned with these things, especially those who produce them.

In 1980, the French/American label ZE produced a compilation with the title *Mutant Disco—A Discolation of the Norm*. Discolation was a play on disco and *dislocation*, an emerging buzzword at the time with a hint of deconstruction. Ian Penman wrote the liner notes. Penman in those days furnished the postpunk press with strange manifestos. Rich in Roland Barthes quotations, they praised the joys of a hybrid hedonism and of seductive, soft singing voices on the far side of protest and expression. It was no fluke that one of his heroes—also featured on *Mutant Disco*—was one Kid Creole, who ran around in the zoot suits favored by those Mexican and Caribbean migrants in the 1940s, whose subversive influence on the morale of All-American kids during World War II caused a cultural crusade to break out on the home front. Yes, gimme juicy ambiguities and creeping, creolized disco music. At that time the term "dance floor" didn't exist as a category, and House Music hadn't remotely been thought of. Prince had barely appeared above the parapet with "Sexuality." In the Paradise Garage DJ Larry Levan was in the process of developing the sound for long, uninterrupted dance nights out of S.O.S. Band remixes. The AIDS crisis prevented this phase of disco music from having any direct influence on the rise of House Culture in the late 1980s.

I was reminded of this record sleeve recently when I visited Isa Genzken's studio. Art spread through rooms and parts of rooms, yet

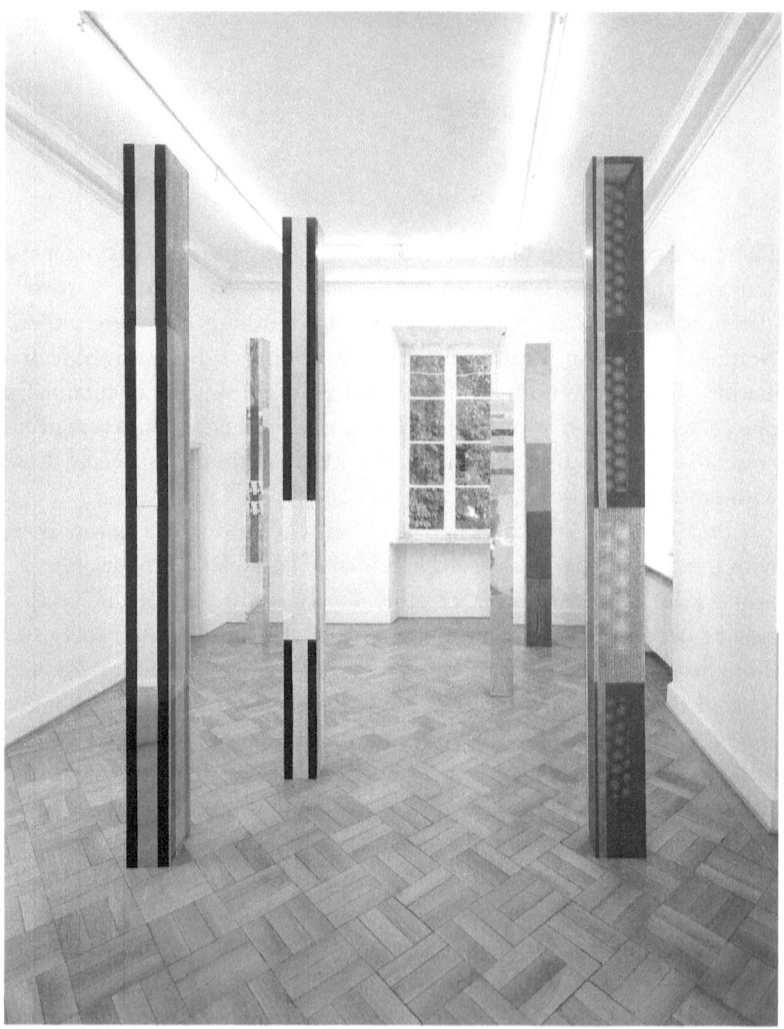

Installation view of *Isa Genzken: Sie sind mein Glück*, Kunstverein Braunschweig, Germany, 2000.

groups of works were left a private space to some degree. In one room, towers, enameled, painted, plastered with patches, and sprayed in different colors, gave me a sudden impression of a three-dimensional version of those skyscrapers, hand-colored with felt-tip marker on the sleeve of the *Mutant Disco* record. And yes, yes indeed, there was a connection between the specific, lurid, partly fluorescent decoration of these serial singles and the concept of nightlife and all-night dancing. These columnar sculptures jutted vertically into the heavens of the studio and at the same time entered into spatial relationships with their neighbors in close proximity. To be self-absorbed, tall and alone, and yet surrounded by others, and to know that these others in their unbridgeable individual ways feel exactly the same—the feeling of community that comes after another feeling of community that tastes of bitter drugs.

In the next room photographs of, in many ways discreet yet decisively decontextualized, Manhattan cityscapes lean against the wall. The right angles often out of kilter, tilted at oblique angles, they seemed curiously stilted, like poses in vogueing—and above all the sharply profiled outlines in the black-and-white photos often looked drawn, or engraved to be precise, rather than photographed. Despite having related subjects (verticalness) these simple-to-crude, mildly tragic sculptures and these elegant city photographs form no recognizable aesthetic connection. Yet they remained closely linked for me.

That houses should dance is an ancient longing. Things petrified are perceived as the converse of anything that might dance. To be set in stone is seen as the opposite of being capable of dance, and we didn't need Marx's bon mot to tell us. So the assertion that skyscrapers can be set in motion as on that record sleeve is in the first instance only one of efficacy: this music is so good that it even reaches its diametrical opposite. But beyond this topos there is another, more specific and deeper relationship between the dance ideas of the last thirty years and skyscrapers, and indeed also tower-shaped sculptures. And this relationship in its turn resembles the one between the psychedelic and the minimalist gaze, which—albeit rarely mentioned—existed in the 1960s, in my opinion.

Many 1960s minimalists, as is well known, took their cue from phenomenology via Merleau-Ponty. Perception had always been affected by diversion, contextualization, and multiple perspectives, and phenomenological reduction proposed its reduction as a means of achieving more concentrated comprehension or perception of the object or of anything taken out of its context in short-lived moments of stability. Minimalist presentation of objects and materials was intended to assist or encourage efforts of perception along these lines on the part of the viewer. This has been much discussed and criticized, defended and discarded, but most writers overlook the fact that psychedelic culture was pursuing a similar program at the same time.

Similar to "phenomenological reduction" in the reception of minimalism—but reducing minimalism's philosophical complexity to a chemically induced concept of decontextualized perception—the "psychedelic experience" focused interest on the world of daily use, on the everyday meaning of random objects, and on the transformation of things limited by function into things transcendental. All apologists of the LSD experience, from Leary to Ginsberg and including mescaline forerunners like Aldous Huxley, describe how magnificent but also how pathetic and ridiculous objects are when totally purged of all worldliness. In contrast to the phenomenological ἐποχή,[2] which consciously excludes or switches off knowledge and all its applications (say the scientific laws of time and space) with the methodical, neutral aim of increased cognition, the psychedelic ἐποχή is not neutral. It is intrinsically connected with a before and an after. It does not suspend in the interest of a pure judgment, but in order to laugh from the "pure" psychedelic standpoint at the world that is temporarily suspended.

This was a laughter that related partly to the contextual residue in a coffee cup or an automobile design, while the context itself—psychedelically and phenomenologically switched off—disappeared. Or it was the contrary—laughing at the briefly induced great void, the absence of context, the real. However there were two links between this experience and the world after it, one political, the other escapist. The possibility of linking the great laughter of contextlessness to the fundamental political insight that all cultural contexts are constructed and alterable was an obvious one in the 1960s. So too was the feeling that the dimensions of the experience were not to be reconciled with the world, not even if one contemplated totally revolutionizing it. On the one hand every ideological neutralization of the world and its condition lost its authoritarian terror and turned into a risible convention, on the other hand the possibility of such a distanciation of the world authority of ideology made many, even after the traditional dissolution of an even greater authority, turn to religion. In the thinking of figures like Allen Ginsberg or in a film like *Zabriskie Point* both possibilities are brought together.

However music as an instance of the *Aufhebung* of psychedelic experiences (i.e., its storing as well as its sublation), but also of debilitating and resocializing them, insinuated itself between these two possibilities, asceticism or revolution. Isa Genzken's Ellipsoids and Hyperbolos are the spatial representation of extreme extension and mathematically sublime curves, of inflation and contraction, and of the collective unconscious of the 1960s. But these are counterpointed by works that conjure up the immateriality of music: ears, world receivers, stereo units. Did music now stand for the loss of the psychedelic moment to an industry—or was the invisible resonance, the transmission of tones through amplifiers, headphones, and aerials precisely the point where something of these moments could survive?

In 1996 Isa Genzken made her own statement on the relationship between her work and music: "I have always thought that the plastic arts were the most important of all art forms. From time to time I have thought it's music, because it's so popular. But I think that the plastic arts are so important precisely because they are basically so unpopular. Because nobody recognizes what is so important, nobody sees it, it's only seen retrospectively…. Music is naturally extremely important too, because it relaxes like a sedative at this level."[3] The polarity between popular and unpopular that she opens up here and sets against another polarity, tension and relaxation, can be readily applied, in my opinion, to my thesis on how phenomenological processes in the 1960s found a pop-cultural echo in psychedelic culture, and how both are related to the problem of storing modes of experience that by their nature really invite the opposite of fixing and freezing.

If on the one hand popular and unpopular stand here for degrees of comprehensibility—how much is understood, and by how many—and if on the other hand we are talking about how one can ideally attain relaxation on the highest level of understanding—through music—then what is being outlined is an ideal of relaxed but intensive understanding, which is normally associated with privileged modes of cognition. That is, with moments of illumination, etc., which are often introduced in order to describe the psychedelic experience, but also to inscribe it in conventional and religious models. But these models involve neither the connection with the minimalist use of phenomenology nor the political dimension of the psychedelic experience, which originally mobilized its own particular privileged understanding in opposition to a world

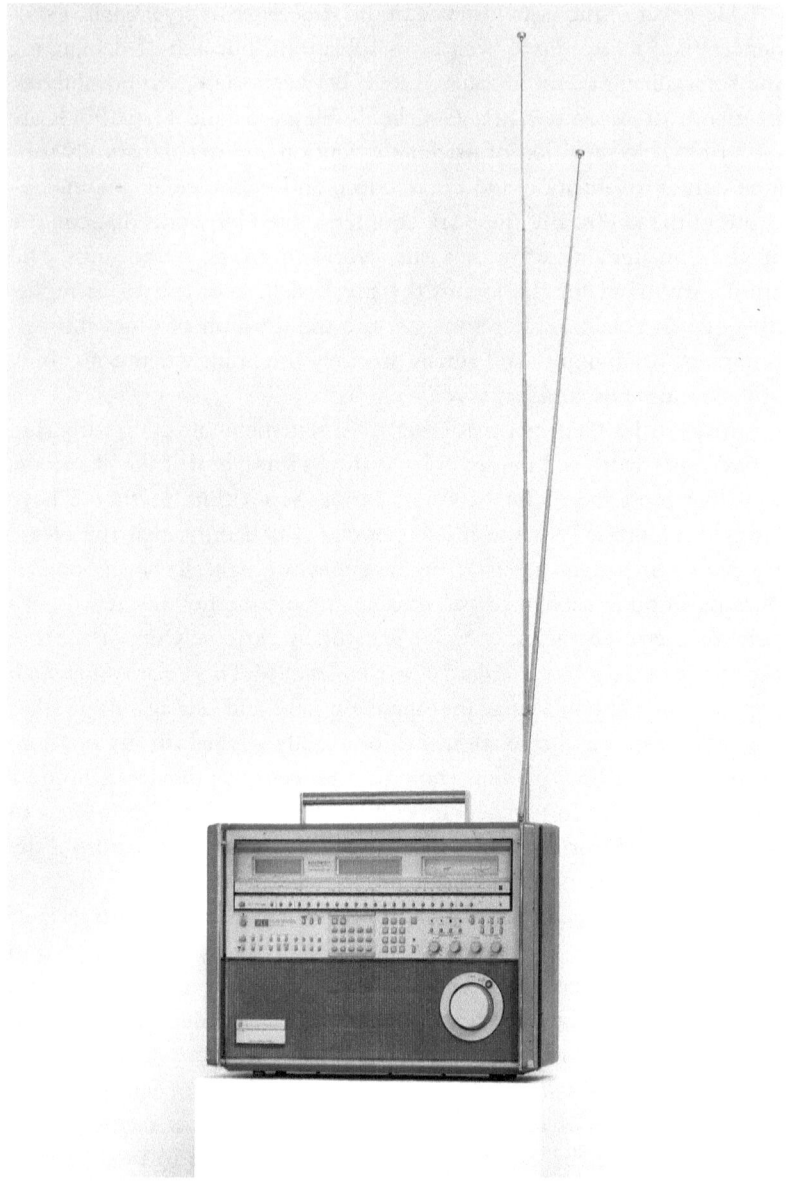

Weltempfänger (World Receiver), 1982. Multiband radio receiver. 37 × 51 × 20 cm.

that—in this reading—unmasked and exposed itself to ridicule with these cognitive and aesthetic weapons.

Genzken's sculptural works are not only distinguished by the combination of machine-like perfection with elements of arbitrariness and singularity. The special feeling for a particularly fine and successful exercise in modernism and for the simultaneous abject failure of that exercise, which characterizes all of Genzken's work, is particularly striking in her presentation of inclusion and exclusion. It is common knowledge that every white cube is ideologically connected to a version of exclusion, which in the course of time has drifted away from its heuristic-aesthetic basis to become convention and conservation. One can only recognize and enjoy art if one combines its reception with a recognizable act of exclusion. There were and are many ways of addressing or attacking this proposition. One of the less well known is the idea of confronting the bourgeois dream of pure cognition and pure art with a factually momentary act of "pure" cognition embedded in an extremely impure, mixed environment—hippie culture, city life, festivities. The idea of the Ellipsoids and the Hyperbolos could well be to freeze the elongation of sublimely failed modernity in a unique, grotesque moment, and to simultaneously celebrate its uniqueness—not as a monument to its failure, but as a psychedelic displacement of eternally growing columns. This displacement totally exposes the symbolic architecture of every white cube to ridicule, while at the same time sizing it up exactly and filling it out. The comic but authoritative solitary ground sculptures, with their virtually unlocalizable points of support and their illusion of permanent "lift," are counterpointed by the fluorescent, technoid finishes and coatings of the verticals. Fluorescent effects and certain strident Day-Glo colors stand for an incredibly cheap and "inadmissible" fixation on the psychedelic in the everyday culture of those worlds and milieus that would like to conserve (and re-sell) the misunderstood but sublime memories of those great moments. In their profane way they mimic the manner in which a garish, burning object approaches the psychedelically sensitized eye; they live on in Ibiza, San Francisco, etc. But these shrouds of the crucified 1960s have contrived to caparison the next, quite different use of psychedelic experiences, which we have known since the late 1980s, and which now comes under the comprehensive heading techno.

Precisely these colors were there from the beginning and were initially for the more extensive process of exclusion and suspension that was at the time called rave. The idea of total immanence for a limited time. A large group of people gathers for as long as possible (the end is left open on the understanding that it will inevitably come) and everything you do is related exclusively to the little temporary world of the rave. The music is so immanent that the only point of reference is the last beat. In contrast to all other arts, nothing on the outside is cited or named. There is no object on the outside, no stars of radio or television appear. All there is is the immanent festivity, and the only thing to relate to: the other dancers. The other column, wobbling, twisting, leaning, now hanging loose, now rigid again, toppling again, falling, and then standing again.

And afterward, nothing in the world has changed. And cultural critics are sometimes right when they say that the subjects subsequently, or after living through a longish phase of exclusive happiness, may even function better in unhappiness. They believe that happiness is based on exclusion and escape. On the other hand, after a rave, the effect of the gaze returns in a much more massive sense to the false world, indeed this is included in the calculation, much more than in the case of psychedelia. The chemically or euphorically oblique but sharper gaze of those who really were somewhere else. For within the psychedelic experience one was above all alone somewhere else, whereas in this case the experience was communal.

Isa Genzken's skyscraper sculptures, clad in technocolor, open up for me the whole connection between the psychedelic ἐποχή and the collective exclusion of world in techno rave. Neither represents escapism, but rather an attempt to raise the intensity of individual living within a ritual in which the impossibility of prolongation is inscribed. The price of intensity is brief duration, which however produces political and aesthetic insights in the moments that follow, and these open up a better view of conditions, one that is superior, new, different, and true. A luxury hangover, supreme heuristics. However much this may seem to smack of artistic romanticism—and this is not propagated in Genzken's work—it is, to a greater or lesser extent, the secret key to a significant part of the countercultural aesthetic philosophy of the last thirty or forty years. In Genzken's case it does not necessarily manifest itself in her method. The artist does not speak of psychedelic

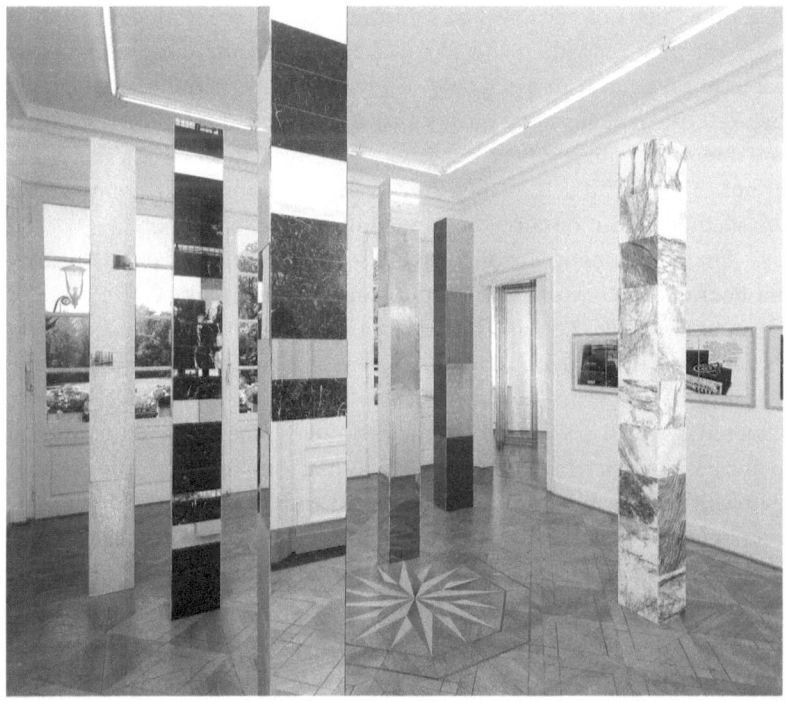

Installation view of *Isa Genzken: Sie sind mein Glück,* Kunstverein Braunschweig, Germany, 2000.

experiences, she prefers to speak of art and music, tension and relaxation. But it occurs in her motifs and in certain fundamental decisions, which, as described above, were already visible in the ground sculptures. There is a line in which their precise, mechanically contrived obliqueness and psychotropic extension combine with the Brancusi-Manhattan verticality and with the implication of an immaterial musical communication between these towering signs of a glorious, failed, admired modernism in retreat.

Step out of the Paradise Garage in 1983, after ten hours under rave conditions, but danced years too early, no alcohol, but drugs: Society is now just a husk, a fixed pose—architecture. The short-lived, intensely experienced, and collective exclusion of the world has made it possible to take precisely this now purely formal look at society. Only the shell of laws and rules is recognizable. These husks, the architecture, the skyscrapers as columns to the heavens dissolve strangely into the dancers, that other series of verticals I was surrounded by just a moment ago. Not only are they individual and identical in kind in the same serial sense, subjects at the end of a flagpole. They also wink at me encouragingly because of a certain tragic quality that is inherent in the project to wear me down to a point where my senses are forced to show me the world as out of joint as it is in reality. But I can see this not because my senses are sharpened, but because they are completely overwrought.

The permanently floating ground sculptures were classically beautiful because they synthesized a quite complex and multi-faceted line of thought in a unified entity. They were orientated to the relation of unity and complexity, which traditionally belongs to the complex of the *Naturschöne* (beauty in nature). The psychedelic culture of the 1960s adopted a similar procedure, often with duller senses, but sometimes in comparable fashion, when it established metonymic connections between objects in nature, often deployed emblematically, and the non-representable psychedelic intimations of ideally decontextualized, ludicrously sublime objects. The last step in this tradition was perhaps the fractal enthusiasm of aging hippies in the early days of techno (for example with The Orb). Genzken did not however proceed in linear fashion from this complex exercise in synthesis, but with her columns and other sculptural works in the 1990s she orientated herself more to simple forms and "low" materials. Solitaries are not better per se. They stand in the series, albeit quite alone and on their own feet, but only for the duration of a night—in order then to cast a glance on their serialized existence that holds them captive by day as well.

To confuse sculptures and people is obviously a peculiarly psychedelic effect, which the author underwent—for a certain time. Verticality remains a joke, as Tati knew long ago. Floating on air is another possibility.

Translated by Hugh Rorrison.

Notes

1. See Diedrich Diederichsen, "Psychedelische Begabungen—Minimalismus und Pop," in *Sharawagdi*, ed. Christian Meyer and Matthias Poledna (Cologne: Verlag der Buchhandlung Walther König, 1999).

2. Edmund Husserl, "Ideen zu einer reinen Phänomenologie und phänomenologischen Philosophie (Husserliana III/1)," in *Gesammelte Schriften*, Vol. 5 (Hamburg: Felix Meiner Verlag, 1992), p. 65.

3. Untitled note in Isa Genzken, *Met Life*, exh. cat. (Vienna: AE-Generali Foundation, 1996).

The Skyscraper at Ear Level

Pamela M. Lee

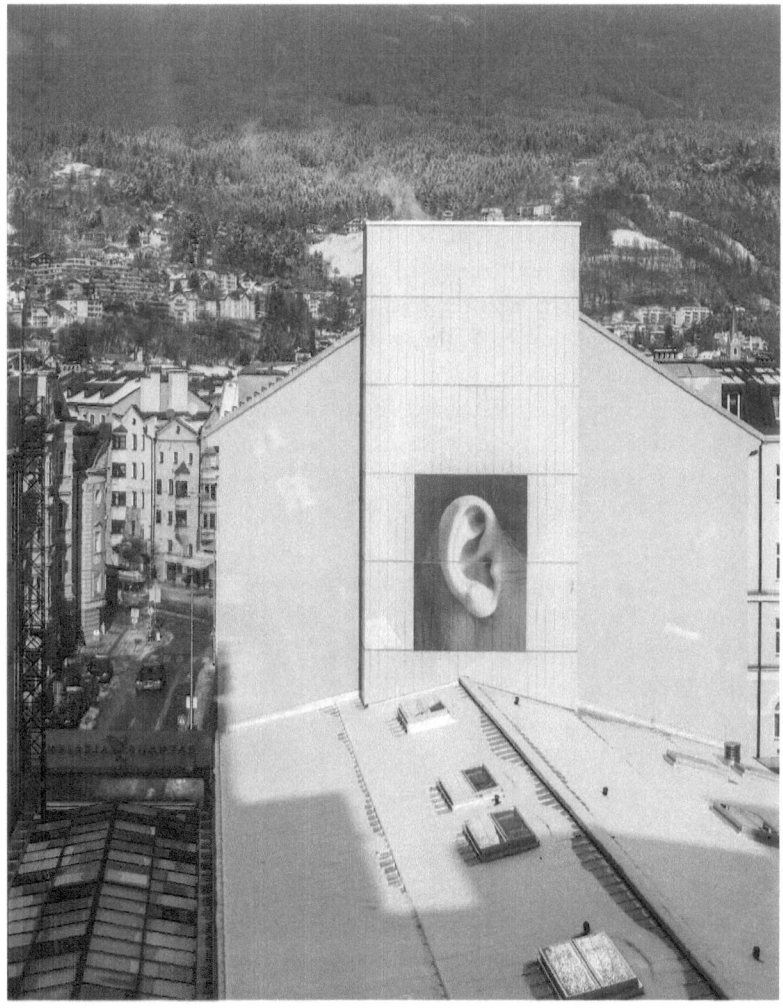

Ohr (Ear), 2002. Digital print on high-performance foil. Installation view at City Hall, Innsbruck, Austria. 580 × 390 cm.

The ear is uncanny. Uncanny is what it is; double is what it can become; large or small is what it can make or let happen (as in laisser-faire, since the ear is the most tendered and most open organ, the one that, as Freud reminds us, the infant cannot close); large or small as well the manner in which one may offer or lend an ear.

—Jacques Derrida[1]

There's an ear on the side of the building. I wonder what it hears. Set flush against a translucent paneled surface, a monumental ear—or rather, a digital print of one—stands several stories high above the city of Innsbruck, as if eavesdropping on some conversation down below. The fleshy lobe, an arabesque wisp of hair, the shadowed recess spiraling into the depths of the tympanum all stand in marked contrast to the featureless stripped-down side of the building upon which it appears. The ear is visible from inside the new, adjacent hotel with its shopping complex on the ground floor but is more difficult to read outside at street level. But whatever dissonance exists between the ear and the building—the one, a delicate, erogenous zone, the other a chill, inorganic presence—we, as viewers, tend to treat the two together. We see them as indivisible. The ear belongs to the building. Or maybe the building belongs to the ear. We don't read the ear as a surface ornament of the building—like the decorated shed of Robert Venturi's postmodern architecture—but somehow, as contiguous with our experience of that architecture. We might call this architecture at "ear level": at the threshold where the interior space of mental life represented by the ear—generally conceived as private—is intertwined with the public space of the architectural environment, experienced in stereo. Somewhere between the inside and out is the space occupied by the work of Isa Genzken, the artist who placed the ear on the building in 2002.

Let's admit the ear seems a strange opening into this discussion. It is strange because, as a motif, its appearance seems out of sorts from what we usually think of Genzken's architecturally-inflected sculpture: her brusque concrete fragments of the 1980s, the minimalist fenestrations from the early 1990s. More lately she has shown fields of "models" on plinths: rainbow prisms of glass, foil, and tape as in the *New Buildings for Berlin* (2001) or the vacation-home-by-way-of-the-fun-house aesthetic suggested by the works in the exhibition *Urlaub* (2000) or the ersatz skyscrapers, noisy with color and junk, that comprise *Fuck the Bauhaus: New Buildings for New York* (2000). And it is the eye, not the ear that we tend to associate with this work. The eye's movement of scanning the horizon of Genzken's sculptural objects seems analogous to the kinesthetic dimensions we bring to our experience of architecture in general. As Beatrix Ruf has persuasively written, "the importance and role of the 'eye level' from which we perceive her sculptures" is that of "a kind of filmic movement of the works themselves."[2] The "eye-level" perspective of Genzken's work, like that of Bruce Nauman's, is the perceptual horizon from which we conceive our individual relationship to architecture.[3]

This is hardly to deny the eye for thinking about Genzken's art, but somehow, in leaving the ear out of the picture, we get only half the story. As Maurice Merleau-Ponty reminds us, it is in the communion and integration of the senses that perception occurs; and the body, as much as it is a seeing body, is also "an object which ...reverberates to all sounds."[4] Attention to the ear might complete an understanding of Genzken's practice. If the eye's relationship to the human sensorium is binocular, facilitating the forward trajectory of our bodies as we move through space, the ear's implication of that space is stereographic, in the round. And because the ear is "the most open organ" as Derrida points out, it is a liaison between the self and the environment that is always porous, always ready to receive. At the same time, Derrida identifies the ear as "the most tendered" organ, suggesting something of the intimacy that it represents. Sensitized to register the external vibrations of the environment, the ear also internalizes the world outside it: it is a figure of the inside out. It is with this kind of perceptual balancing act (as Rita Kersting observed of Genzken's art, the ear is an instrument of balance[5]) that we begin to grasp how Genzken appeals to the gendered dimension of architectural space relative to the mythic divide between public and private.

Making that leap demands a brief review of the ways in which Genzken both inherits and departs from minimalism and the generalized diswreferences to architecture. Indeed, following Carl Andre's call for "sculpture as place" minimalism was necessarily an art of location: of the ways in which the body calibrated space as it was shaped by those sculptural objects in the museum or gallery or outdoors. The movement of the body in space served to register that relationship, which shifted continuously depending on the range of environmental and temporal conditions informing the encounter.

But critics of the minimalist legacy have argued that the body relating to that space was largely represented as an idealized or neutral (perhaps neutered) body. If spatial perception was contingent on the ever-changing conditions of the environment, the body was nevertheless regarded as socially unmarked, without gender, ethnicity, or class. Even still the contemporary criticism around minimalism pointed the way to that thinking by alluding to the terms of public and private space in the work's reception. Genzken's art insists upon the shifting values of public and private; and the artist advances this critique in thematizing minimalism's architectural dimensions. An ear-level perspective of her work gains particular access into that space.

Consider, for instance, a few of Genzken's extra-architectural works, the things that don't immediately fall under the rubric of "architecture," or "buildings," or even just plain old "space." These objects, which include chairs, videos, and clothes, constitute a considerable part of her oeuvre and cannot be merely dismissed as one-offs relative to the rest of her practice. This is especially so with her photographs. Genzken's first venture into the medium in 1979 included (and not incidentally) pictures of hi-fi systems appropriated from newspaper advertisements, which she described not only in terms of sound and music but also "their very own strong form."[7] But the photographs that followed in 1980 more pointedly call up the problematic of inside and outside, private and public coextensive with her more architectural work. It was a series of women's ears. Walking down the streets of New York, a city she loves well for its skyscrapers, Genzken would ask random women pedestrians if she might take a picture of their ear. None, she claimed, refused or was offended by the odd request. For Genzken, the images represented "Something organic. Something from the inside out. Coming from the head."[8] The photographs engender a paradox: Genzken asked women strangers to expose their ears, a rather delicate organ, as she encountered them on the highly trafficked, expressly public streets of Manhattan. The identities of the women pictured are anonymous, but there's a certain intimacy in the ears represented: each is different, some sport distinctive earrings, a tendril of hair suggests the pedestrian's overall appearance.

Genzken's ear-level photographs play upon this oscillation between inside and out, or what feminists describe as "the intimate public sphere." These pictures stage the precarious threshold between public and private life, captured on the very streets lined by the architecture Genzken so admires. It's not surprising that Genzken followed this series with "self-portraits" of a kind—x-rays of her head—along with photographs of the facades of New York buildings. Both represent dialectical flipsides of the same spatiotemporal coin: here an image of the head as an internal landscape, a "globe" as she called it, is poised in relation to the blunt frontality, the external surfaces, of New York's architecture.

Much of Genzken's work of the last few years has progressively collapsed these two registers of spatial experience. With the *Strandhäuser zum Umziehen* (Beach Houses for Changing) series, Genzken offers a perspective into the intimate workings of domestic life and its phantasmatic projections; here, the external constructions of vacation homes act as inverted screens or mirrors for psychosexual desire and fantasies of retreat from the world outside. In brilliantly colored sculptural columns named after friends and associates from 1999—Karola, Daniel, Lawrence, Isa herself—Genzken further meshes the social world of the intimate sphere with forms evoking its architectural surround. For Genzken, those spaces are of the same phenomenal and perceptual plane: they are not oppositional but contiguous.

Perhaps this is why one of the ears from 1980 made an uncanny return of sorts, monumentalized on the side of a hotel in Innsbruck. That work, simply called *Ohr* (Ear), recalls one of Genzken's most oft-repeated remarks: "Everyone needs at least one window." It's hard not to take this mandate literally as a call to spatial poetics (and even politics) as determined by the accessories of architecture. To treat Genzken's work from the inside out, however, suggests a different vantage point altogether. She lends us a window in the form of an ear.

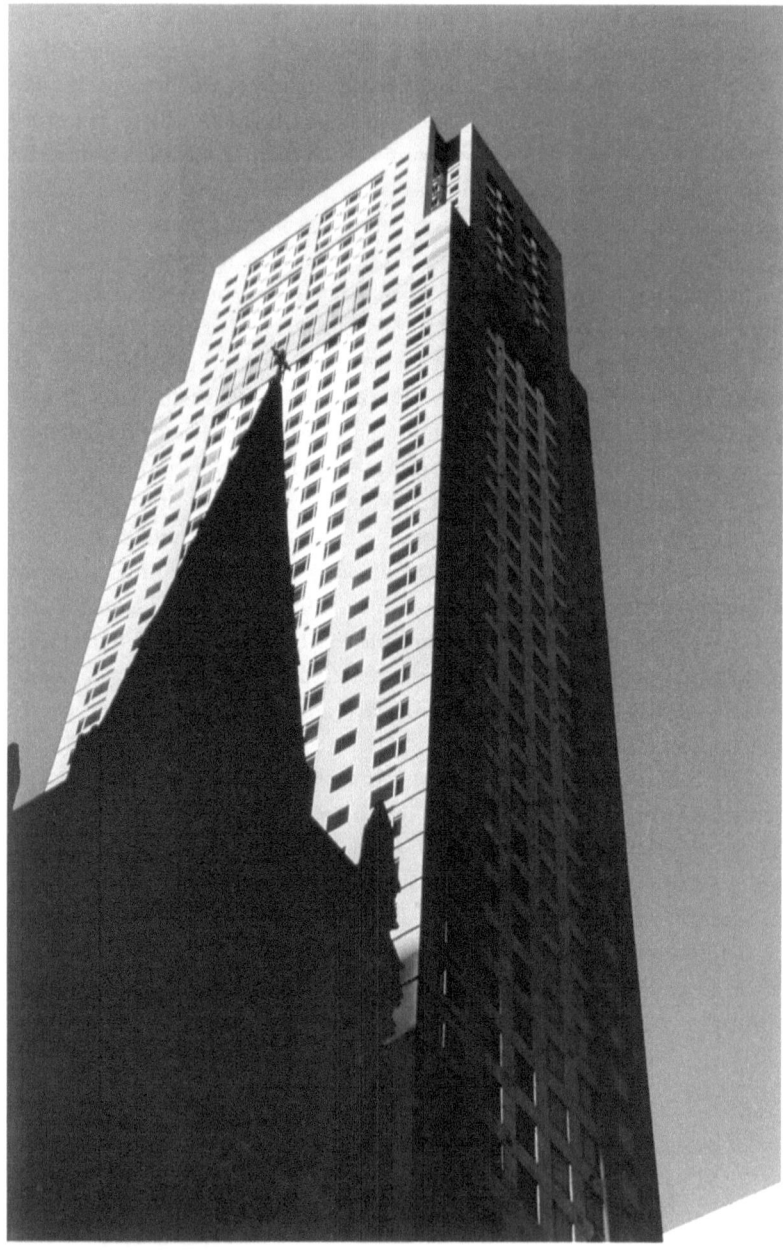

New York, N.Y., 1998/2000 (detail). Chromogenic color print, from series of fifteen photographs. 60 × 40 cm.

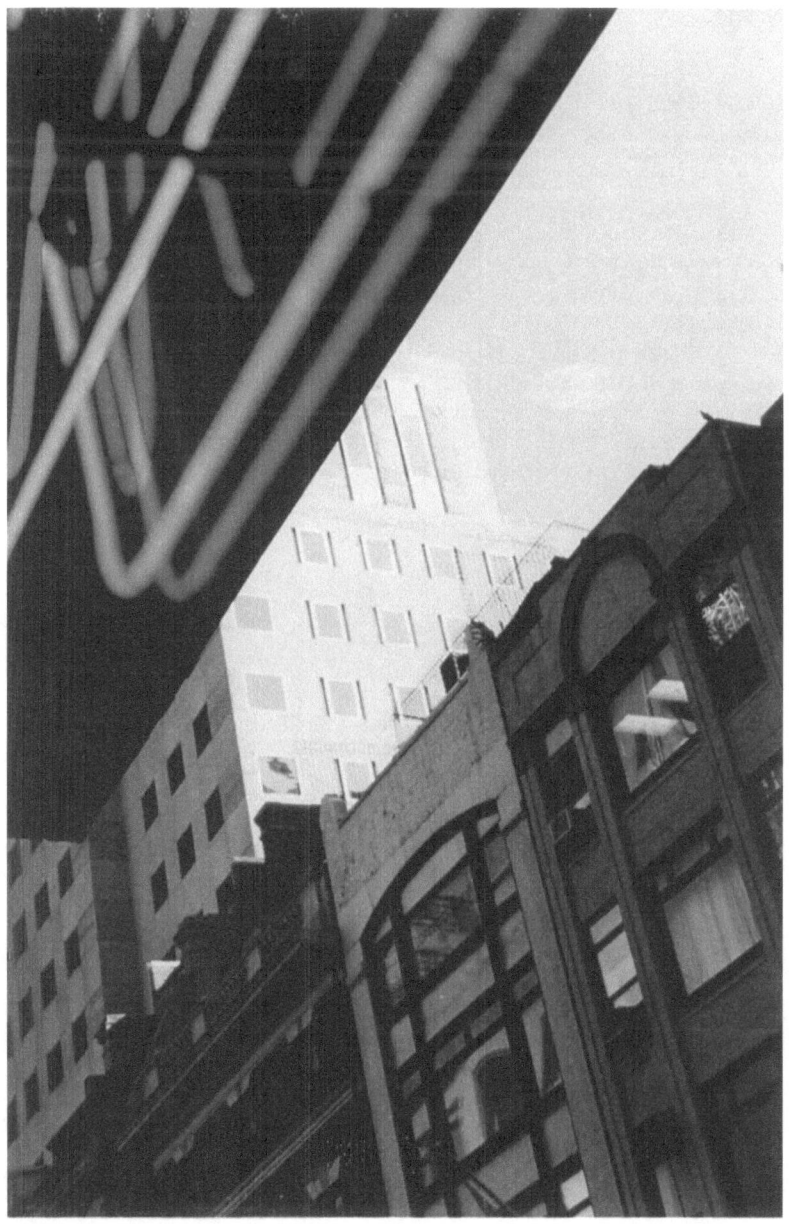

New York, N.Y., 1998/2000 (detail). Chromogenic color print, from series of fifteen photographs. 60 × 40 cm.

Notes

1. Jacques Derrida, "Otobiographies," in *The Ear of the Other*, trans. Peggy Kamuf (Lincoln, Nebraska, and London: University of Nebraska Press, 1985), p. 33.

2. Beatrix Ruf, "Contact," in *Isa Genzken: 1992–2003*, exh. cat. (Cologne: Verlag der Buchhandlung Walther König, 2003), p. 11.

3. Ibid.

4. Maurice Merleau-Ponty, *Phenomenology of Perception*, trans. Colin Smith (London: Routledge, 1989), p. 236.

5. Rita Kersting, "Ellipsoids and Grandparents in the Bavarian Forest—Unsuspected Conjunctions," in *Isa Genzken: Sie sind mein Glück,* exh. cat. (Ostfildern-Ruit: Hatje Cantz Verlag, 2000), p. 51.

6. Benjamin H. D. Buchloh, "Isa Genzken: From Model to Fragment," in *Isa Genzken: Jeder braucht mindestens ein Fenster*, exh. cat. (Cologne: Verlag der Buchhandlung Walther König, 1992), pp. 135–141.

7. Isa Genzken, "A Conversation with Wolfgang Tillmans," *Camera Austria*, no. 81 (2003), p. 17.

8. Ibid.

All Things Being Equal

Benjamin H. D. Buchloh

To situate sculpture between two mutually exclusive discursive conventions, or between two equally intolerable governing conditions, has been one of the motivating principles of Isa Genzken's sculpture from the very beginning. It is hard to trace the prohibitions, geopolitical or gendered, that posed the most obdurate barriers Genzken would have to scale when starting to sculpt in the mid-70s, against all odds. After all, sculpture had not been made in Germany by women (no Hepworth, let alone a Hesse, to draw upon). And if any influence from prewar sculpture had carried over into postwar practice, it was that of Arp. Worse yet, if prewar Constructivism turned into cold-war constructivism, it was the kind of sculpture that decorated the new corporate office towers of Frankfurt and Düsseldorf—what Joseph Beuys once called, inimitably and untranslatably, "*Stahl-und-Eisbein Skulptur*" (steel-and-pig's-knuckle sculpture).

So Genzken situated herself (as did Blinky Palermo, whom she encountered at the Kunstakademie Düsseldorf in 1973) between Beuys on the one hand and Barnett Newman and Ellsworth Kelly on the other, to confront the massive onslaught of minimalism. It seems that only artistic dialogue and aesthetic reception are capable of synthesizing profoundly incompatible epistemes, as is evident once again—to cite a more recent example—in the fusion of Beuys and Warhol in Thomas Hirschhorn's current work, whose idiom of chaos sculpture Genzken would seem to have anticipated in certain ways.

In her almost herculean ambition to bridge the chasm that separated the absence of sculpture in Germany from the affluence of sculpture in American minimalism, Genzken emerged as one of the most serious artists after the famed generation of Palermo, Polke, and Richter. Undoubtedly, the strain to be accepted by that generation drove her sculptural projects into considerable dimensions. One of her ambitions was a programmatically antimasculinist idiom of sculpture. Its extraordinary fusion of stereometrical and biomorphic forms resulted from Genzken's radical decision in 1975 to deploy computer design to create the extremely elongated curves first of her Ellipsoids (1976–82) and later of her Hyperbolos (1979–83), mathematically exact sinuosities that seemed to suddenly stand the techno-scientistic minimalist boxes on their male blockheads. Genzken produced these complex ellipsoids and mathematically polymorph models of stereometry by computer twenty years before Richard Serra discovered Frank Gehry's tool kit. Unfortunately, these wooden hulls rarely crossed the Atlantic (her 1992 retrospective at the University of Chicago's Renaissance Society having remained exceptional in every regard). It must have taken no less of a herculean hysteria to actually assemble and enunciate a vocabulary of feminist sculpture in the land of the Masters—a task that Genzken performed with a dogged and eventually triumphant obstinacy that associates her with her admired fellow Hanseatic elder Hanne Darboven. Yet, typically, just when Genzken had fully formed that vocabulary in her wooden hybrids—ranging from paeans to the utopian promises of luminously colored biomorphic abstraction and proto-utilitarian mechanomorphic devices for submarine and extraterrestrial locomotion—she abruptly canceled all continuity and abandoned the holistic splendor of her immaculate conceptions in favor of an aesthetic of rupture, rubble, and architectural fragments (at the very moment that her work— included in 1982's Documenta 7—had finally become widely visible).

This sudden inversion signaled yet another schism, or a double reversal, in Genzken's sculpture. First of all, her new work now negated the constructivists' confidence in an alliance of sculptural and techno-scientistic rationality that American minimalism had proudly presented as salvaged. In acts of almost programmatic disidentification, Genzken now severed all ties with American-type abstraction, its colors and its morphologies. Negating her sculpture's perfectly executed stereometrical forms, she opted in favor of an aesthetic of dispersal and dissemination (of monochrome gray matter such as cement and concrete) and of architectural fractures. These were the very principles and materials she now rediscovered as having governed atopian objects and spaces from Kurt Schwitters to Beuys.

Genzken's return to the local idioms was prompted furthermore by the fact that her once-utopian models had reached the size and scale of public space and the condition of simultaneous collective perception that all serious sculpture in the twentieth century had aimed for. Probing the credibility of her commitment to such utopian aspirations under the conditions of postwar Germany, Genzken now reverted to the melancholy of ruined interiors and fractured bunker shards. Not only negating any notion of an innate sculptural dynamic toward architecture and collective public experience in the present, her ruinous refusals assaulted the governing codes and prevailing conditions of German reconstruction architecture in all its misery.

Her early forays into photography were equally astonishing and even less recognized. Having been engaged at the academy in dialogues with the soon-to-be-prominent members of Bernd and Hilla Becher's class—in particular, Candida Höfer and Thomas Struth—Genzken produced Hi-Fi (1979), an extraordinary series of photographs that presaged her future deployment of endless accumulations of mass cultural imagery in collage books as an integral complement to her sculptural disarticulation of the terror of the daily object-world. In this series Genzken traced the most seductive—i.e., rigorous—designs of what was then-contemporary Japanese stereo equipment (in manifest opposition to the Becher school's fixation on architecture) as a visual regime in which all avant-garde aspirations for the transformation of everyday life now lay entombed. In a second series (from 1980), strangely complementary to the first in its focus on aurality, Genzken photographed the ears of friends in large-scale color close-ups. These metonymies of the ear, strangely echoing and displacing both constructivist metonymies of the hand and Surrealist metonymies of the foot, not only demarcated Genzken's departure from her preoccupation with sinuous organic forms in her sculpture but also responded to the increasingly reactionary resuscitation of photographic portraiture by her peers. Shifting the portrait genre to the physiognomic (and criminological) bodily detail of utter singularity, Genzken's photographs pointed simultaneously to the infinite differentiation of subjectivity and to the determinism inherent in

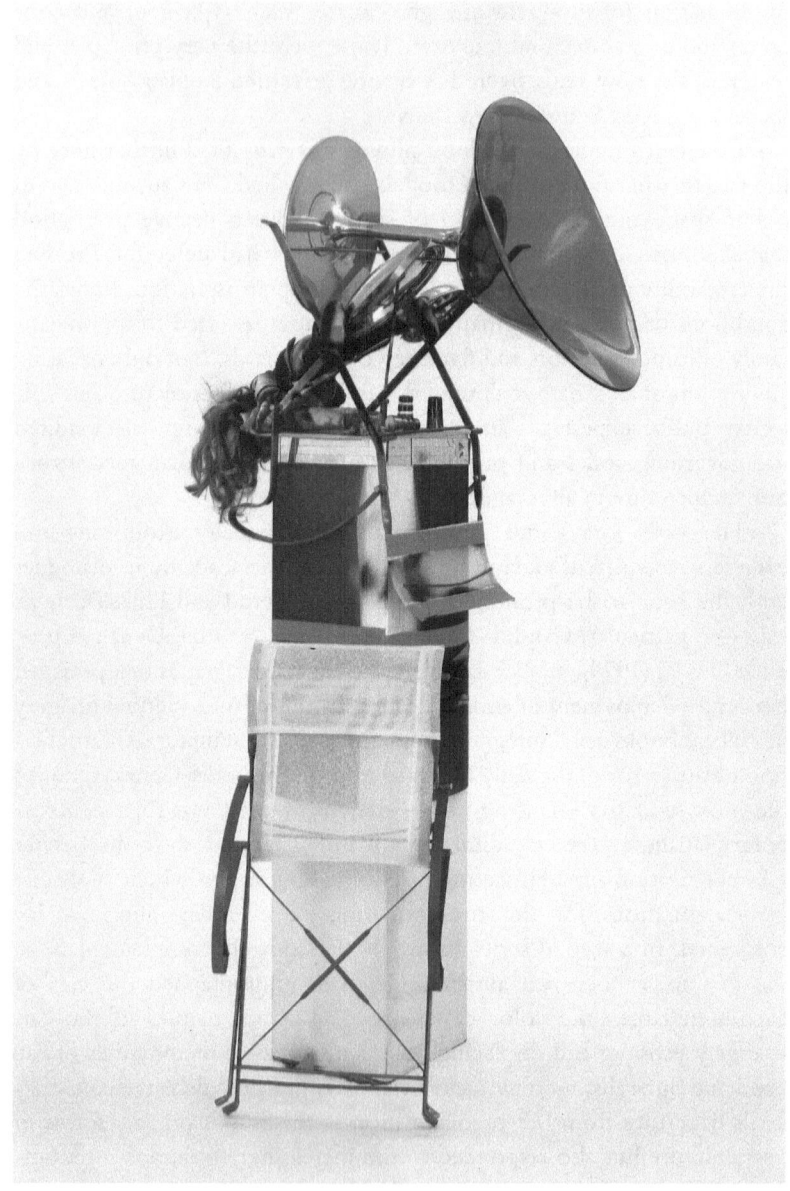

Geschwister (Siblings), 2004. Plastic, lacquer, mirror foil, glass, metal, wood, and fabric.
220 × 60 × 100 cm.

the mythical claim that subjectivity could in fact still be recorded in a photographic portrait.

In her most recent work, Genzken confronts one of the prime calamities of sculpture in the present: a terror that emerges from both the universal equivalence and exchangeability of all objects and materials and the simultaneous impossibility of imbuing any transgressive definition of sculpture with priorities or criteria of selection, of choice, let alone judgment (be it artisanal skills, choice of objects or materials, or the analytical intelligence to identify the specific structure of a contextualized readymade). To have the self succumb to the totalitarian order of objects brings the sculptor to the brink of psychosis, and Genzken's new work seems to inhabit that position. However, since total submission to the terror of consumption is indeed the governing stratum of collective object-relations, that psychotic state may well become the only position and practice the sculptor of the future can articulate.

A Conversation with Wolfgang Tillmans

WOLFGANG TILLMANS: Chicago was the first city to have skyscrapers?

ISA GENZKEN: Chicago was the birthplace of skyscrapers. There was a big fire once that destroyed almost all the houses—at one fell swoop—and then they started building up. That's how the first skyscrapers came about. Earlier than in New York.

TILLMANS: It was because they invented lifts, wasn't it?

GENZKEN: Yes.

TILLMANS: I remember reading that once. Otis invented them, I think, and that's why there just weren't any skyscrapers before that. But skyscrapers have always taken your fancy, haven't they?

GENZKEN: I was twenty-one when I first went to New York, and I was so fascinated by the architecture and glad that something like that existed and that I was able to have this visual experience that I thought to myself, this is where I want to live. To me, New York had a direct link with sculpture—that must have been it. Although at twenty-one I wasn't a sculptor yet, I was just starting my studies and I didn't even know what I wanted to do. New York is a city of incredible stability and solidity. And then the height of the buildings—that impressed me, like the people who always seemed a bit happier than the Germans in the street. When I came back to Germany it seemed to me that it wasn't particularly nice, my visual surroundings—it was all so dreary. And modernism hardly features at all in Germany. OK, there was the

Bauhaus and there was this and that, but modernism is practically non-existent in architecture. You can see loads of modern architecture in New York: there was the Empire State Building in the 1930s, then there were the Twin Towers…. I mean, the Twin Towers were extremely modern…. The awful thing about architecture here is that everything, almost everything, is done in the cheapest construction style, the cheapest. They don't make sure people use the best materials, they just use what's cheapest. Just look at Potsdamer Platz, it's like a piece of scenery! It's all done so cheaply, it could be in Cologne or in Tenerife…. They would never allow something like that in New York, they just have an incredible sense of quality.

TILLMANS: Well, perhaps one reason is that Americans don't have a fear of wealth…. They don't have any problem building something really expensive, do they?

GENZKEN: No, not at all. Conversely, I always have to fight with cheap materials here and now…because I live here and I can't just pretend I'm in New York. Incidentally, Josef Strau realized an outdoor sculpture for me recently, and a lot of young artists were really enthusiastic about it at the opening. I certainly hadn't expected that, because I had just thought it would be a good idea to do something simple for a change. But that's exactly what appealed to them: something can be relatively big but still cheap. Of course, Americans are totally different in this respect. They love seeing that something is expensive. I was lucky with my exhibition *Fuck the Bauhaus*,[1] in New York in 2000, because I exhibited some sculptures made of cheap materials, and the show was still a big success. Maybe it's just that Americans can really relax when they see something simple for a change. Do you see what I mean? Something no one expects to see in America.

TILLMANS: But the work with Josef Strau is really beautiful, too. How did you get the idea for something like that?

GENZKEN: Well, at first I wanted to put blinds on the building. But when I do something I've already done before, I sometimes have a certain feeling of uncertainty. Although I am falling back on something that I know is safe and pretty good. But then it was all too expensive. I had seen glowing green, fresh bamboo at the KaDeWe store. It had attracted

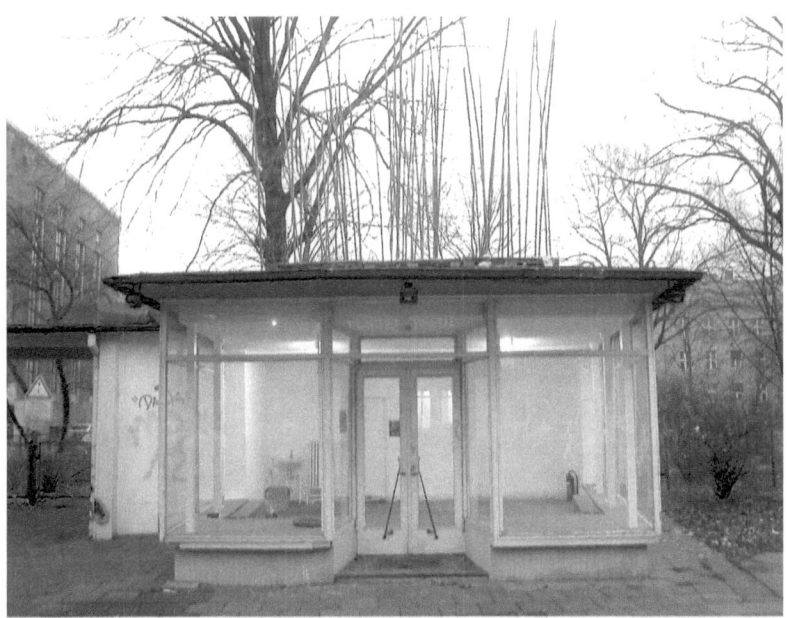

Haare wachsen, wie sie wollen (Hair Grows However It Wants To), 2002. Outdoor project, Galerie Meertisch (Josef Strau) in the Glaspavillon at the Volksbühne, Berlin. Bamboo construction.

my attention and I thought it would be nice to do something with it. Back home, sitting over the photo, drawing some things on it, I remembered this lovely green bamboo again and also that there was this fascist building—or partly fascist building—next to the store, a theatre, an ugly building. And then I thought, bamboo is politically correct, that's just the thing. But I also think it's visually beautiful. Simple. The work is called *Haare wachsen, wie sie wollen* (Hair Grows However It Wants To), and it matches the little pavilion quite well.

TILLMANS: And the bamboo, did you actually get it from KaDeWe?

GENZKEN: No. But it's turned gray now, that looks quite nice, too. Bamboo is normally yellow, and there's something cheap about it, something touristy—bamboo yellow. And now the weather has turned it gray—from green to gray. I've never seen anything like it, this coloring. The coloring gradually adapts to the surroundings, that's good.

TILLMANS: You over-painted a photo for this project?

GENZKEN: Yes.

TILLMANS: Are photos often the starting point for ideas?

GENZKEN: Yes, for outdoor sculptures.

TILLMANS: Always?

GENZKEN: Yes, almost always. You take a photo of the situation and then you think about what's missing.

TILLMANS: And is it important that they are your pictures? I mean, that they are your views of the situation that you work with? Or could people send you photos, too?

GENZKEN: It's better for me to see the situation and take the photo myself.

TILLMANS: I am always astonished just how little you can see in professional interior views of museums and so on. Although you are familiar with the rooms, the photos don't mean anything to you. Although they are usually perfectly done. I prefer to work with a casual snapshot I've taken myself. How often do you have your camera with you?

GENZKEN: Well, when I get invited to do something, I pick it up and take it with me.

TILLMANS: And other times? In the studio? Do you have a camera there?

GENZKEN: Very rarely. I have to really force myself to take photos of my new sculptures.

TILLMANS: As notes?

GENZKEN: Yes, because that's important, too.

TILLMANS: To see how far you are?

GENZKEN: Yes, I recently found some photos of my glass sculptures that show the ideas I started out from. It is interesting to see.

TILLMANS: Have you always taken photos?

GENZKEN: What do you mean?

TILLMANS: Well, I know you were already taking photos in the 1970s. Did this medium play a particular role for you? Or rather, did there come a point when you realized that it might be for you, too?

GENZKEN: If you have an idea to photograph an ear or hi-fi equipment... that's a big difference from the pictures I take now when I'm working on a project.

TILLMANS: Well, I realize that. But what I'd like to know is what photography does for you in concrete terms...

GENZKEN: I think that photography has a lot to do with sculpture— because it is three-dimensional and because it depicts reality. For example, I have always been able to relate to photography more than to painting. When I was photographing the hi-fi adverts I thought to myself, everyone has one of these towers at home. It's the latest thing, the most modern equipment available. So a sculpture must be at least as modern and must stand up to it. Then I hung the pictures on the wall and put an Ellipsoid on the floor and thought, the Ellipsoid must be at least as good as this advert. At least as good. That's how good a modern sculpture has to be. Do you see what I mean? That was the dialogue...

TILLMANS: So, really, the real world is always your point of reference...

GENZKEN: Yes, and I have always said that with any sculpture you have to be able to say, although this is not a readymade, it could be one. That's what a sculpture has to look like. It must have a certain relation to reality. I mean, not airy-fairy, let alone fabricated, so aloof and polite.

TILLMANS: So it's not simply pure will that induces you to juxtapose forms with the real world. The Empire State Building, for instance, acts as a kind of benchmark, a yardstick.

GENZKEN: Precisely. And I don't see this aspect in many artists' work. Often, my feeling is that they think something up that is supposed to be art. That's not what I want at all. Rather, a sculpture is really a photo—although it can be shifted, it must still always have an aspect that reality has too.

TILLMANS: That's what I like about the medium of photography as well. That it has a certain economy. That it is unobtrusive and unpretentious. You could put a pair of jeans above a doorpost and put it all somewhere in all its 3-D glory. But I find it much easier to photograph it. As a gesture, it is somehow less pompous. Because the photo creates a kind of universality or accessibility.

GENZKEN: Something that bothers me with some of my students is that their works are so cold toward the viewer. I have always told the students that they have to imagine how the viewer sees something, too. You've got to put yourself in the viewer's shoes when you do something. That's important to me. It may be complicated, but it's important to me. Otherwise I find it too cold or too arrogant.

TILLMANS: In the sense that I can do something you can't?

GENZKEN: Precisely.

TILLMANS: So in that respect, you also see the photo as an economic means of conveying something that exists and that interests you?

GENZKEN: Yes. Basically, I can read your photography and see what moves you. What really moves you and not just faked emotion. I don't think it's good when it's like that in art—but unfortunately it often is. That's why I like Bruce Nauman, for example, as a sculptor. With his work, sometimes I have really thought to myself, that's simply beautiful.

TILLMANS: Because he is someone who potentially always uses means that are already there? Because his works are not made up of imaginatively devised forms...

GENZKEN: Above all, it is difficult enough to depict something that moves you deep down inside. But that's ultimately what art is all about, and that's also what appeals to people—if an artist can do it.

TILLMANS: And when the will to create art isn't the first thing you see, but rather...

GENZKEN: Yes, exactly.

TILLMANS: ...but rather when someone is really interested in something. That's much more exciting, when someone is interested in something, than when someone is only interested in the will to do something. And, essentially, you can divide art into these two groups. One consists in the will to show: I am making something. And the other arises from an immediate interest in the world and things.

GENZKEN: ...I don't know how to put it...it's not easy to express it all, but...that's why I don't like to give interviews, either...

TILLMANS: What I just said, for example, is extremely trivializing, when you think, good grief, can you really say that? But when I look at art, that's basically the way it works for me. Is it conceptual art or not? Is it conceived or is it not conceived? Really, these are taboo areas that this takes you into. Because you are not really supposed to say that...

GENZKEN: But I think we're a bit similar in that.

TILLMANS: Do your photographs have a formal structure?

GENZKEN: The first pictures I took were the hi-fi systems, and obviously they're connected with sounds and music, and they have their own very strong form. Next I photographed the ears. Something organic. Something from the inside out. Coming from the head. I did this ear series in New York and I asked people, women, on the street if I could photograph their ears. Not a single woman said no. Because I didn't ask for their face, but for something largely anonymous.

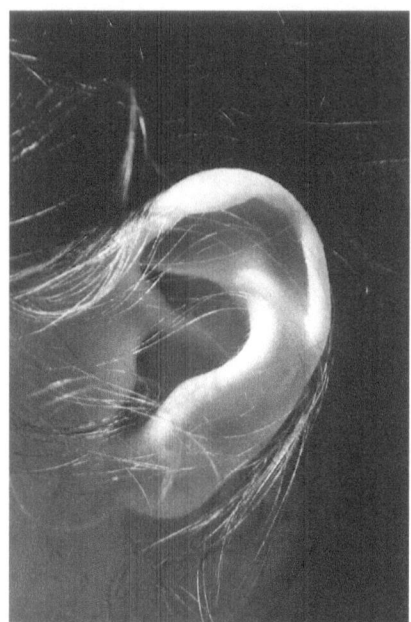

Ohr (Ear), 1980. Color photograph. 175 × 118 cm.

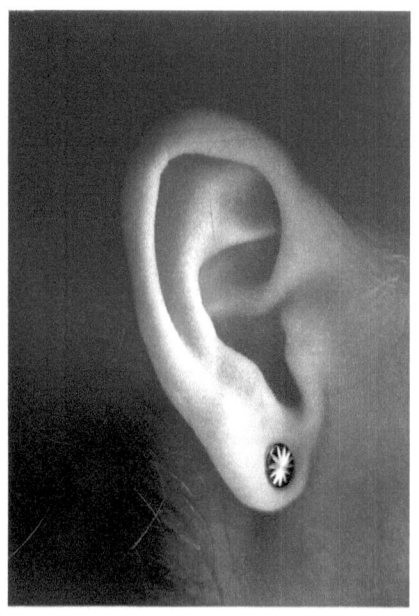

Ohr (Ear), 1980. Color photograph. 175 × 118 cm.

TILLMANS: What kind of women were they?

GENZKEN: Well, just women on the street.

TILLMANS: Women, then, you hardly knew and whose ears you photographed right there and then?

GENZKEN: Yes.

TILLMANS: I see. Really? On the street? Or did you arrange to meet them?

GENZKEN: No, on the street. It only took a moment. The women always said, what, my ear? Sure! But I never offended anyone by examining them. It was just the ear. And everyone thought that was great. That was a nice experience. For me as a photographer, too. Of course, I did work with some light and hair shining in the sun.... I tried to make the situation nice for the ear.

TILLMANS: What role does self-portraiture play?

GENZKEN: I did the *X-rays* after the hi-fis and the ears. Do you mean them?

TILLMANS: Are they the first self-portraits? Because you've also got the photos in the clinic, those black-and-white pictures.

GENZKEN: Oh, them. I had just had an operation, I was totally bored and so I just took my camera and took some pictures of myself. Out of boredom. I only realized afterwards that this work was something special. Taking photos in the clinic and publishing them in a catalog...it suddenly took on a kind of seriousness. Everyone's scared of clinics, and no one wants to see what a clinic looks like from the inside. Well, not really. And everyone's a bit scared of having to go there themselves. And there I was in there. And I stood by it. And I used the clinic as a studio and started taking photos. And then I felt better. Just because it let me do something. Well, and the *X-rays*.... I was just interested in seeing what it looks like inside my head—and the idea that they could just examine the inside of my head like a globe. And then I photographed the facades in New York.

TILLMANS: That was at the end of the 1990s, wasn't it?

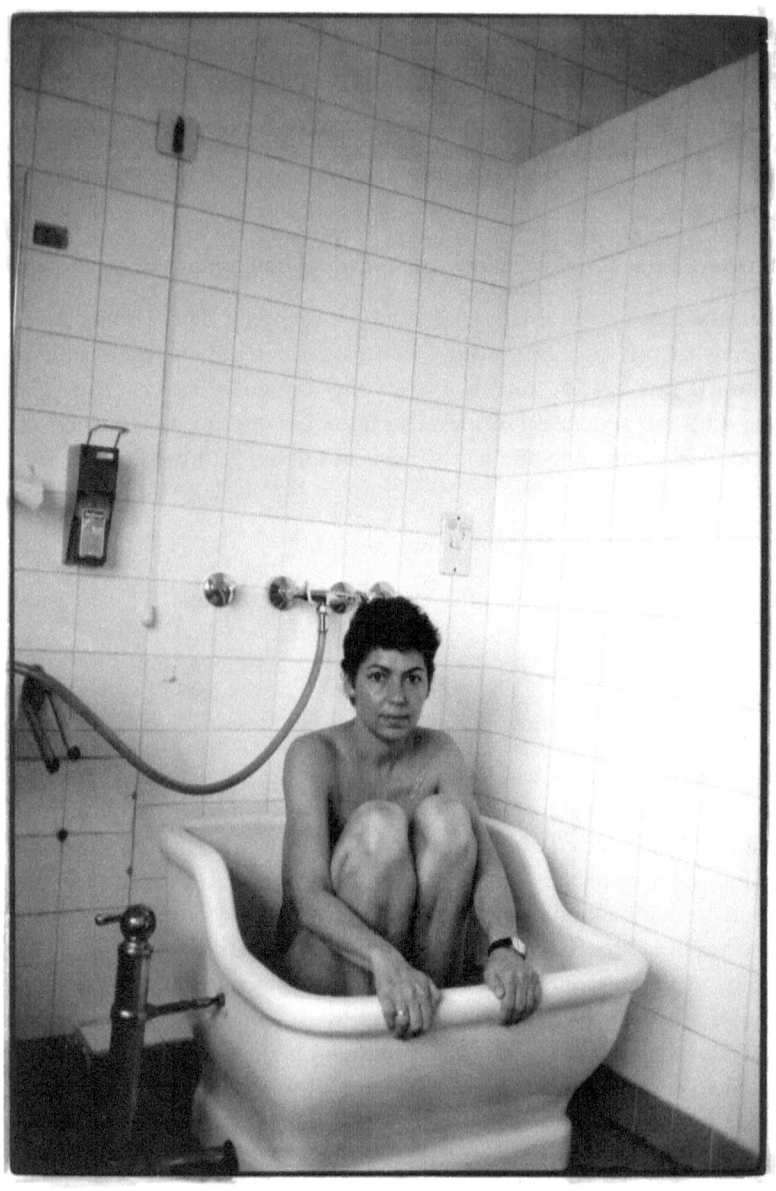

Krankenhausfoto (Hospital Photo), 1991. From series of gelatin silver prints published in the
exhibition catalog, *Jeder braucht mindestens ein Fenster*, 1992. 30 × 24 cm.

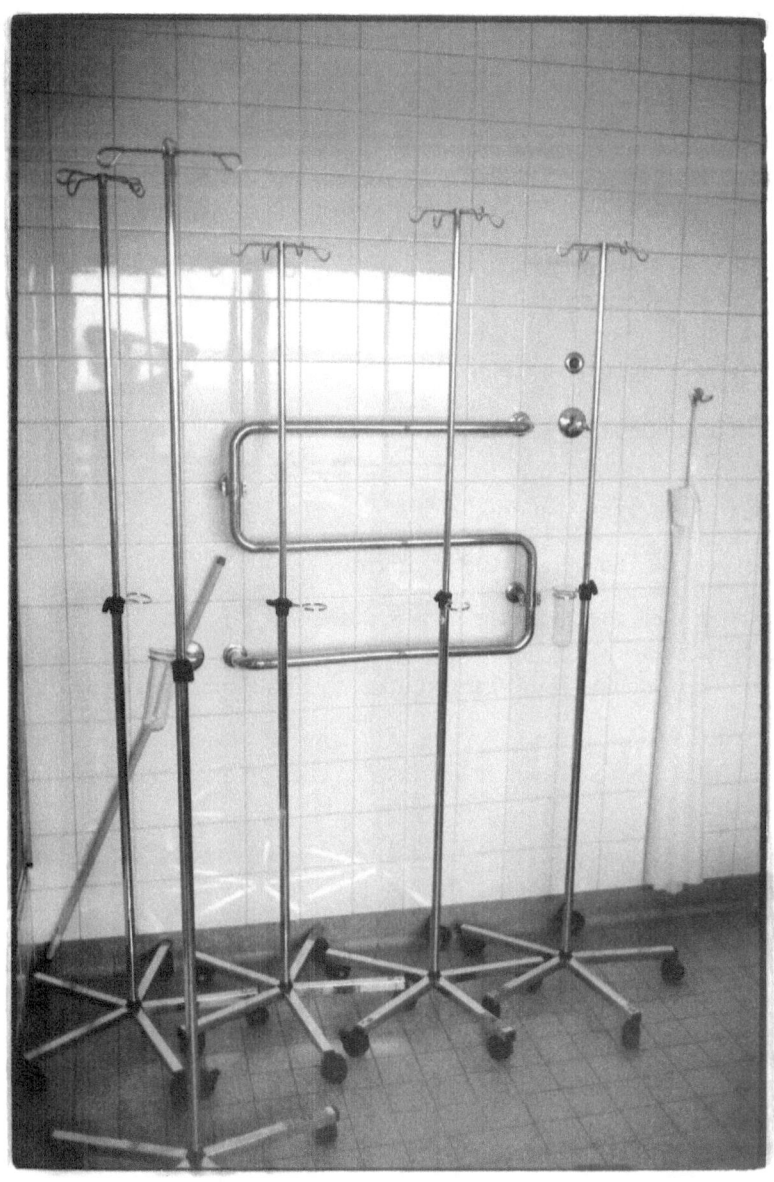

Krankenhausfoto (Hospital Photo), 1991. From series of gelatin silver prints published in the exhibition catalog, *Jeder braucht mindestens ein Fenster*, 1992. 30 × 24 cm.

GENZKEN: Yes. I did the books at the end of the 1990s, and I did the facades shortly after that.

TILLMANS: And you also did the photos in connection with the books because of an economy of means, didn't you?

GENZKEN: Yes.

TILLMANS: So it was like in the clinic, there was no studio, just the camera.

GENZKEN: Yes, exactly. Because I'm a person who always has to do something. If I cannot do anything, I'm in a very bad way. But really I'm always working on something. And I always want to work, too.

TILLMANS: Perhaps that's another thing we have in common? A certain obsession...

GENZKEN: Yes, I think so, too...

TILLMANS: But perhaps all artists are like that...

GENZKEN: Well, the few artists I know really well, they are all so.... It's a really bad block when you think, right, now I've got to do art. It really is very important to learn that that is not the most important thing.

TILLMANS: "*Hier und jetzt zufrieden sein*" (Be satisfied here and now),[2] that's what I have to keep telling myself. Then art will just come along on its own.

GENZKEN: Yes, it'll come along.

Notes

1. Part of the title, *Fuck the Bauhaus/New Buildings for New York*.
2. Part of the joint title, *Science Fiction/Hier und jetzt zufrieden sein*.

DIEDRICH DIEDERICHSEN: In the short video by the artist Kai Althoff in which the two of you are shown in conversation, he asks you why you have such an aversion to interviews. You explain that answering questions represents exactly the opposite of artistic work—of making decisions for oneself. It sounds as if, to you, creating art is like being on holiday, without any pressure, while making concrete statements in a conversation is like work. But people send postcards home even when they're on holiday. Perhaps it would be possible to view an interview as a sort of postcard?

ISA GENZKEN: Actually you only think you're not under any pressure when you make art because there's nobody telling you what you're supposed to do. But you have to find everything within yourself and make each decision on your own. And though there's nobody forcing you to do anything, it can nevertheless turn into a disaster. In the creative process you're very much on your own. You can't simply call someone up and say, "Have a look at this."

DIEDERICHSEN: And do you have imaginary conversations with other artists—people whom you know or don't know? Do you ever ask yourself, "What would so and so think of that?"

GENZKEN: No. I don't do that sort of thing. My experience is that the artists I appreciate seldom approve of things made by other artists. I don't often speak with other artists the way I do with Kai in the video, especially since we weren't talking about my art, but rather something we created together—namely this short film. What was interesting was that we didn't plan our conversation.

DIEDERICHSEN: He asks you what you mean when you say that your work must be "modern." You reply that it is precisely this aspect of interviews that you dislike: instead of being able to digress, the questions tie you down.

GENZKEN: I gave him a completely unrelated answer.

DIEDERICHSEN: I thought his question was very interesting. The word "modern" has, of course, two meanings. One pertains to things that are topical and contemporary, the other to the historical movement of modernism and modernity, which in a certain way is no longer contemporary. But I suppose that's debatable. In any case, I have the feeling that your work is concerned with both. First, you incorporate contemporary symbols, products, objects, fetishes in your work, but you always make reference to the historical movement as well.

GENZKEN: Yes, that's true. But I don't want anything to do with traditional elites and their self-awareness. That's too rigid and boring. I focus on completely different sensibilities in my work. "Topical" is perhaps a better description than "modern." But that doesn't mean I don't want to be modern. My work is modern.

DIEDERICHSEN: There's certainly a sub-movement within historical modernism to which you make reference in a number of ways: the idea of the "social" work of art that both incorporates and influences its surroundings. This is something you've referred to often lately, even if in a critical fashion. *Fuck The Bauhaus* (2000) and *New Buildings for Berlin* (2001–2004) come to mind.

GENZKEN: Yes, although in the last year and a half I've become more interested in a formal language of cheap materials and cheap production. I'm not talking about cheap, hand-made objects, like the self-modeled stuff that's so amateurish you can see it a mile off. When I say "cheap materials" I mean industrially fabricated sculptures that are very interesting as sculptures in their own right. A year ago I started on the series *Empire/Vampire, Who Kills Death* (2002–2003) using small plastic objects, figures, toy tanks, and so forth. At the beginning, the topic of war was uppermost on my mind because the conflict had just started up in Iraq. But then the objects I'd bought became much more important in themselves, and I started working with them more and more. For example, that hippopotamus figure you see over there and the small iron next to it: I specifically bought things that were cheap, both in terms of how they were manufactured and their retail price. They were things I'd never be able to create with my own hands. If I were to model a hippopotamus it would never look like that—and I wouldn't be capable of doing it anyway. It looks so good, not even Stephan Balkenhol could achieve it. But I think I succeeded in creating something completely different. There's no longer any mediocrity, but it's important that it's based on "everyday beauty." Nowadays there are more and more shops that sell these really cheap items. That's where I found all of these figures and objects. I'm not only interested in what they portray, but rather in the formal aspect of how they were made. And they come from all over the world: one component is from Taiwan, the next from Mexico, and the third from somewhere completely different. As I said, I'm not speaking of poor quality. You find "poor" quality in Markus Lüpertz or Balkenhol and in many other areas of sculpture. I combined cheap things with expensive things—for example very expensive glasses, figures from film modeling workshops, or the costly reflective foil used in architecture. These are all mass-produced, assembly line materials, which I then altered with color or through their placement in unusual combinations.

DIEDERICHSEN: A global taste of mass reproduction, yet characterized by exceptional formal qualities.

GENZKEN: Yes, but I tried to place everything in a different artistic context. What appealed to me was that they could be movie scenes. The works should function as motion pictures rather than sculptures. You see a new picture from every different angle. Nothing is rigid or two-dimensional, but cinematic.

DIEDERICHSEN: These cheap figures are also often described as emotionally moving. One sees an effort that's futile—toward a totality of form and completeness that's doomed to failure. It's poignant somehow.

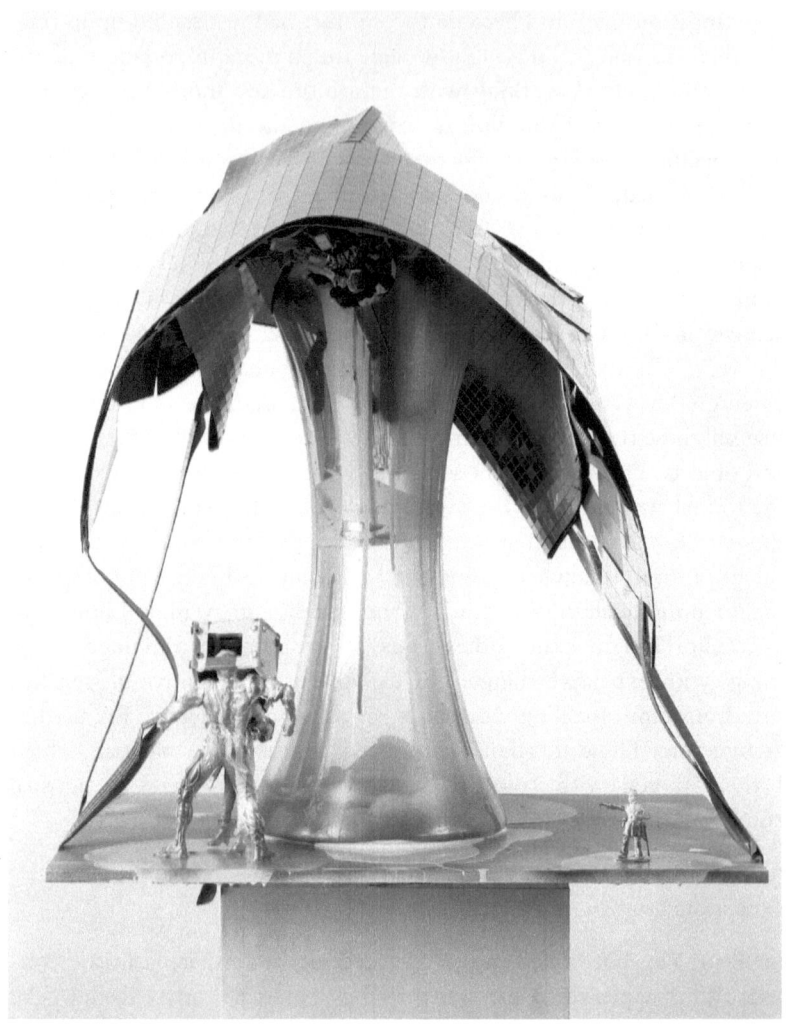

Empire/Vampire, Who Kills Death, 2002/2003 (detail). Mixed media, one of twenty-two parts.
193 × 62 × 45 cm; installation dimensions variable.

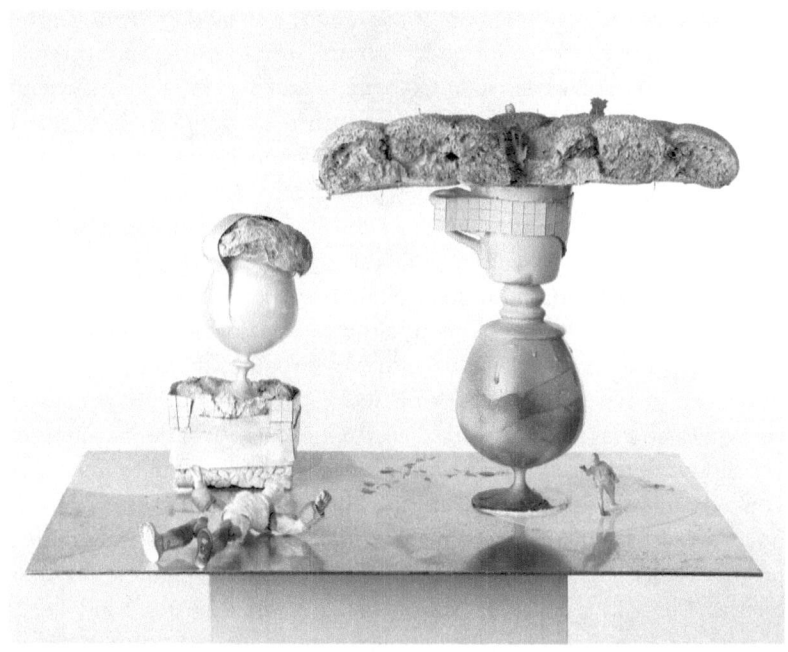

Empire/Vampire, Who Kills Death, 2002/2003 (detail). Mixed media, one of twenty-two parts. 193 × 62 × 45 cm.; installation dimensions variable.

GENZKEN: I disagree—that's not well thought out. The work doesn't fail in any way, and audiences react well; they're perplexed. If you walk around my works and pay attention to the scenery, something different always emerges and you can always discover something new and sympathize with it. That's the opposite of the tradition that began with the *Black Square* (Kazimir Malevich, 1915). This has been abused since the 1960s. Jackson Pollock, Barnett Newman, etc.—I think they're great. Conceptual art, too. That's more where I fit in. But I didn't want these modernistic, flung-down objects that strive to avoid all content. Benjamin Buchloh criticized my Ellipsoids for having too much content. He said to me, "You haven't even understood Carl Andre yet." I said, "Of course I understand him. But I can hardly try to outdo Carl Andre." Of course, it was exactly this "content" that I wanted to bring back into the Ellipsoids so that people would say, "It looks like a spear," or a toothpick, or a boat. This associative aspect was there from the very beginning and was also intentional, but from the viewpoint of minimal art it was absolutely out of the question and simply not modern. And yet the Ellipsoids made reference to modernism in terms of media and material. I had to go to the University of Cologne, where I knew a physicist who calculated and drew all of the diameters on the computer. After that I had to build it so that it would gain this horizon-like quality. I was influenced by Bruce Nauman. They were tremendously complicated to produce in terms of craftsmanship. I did it all by hand, but I wanted them to look—plop!—right out of the machine. People have always thought they were machine-made, but I wouldn't have been able to afford to get them produced in an airplane plant or wherever you can have things like that made. I was also very proud of them because they helped me achieve a level of craftsmanship that many of my American colleagues no longer have. With the exception of my outdoor sculptures I've always done everything by hand anyway. I don't mean to insist that you have to do it that way, but it can't hurt. The modernists might see it differently. László Moholy-Nagy, for example, made pictures by calling up the factory and describing his images over the telephone. That was seen as especially advanced. And it was. But times change, and today everything is outsourced. And it's also more interesting to develop things yourself. Many contemporary artists do it. My colleagues in my gallery share this inclination. Whatever "modern" means, I don't reject the term. On the contrary, for me, "modern" means progress in social and aesthetic terms, but as a wanderer within diversity.

DIEDERICHSEN: You said there was this moment at the beginning of your artistic development where you departed from minimalism and connected it with "content"—does that also have something to do with the almost involuntary way that minimalist objects can have "content," that they seem to look at you in an uncanny way? They have something like a psychotropic, psychedelic side, and can suddenly appear to have a soul—and this precisely because they aren't supposed to have one. I was just thinking of how you've also given many of your objects proper names.

GENZKEN: That way I always know exactly which is which. Over the years I've created many objects that, though diverse, look very similar. Because they carry the names of certain people I thought about during my work—*Mies* or *Schindler*, names of architects, or *Schönberg*—I can identify them precisely and know by heart how they look in detail.

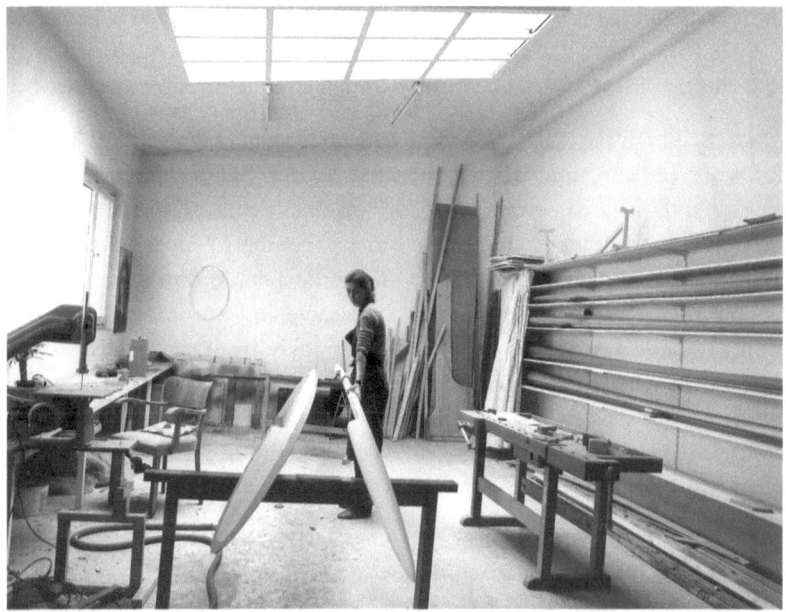

Genzken working on *Rot-gelb-schwarzes Doppelellipsoid 'Zwilling'* (Red-Yellow-Black Double Ellipsoid "Twin") in her studio in Düsseldorf, 1982.

What else can you do? You could number your pictures like my ex-husband did, but he didn't know by heart which picture went with which number.

DIEDERICHSEN: Yes. But those are just series when you number them like that. When you assign names, then we're not talking about objects in a series anymore, but rather about a specific type of logic, about something that must have been intended that way.

GENZKEN: It's always closely related to my feelings at the time. Back then I visited Lawrence Weiner, who had a boat in Amsterdam called Joma. I was invited to the boat and had such a nice evening that I used this name as the title for a work of 1981. And now I can always say exactly how that object looks. Later, I named the pillars after friends, but even then, I know exactly which pillar is *Wolfgang* [Tillmans].

DIEDERICHSEN: So the sculptures have a sort of physiognomy? They may belong to a genre, a series, but are they nevertheless individual beings that can be differentiated according to their unique physiognomies?

GENZKEN: There have always been series, such as *30 Ellipsoids* (1976–82). I'd work on one thing until it became boring. Simply continuing the series would lead to certain ideas, which then provided the foundation for a new kind of work and a new series altogether. This would happen almost automatically. And that's what some people don't understand. People used to accuse me of being indecisive and not knowing what I want, because I was able to change so quickly from one genre to the next: "First she creates such elegant things and then goes on to make these strange plaster objects." Honestly, though, I think people have always given me credit for being able to move on. In my life, I've always been concerned with fluidity and opposed to rigidity. That's been automatic—I've never had to think about it.

DIEDERICHSEN: The elegant Hyperbolos and Ellipsoids were, of course, the things that put you in the spotlight. It's clear that people wanted to associate you with "elegance." It was something new in the late 1970s. I feel that your subsequent works in plaster and cement were, in part, a deliberate attempt to thwart this association.

GENZKEN: Absolutely. I really wanted a change—and to get away from the drudgery of the early works; they were incredibly difficult to make. So I went to a plaster workshop in Düsseldorf. I'd never been there before. When I arrived, I realized immediately: I really like this. It was something completely different from the places I'd been before, where we were working with wood. Then I played around a bit with the plaster and suddenly had the feeling, "Hey—this is easier than I thought!" I felt like a real sculptor [laughs]. Even so, making my way from plaster to cement was a longer road than I'd imagined.

DIEDERICHSEN: And now your studio is located next to the city's plaster molding workshop.

GENZKEN: I find that almost romantic. And there's the Charlottenburg Palace next door and its lovely park. I've never been to the workshop, but I'll go some time. I wouldn't want to buy the Nefertiti they make there, but I'd gladly go and find out how a Nefertiti sculpture can be made really well.

DIEDERICHSEN: Or they could make casts of your works.

GENZKEN: Yes, but I've only made two bronzes in my life. I was at the best bronze foundry in Düsseldorf, and in the process the plaster molds were ruined. That was terrible for me because I thought the plaster forms were much nicer. The bronze had lost something. I'd never do anything like that again. It would destroy the original. This being said, one thing I believe about my works so far is that I've been able to do justice to whatever material I'm working with. I'm able to make the best of it. For my London exhibition (*Wasserspeier and Angels*, 2004), I worked with this special sort of foil that's very strong and stable. I rounded off the forms with it, and the light shined through. You can incorporate "inside" and "outside," and everything appears so colorful and cheerful. But the decisive thing about working with the material was to create something round with it. That's always the most difficult aspect of sculptures, and with this material you can do that.

DIEDERICHSEN: How did you come up with the idea to create the sculptures you call *Wasserspeier* (gargoyles) for this London exhibition?

GENZKEN: Whenever I'm in Cologne I go to the cathedral there several times a day because I find it absolutely magnificent inside. I've even referred to it before as my "atelier." Wolfgang Tillmans did a photo series there with me. And there's the famous masonry shop there. It's the workshop for the cathedral, a large area that you can look into from above, where they work on the stones. And that's where I discovered the gargoyles, which are normally on the outside of the cathedral. They were being restored. I saw their wide-open mouths, their terrible faces—they're total figments of the imagination. They're meant to pro-tect the building; the rain water and filth flow from their mouths, away from the church, which is important for the upkeep of the building. I thought to myself that it would be good to take them to London. I tried to convince the cathedral's master builder of the idea, but he wouldn't have any of it. "Out of the question," he said. "They belong to the cathedral here in Cologne and nowhere else." "But I just want to borrow them." "No, that won't be possible." I think they would have fit in well in London because there's a certain architecturally similar "heaviness"—both in London itself, in the architecture of the city, and in the churches. For me, the gargoyles of Cologne were simply

"English." So I made these photos for the invitation card, which—as someone there told me—was "very British" in itself. And for the London exhibition I created my own gargoyles.

DIEDERICHSEN: The *Wasserspeier* are also active sculptures—where the name itself [literally, "water-spewers"] expresses an activity. The same applies to your works all the way back to the *Weltempfänger* (World Receivers) (1987–92), where sculptures have a function, an activity. Yet at the same time, in that case, the activity is the act of receiving—so you have activity and passivity all in one. For me, that's a very good description of the art of sculpture: held as if by magic in a concrete form, but always having something to do with the possibility of activity and passivity, which reveals itself in titles, contexts, etc.

GENZKEN: Before the *Weltempfänger* I made the pieces about hi-fi systems—or rather, the sculptural aspect of hi-fi equipment—which I photographed in 1979. Then, as usual, I built my own devices and called them *Weltempfänger*—even though you couldn't hear anything. I found that aspect pleasantly absurd. They were made out of cement, but had small, real antennas. At the Frankfurter Kunstverein, Nikolaus Schaffhausen had recently put together an exhibition on Theodor Adorno. He displayed my *Weltempfänger* along with similar looking works by Bruce Nauman. Bruce had made casts of small cassette recorders. My antennas were also meant to be "feelers"—things you stretch out in order to feel something, like the sound of the world and its many tones. But, of all things, some people took offense at the feelers.

DIEDERICHSEN: Too concrete, too literal?

GENZKEN: Yes, but people were really disconcerted. And I was upset that they'd taken offense. But in the end they were pleased with my invention.

DIEDERICHSEN: It's no surprise that aficionados of "pure sculpture" thought you were making a joke about their artistic beliefs by using these very literal, "quoted" antennas in otherwise highly formalistic sculpture. On the other hand, and in contrast to other artists of the early 1980s, the works don't only strike a humorous note. Their sober, "pure" aspects are no less important than the more literal, humorous "quotations."

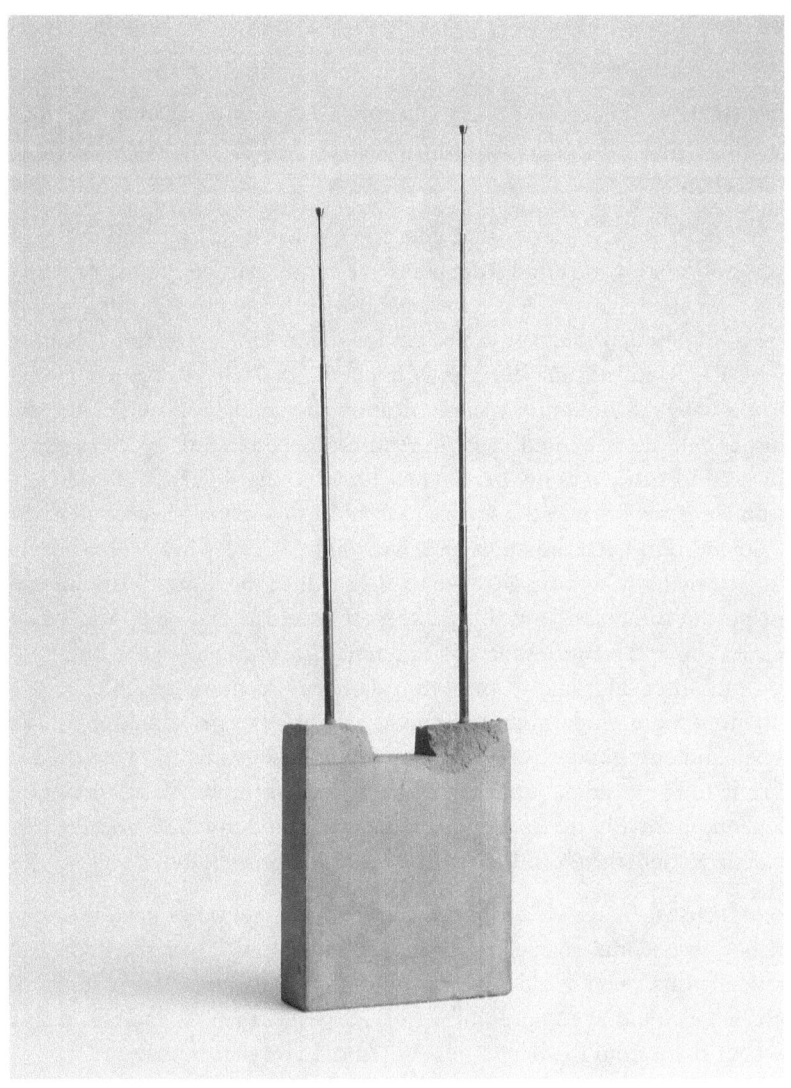

Weltempfänger, 1987 Concrete and metal. Concrete block 16.8 × 13.8 × 4.3 cm; installation dimensions variable.

GENZKEN: I didn't even want to create such a contrast, or play one aspect off against the other.

DIEDERICHSEN: There are many allegories of communication in your works, along with references to the outside world: windows, transmitters, receivers.

GENZKEN: Yes. The idea is that you open yourself up and find different ways of looking at things; that you have more than one frame of reference for the sculpture. Take for example the sculpture I did in a public space in Munich (*Untitled*, a project for the award International Kunstpreis der Kulturstiftung der SSK München, 2004). It also has something to do with this notion of communication. It's as big as possible, but still just as delicate as I could make it. And it takes up as little space as possible. (El Lissitzky was my hero when I was young.) There's an old cast-iron lamp, very tall, in the square in front of the Lenbachhaus. I attached a flower to it. Even though it looks very light, it's very heavy—so heavy, in fact, that you'd normally have to anchor it to the ground. But instead of putting supports beneath it, like you would with a tent, I attached cables above the entire square in different directions and to the buildings on the other side: one to the Propyläen, one to the Lenbachhaus, and one to a more modern street light. As a result, you get something that's open and communicative. A structural engineer would have attached it firmly to the ground, but this way it's held up securely but still draws in, and engages with, the entire square and the other buildings, and the cars can drive underneath it. Pedestrians can walk under it too.

DIEDERICHSEN: As we've already discussed, your sculptures have this tendency to become characters, as if they had a soul. Over the course of several years, even decades, you seem to have developed an ensemble of characters. And at some point a story, a plot, began to emerge. But it wasn't there from the beginning. When did you start to narrate?

GENZKEN: I always have, but not to this extent. At some point—with the New York books (*I Love New York, Crazy City*, 1996)—I started doing it more and more. I wanted to move to New York. In the beginning I didn't have a studio and lived in a hotel, so I took pictures. I've often taken photographs when I don't have a studio—for example, the *Ohr* (Ear) (1980) photos, where I took pictures of women on the streets of New York. I didn't have a studio then either. And at one point I put them together and pasted them into books. The idea was to make a guidebook for New York—not a normal one, but something for people who wanted to experience New York differently for a change: a lot crazier, more special, more multifaceted and beautiful.

DIEDERICHSEN: An atmospheric guidebook? And how did you make the transition from the narration you get from turning the pages of a book to the sculptural narration you practice today? How did you make that step to the "cinematic" works?

GENZKEN: I'd already made works in concrete that look like churches, ruins, and bombed-out buildings. These have a bit of this feeling to them. If you walk around them, you can discern different stories, find hard-to-reach nooks and crannies, areas that feel more secure. I was also quite explicitly playing with the idea of ruins and a Caspar David Friedrich kind of mood. So these works already had something narrative about them. I also placed small figures in them and, piece by piece, this just continued to develop. When I was in New York I felt this compulsion to make a feature film. That's where the title *Empire/Vampire, Who Kills Death* comes from: a screenplay I wrote at the time; but it was very difficult and I never published it. However, ever since then, the idea of narration has been a latent aspect of my work. I can make relatively small sculptures that go on to attain a large, relative monumentality. That's a rare attribute. It never has a 1:1 effect, but rather the quality of a model. The true size is only realized in the viewer's imagination.

DIEDERICHSEN: Every narration has a punch line or an otherwise meaningful end. What is it in your story?

GENZKEN: Humor, Cupid, love, and surprise are the future of modern art. How should I close? Many people are unhappy, and I think that sucks.

Translated by Matthew Gaskins.

Make Life Beautiful! The Diabolic in the Work of Isa Genzken
(A Tour through Berlin, Paris, and New York)

Lisa Lee

A total absence of illusion about the age and at the same time an unlimited commitment to it—that is its hallmark.

Walter Benjamin, "Experience and Poverty"

Subtle gray gradations—dove, ash, lead, silver, pewter—tinged with brown or blue, marked by wooden molds, speckled and streaked with uneven sediment, pockmarked with air pockets: Isa Genzken's concrete sculptures of 1986–90 exploit the irregularities of the material, further exacerbating its grittiness with raw edges and uneven horizontal breaks. Titles like *Zimmer, Saal, Halle, Kirche, Hochhaus, Korridor, Welle,* and *Bühne* demonstrate that Genzken's reference points are clearly architectural, though the roughly model-scaled works seldom mimic the morphology of specific architectural typologies. With the exception of a few early examples, the rectilinear structures in Genzken's works are never sealed or solid but instead roofless walls that delineate space. Breaks in the outer walls reveal dark corridors and niches partially lit by slanting rays that snag on concrete ridges. The pieces are lifted on their bases to eye level, and the viewer's wandering gaze navigates those corridors and occasionally encounters corners that cannot be turned. The pleasures of parallax are economically produced, as a walk around the sculpture opens up new lines of sight previously unmappable.

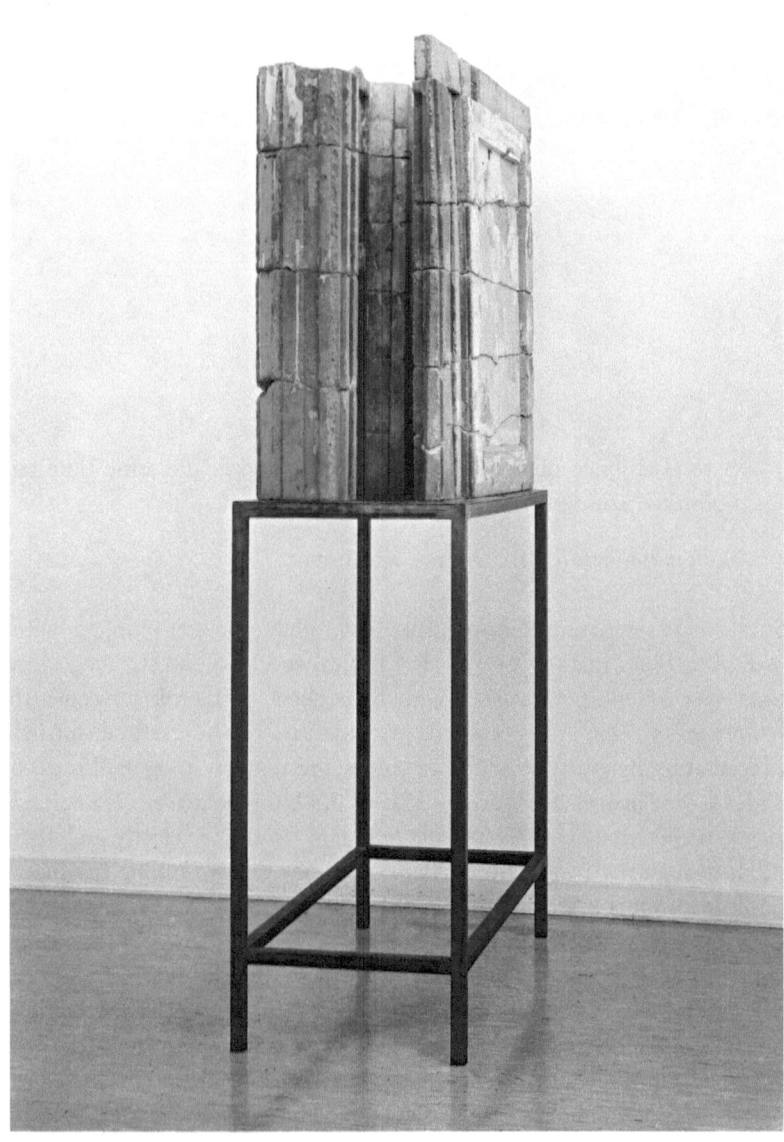

Dom (Cathedral), 1990. Concrete and steel. 280 × 151 × 67 cm.

Much like the different pourings of cement that make up the structures, or like their compositional compounds, layers of often conflicting references settle and aggregate in these concrete sculptures. The hulking masses conjure derelict and dimly lit housing projects and bombed-out buildings. (Genzken does not shy from explicit content or associative properties.[1] She one-ups her minimalist forebears, whose polished metal cubes and tiles look designed and hermetically sealed compared to her construction-site frankness.) Simultaneously, the concrete works rise like pseudo-romantic ruins, gaping structures that speak eloquently of a grandeur that has succumbed to the ravages of nature and time. For Robert Morris, the ruin straddled the sculptural and the architectural, a condition of liminality that aptly describes Genzken's works, the size of which belies their palpable presence. Morris writes, "But whether the gigantic voids of the Baths of Caracalla or the tight chambers and varying levels of Mesa Verde, such places occupy a zone that is neither strictly a collection of objects nor an architectural space."[2] Genzken's concrete works exert a spatial power akin to architecture rather than to scale models (as such, they act less like miniatures than metonyms for architectural presence). This is true even as they maintain sculptural intimacy, upheld, so to speak, by her attention to their attenuated steel pedestals, which raise the sculptures to eye level.

Additional conflicting meanings inhere in the sculptures' material. Sigfried Giedion's nearly alchemical view of concrete's possibilities (1928) speaks to its original promise:

> From slender iron rods, cement, sand, and gravel, from an "aggregate body," vast building complexes can suddenly crystallize into a single stone monolith that like no previously known natural material is able to resist fire and a maximum load. This is accomplished because the laboratory intelligently exploits the properties of these almost worthless materials and through their combination increases their separate capacities many times over.[3]

But even as concrete evokes early and mid-twentieth century utopian aspirations for air- and light-filled spaces, and even as Le Corbusier's *Unité d'Habitation* in Marseilles compellingly reimagined flexible mass housing in undisguised concrete, we have now come to know it better for its degraded manifestation in postwar low-income housing the world over. The more immediate referent in postwar Germany would be the ubiquitous prefabricated concrete slab structures built beginning in the 1960s throughout the German Democratic Republic. Once embodiments of socialist ideals of progressive housing, the large developments of GDR prefab apartments, nicknamed *die Platte* (the slab), were notorious after the fall of the Berlin Wall for their lack of infrastructure.[4] So if Genzken's sculptures cite concrete's utopian promise, their bulky masses aspiring to lightness on thin legs, they simultaneously bring home its failure to make good on that promise. Yet far from any simple melancholic reflection of failure, Genzken's project keeps the original optimism intact and in play. Utopianism in her work cannot be pried apart from its perversion. This is clear in the importance to Genzken of Joseph Beuys, for whom an expanded notion of sculpture as social activism was bound up with a hyperinvestment of his self with shamanistic power. The steel bases of Genzken's concrete sculptures pay homage to Beuys's vitrines, even as her choice of concrete stoically refuses any of the properties suggestive of transformation and energy transfer that Beuys favored (fat, felt, and beeswax).

Benjamin H. D. Buchloh writes that Genzken's sculptural work in concrete "insists conspicuously and consistently on addressing the collective conditions of existing in architecture."[5] She shows these collective conditions to be deeply conflicted. In Genzken's works the same stony face of concrete reads as Kantian sublimity, Brutalist *Je-m'en-foutisme*, Corbusian harmony and airiness, GDR drab, and Giedionesque technological optimism. The suggestive power of Genzken's sculptural practice is precisely a richness of reference irreducible to a single position. Furthermore, hers is an exploration of those positions and possibilities active in the present—as legacies to be reckoned with, tested against one another, deployed, or transformed. More specifically, in the case of the concrete series and the *New Buildings for Berlin,* the present to be explored would be Germany's in the decades leading up to and after reunification.

Like the GDR *Platte,* the Berlin Wall—first a literal barrier and then a differently insurmountable "wall in the mind" post-1989—can be seen as an unavoidable point of reference for Genzken's concrete works, executed between 1986 and 1990. The works are by no means tediously editorial or merely topical, however, but complicated by myriad references and positions and by their sculptural integrity. In their fissured and

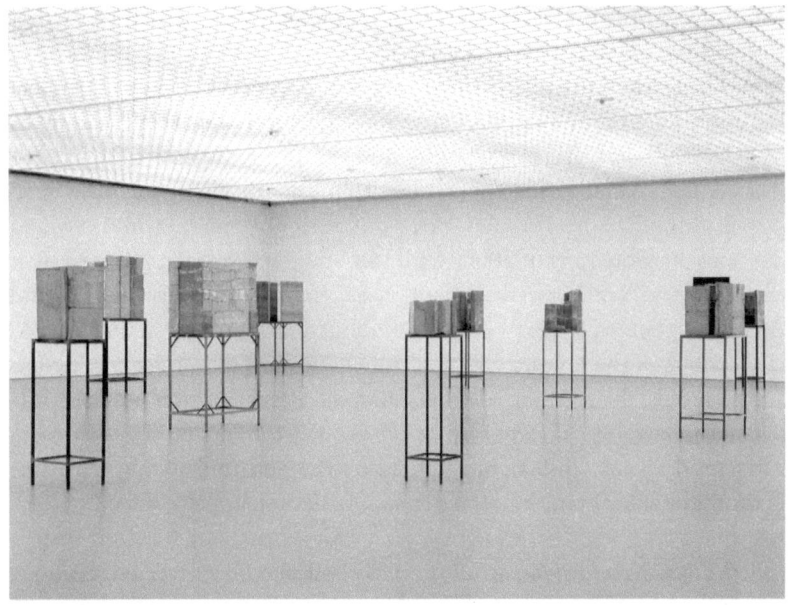

Installation view of *Isa Genzken: Sculptures 1978–1989,* Museum Boijmans Van Beuningen, Rotterdam, 1989.

ruined states, Genzken's sculptures suggest a rupture of circumscribed space and a breakdown of inside and outside, interior and exterior. The emptiness emphatically articulated by the structures and their brutal and unyielding permanence nevertheless speak poignantly about "existing in architecture," as Buchloh put it, and specifically that formidable piece of architecture that was the Berlin Wall.

Rapidly removed, auctioned, or chipped into memento-ready chunks, little was left of the Wall by 1991. In its absence a large swath of no-man's-land cut through the center of the city from the Brandenburg Gate to Potsdamer Platz, Leipziger Platz, and beyond.[6] But the voids, about which Andreas Huyssen has eloquently written, were destined to be patched in a rushed and uncoordinated manner, with corporate entities and private developers vying for spots in the new *Weltstadt.* Potsdamer Platz, a primary node of activity until it was devastated in World War II, was transformed from a thriving center to a barren periphery by the erection of the Berlin Wall. The fall of the wall prompted frantic efforts to reinstate Potsdamer Platz as the symbolic center of Berlin. Even in the months before the fall of the wall, the city government of Berlin negotiated the sale of fifteen acres of Potsdamer Platz to Daimler-Benz at a fraction of their market value. The controversial sale was finalized in 1990 and site work began in 1992 in accordance with Renzo Piano's prizewinning scheme. Only around 1995 were structures seen above ground.[7] The Daimler-Benz building was finished in 1998 and the Sony headquarters in 2000, with still other buildings in progress over the next few years. Friedrichstadt Passagen, Checkpoint Charlie, and Alexanderplatz were also being reenvisioned as commercial and corporate centers in these years. With considerable leeway in regard to design and materials, the first of these, Friedrichstadt Passagen, was built according to the envelope dictated by *berlinische Architektur,* a policy of conservative and illusory historicism upheld by the Senate Building Director, Hans Stimmann. Francesca Rogier summarizes the policy thus:

> *Berlinische Architektur,* an allusion to classical convention, is a homogenization of Prussian tradition blended with the severe architecture of the Third Reich.... *Berlinische Architektur* is, in practice, a rudimentary formula of closed, squat volumes with cornice lines at twenty-two meters and roofs no higher than thirty meters; sober punched-window façades, restrained ornament if any, and preferably drab materials such as stucco or stone.[8]

Alexanderplatz, with little surviving "historic fabric," was exempted from these regulations. (Its more recent history as the rebuilt center of East Berlin was all too readily dismissed.) Against the bitter protest of community groups, big business representatives dominating the Alexanderplatz jury rallied behind Hans Kollhoff and Helga Timmerman's winning scheme, which proposed the construction of thirteen high-rises and garnered the nickname "Little Manhattan."[9]

Critics have described the post-Wall refashioning of Berlin's image, with faux-historicism on the one hand and corporate "modernism" on the other, as a making of a theme park, media city, and *Schaustelle* (site of viewing and spectacle); as a sign of willed ignorance of Germany's Weimar-era legacy of advanced architecture by figures like Ludwig Mies van der Rohe, Walter Gropius, and Bruno Taut; as a troubled reckoning with the Nazi past; and as a stale debate between *berlinische Architektur* and *kritische Rekonstruktion*—stale because both positions ultimately reduce to a fictionalized notion of an European city of uniform building structures.[10] It is against this backdrop of architecture as image and of reconstruction as theater that we must see Genzken's series *New Buildings for Berlin,* begun in 2001 and continued in 2002 and 2004. Rectangular strips of jewel-toned, clear, and textured glass, eighty centimeters high, lean one against another like Richard Serra prop pieces made luminous (if precarious) skyscrapers, or like streamlined descendents of Vladimir Tatlin's *Monument to the Third International* (1919). But are these Serras made luminous or simply Serra "lite"? After all, Serra's meticulous architectonics of gravity and weight hold hefty slabs and plates in perfect suspension—and we feel this tension. Genzken's *New Buildings,* on the other hand, are held together with sticky tape and silicon. (She asks us to move, in other words, from heavy industry's mills to the organized rows of Home Depot—or of Bauhaus, by which I mean Germany's version of DIY heaven.) Genzken pays homage even as she travesties Serra's work, taking to task the hyper-masculine tendencies and blue-collar pretensions of some of the rhetoric surrounding it. This element of travesty is characteristic of many of Genzken's works: Tatlin's *Corner Reliefs* made flaccid, jangling mobiles of mangled cake pans, rakes, and other household wares, for instance. Or Genzken's *Soziale Fassaden* (Social Facades) (2002), compositions on panel of mirror foil in saturated color and disco-ready finishes, which suggest gleeful perversions and amped-up iterations of abstraction's opticality. Gridded foil taunts the stoic modernist grid; the purported non-referentiality of geometric abstraction gives way to glittering facades; and sublime uplift is trumped by the specular ecstasy of the dance hall and club culture. Consider also Genzken's public sculpture for Leipzig, *Rose*—an eight-meter tall stainless steel, aluminum, and lacquer rose, which could be read as a kitschy, banal, and ludicrous literalization of Beuysian utopianism à la *Rose for Direct Democracy,* in which a fresh bloom in a graduated cylinder enlivened each of the one hundred days of Documenta 5 in 1972. Beuys writes, "Bud and bloom are in fact green leaves transformed. So in relation to the leaves and the stem the bloom is a revolution, although it grows through organic transformation and evolution."[11] The revolution is arrested in Genzken's *Rose,* a steely column memorializing the loss of transformative potential, a public punch-line to Beuys's outsized romanticism. With sculptural intelligence and keen wit, Genzken balances her objects on the line between homage and travesty—a line she shows to be remarkably fine.

In the 2006 Phaidon monograph on Genzken, the artist included Charles Baudelaire's prose poem, "The Bad Glazier," from his collection *Petits poèmes en prose,* alongside reproductions of 2004 versions of *New Buildings for Berlin.* The poem begins, "There exist characters, purely contemplative and completely unsuited for action, who, however, influenced by a mysterious and unknown impulse, sometimes act with a speed of which they would not have believed themselves capable."[12] The narrator proceeds to relate instances of "harmless dreamers" "abruptly hurled into action by an irresistible force," finding an "excess of courage for executing the most absurd and often even the most dangerous acts." He ends by retelling his own brush with demonic inspiration. Flinging open his window to the grimy Parisian air, he hears the discordant cry of a glazier hawking his wares. "Seized by a hatred for this pitiful man as sudden as it was despotic," the narrator calls the glazier up to his room, up seven flights of narrow stairs. Examining the fragile wares, the narrator cries in disbelief, "What? You have no colored panes? No pink panes, no red, no blue, no magic panes, no panes of paradise? You are shameless! You dare walk through poor neighborhoods, and you don't even have panes which make life beautiful!" Having wrestled his wares back into the street, the disgruntled glazier is knocked on his back by a falling flowerpot, his precious cargo crushed. The narrator, perpetrator of senseless violence, recalls, "drunk with my madness, I shouted at him furiously, 'Make life beautiful! Make life beautiful!'" Whether or not Baudelaire's poem directly proposed the terms for *New Buildings for Berlin,* it describes an aesthetic attitude critical for understanding Genzken's work, and particularly its development into the twenty-first century. Baudelaire deftly illustrates that the call for beauty and for life's betterment is implicated in violence, irrationality, and intoxication *(ivresse);* that the dystopian inheres in its more idealistic opposite; and that advocacy may erupt in antagonism.

Baudelaire describes the clamor of the glazier's crushed glass as "the brilliant sound of a crystal palace smashed by lightning," a likely reference to the Crystal Palace built for the 1851 London exhibition. Dolf Oehler extends the link to the rapid changes to the Parisian urban fabric brought about by Baron Haussmann's impetus to modernize, sanitize, and make rational the medieval city.[13] For my part, I relate the

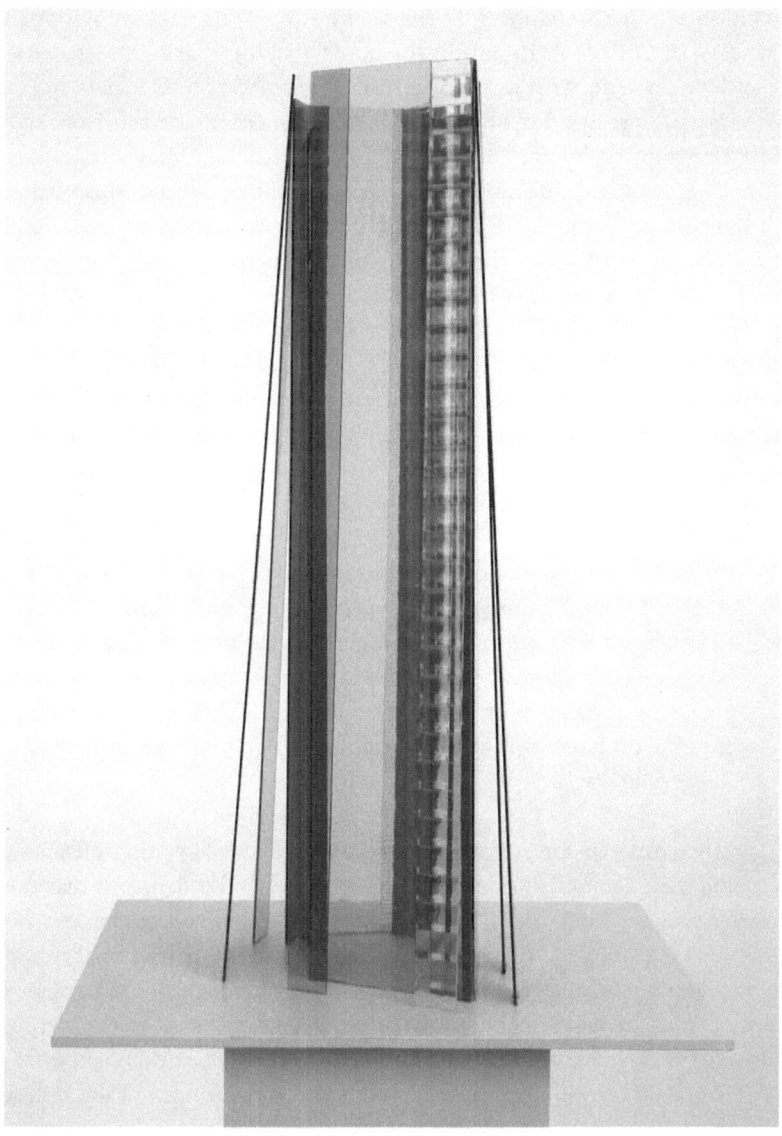

New Buildings for Berlin, 2004 (detail). One of five parts. Glass and epoxy resin on wooden pedestal. 220 × 60 × 45 cm.

wholesale reconfiguration of Baudelaire's Paris to the reenvisioned *Stadtbild* of Genzken's Berlin. In the context of the Friedrichstadt Passagen development, with its strictures of false historicism, Genzken's glass towers raise the specter of Mies's 1921 competition entry for Berlin's first skyscraper, also to be built on Friedrichstrasse. Mies's crystalline structure, with its expressionist, skyward thrust, bespoke a utopian belief in transparency brought about by technology: steel construction would free the glass walls from their load-bearing function. Mies's fascination with "the rich interplay of light reflections" is mirrored in the shifting perspectives offered to the ambulatory viewer of Genzken's *New Buildings,* which additionally offer the delights of shifting colors and texture's subtle distortions. Genzken could be said to give us a taste of glass architecture as figured in Paul Scheerbart's ecstatic vision of "the Earth clad... in jewelry of brilliants and enamel."[14] Writing in the 1910s, Scheerbart imagined the opening out of living spaces

> through the introduction of glass architecture that lets the sunlight and the light of the moon and stars into our rooms...simultaneously through the greatest possible number of walls that are made entirely of glass—colored glass. The new environment that we shall thereby create must bring with it a new culture.... Then we shall have a paradise on Earth and would not need to gaze longingly at the paradise in the sky.[15]

Does this call for cultural change through the liberating effects of colored glass remind us of Baudelaire's narrator, who demands that the glazier remake the world in rose-tinted lenses? ("No colored panes...no magic panes, no panes of paradise?" he asks.) Deliberate irrationality and perversion quickly become nastiness; soon prismatic hopes shatter into shards. In Genzken's work, too, we begin to wonder if the glittering facets of color circumscribe emptiness. For even as Genzken's kaleidoscopic towers invoke glass architecture's utopian promises, they reflect the evacuation of Miesian optimism and rigor from the ubiquitous curtain walls of the anonymous corporate structures such as those rising rapidly at Alexanderplatz and elsewhere in the city. Colin Rowe diagnosed commercial architects' deployment of the curtain wall as the creation of "a suitable veneer for the corporate activities of 'enlightened' capitalism."[16] Taking Genzken's title literally, for a moment, might we suspect that her "buildings" offer us pure veneer, empty of function or program? If architect Dagmar Richter perceives "that Berlin will become the first state-organized media city of surface," surpassing even "our expectations of Las Vegas, Disney, and City Walk," do Genzken's glass facades reflect the apotheosis of image culture, of surface pure and simple?[17] Does Scheerbart's vision of culture reconfigured by glass architecture morph into the nightmare of culture dulled by flickering lights and image saturation? Does Genzken show glass to be a cut-rate substitute for an authentic "jewelry of brilliants"? Or, alternatively, could she be seen to pointedly literalize the recent trend among star architects to wed literal and phenomenological transparency into sculptural preciousness, as diagnosed by Hal Foster?:

> Sometimes…skins and scrims only dazzle or confuse, and the architecture becomes an illuminated sculpture, a radiant jewel. It can be beautiful, but it can also be spectacular in the negative sense used by Guy Debord—a kind of commodity fetish on a grand scale, a mysterious object whose production is mystified.[18]

Of Baudelaire, Walter Benjamin wrote, "To interrupt the course of the world—this is Baudelaire's deepest wish…. From this wish sprang his violence, his impatience and his anger. From it too sprang the ever renewed attempts to strike at the heart of the world, or to sing it to sleep…."[19] Not prone to lullabies, Genzken's impulse to burst the glass bubble of our complacency cannot be extricated from an urge to effect change. However, to "strike at the heart of the world" is an ambivalent motion that can either still the life-sustaining organ or induce it to beat again. The dialectical tension between destruction and construction propels effective action—"*to see, to know, to tempt fate*," as Baudelaire's speaker says—while the alternative is ineffectual ennui.[20] Richard Burton articulates the coexistence of opposing forces in Baudelaire's poems thus:

> The appalling fascination of "Le Mauvais Vitrier" and "Une mort heroique" lies in their insinuation that creation and destruction, the urge to bind, combine, and unite and the counter-urge to break, draw ultimately from the same reservoir of energy…. For Baudelaire, it cannot be stressed too often, is both the *vitrier* and his

tormentor...sado-masochistically united in their very dividedness
and opposition, a congeries of antagonistic urges whose truly explosive conflicts are acted out on and beneath the textual surface of the
Petits poèmes en prose.[21]

If Genzken's sculptures in concrete and glass hold the two poles in balance, or at least refuse to tip her hand, it is partially due to their
restrained visual vocabulary and limited materials. Substantial and conflicting stakes play themselves out on the gritty surface of concrete and
across the glossy planes of glass, but the forms are more or less articulations of post-minimalist and architectural structures. Even the object-
pedestal distinction of traditional sculpture is clearly maintained.

For those viewers most familiar with Genzken's early series in concrete and glass (as well as her other sculptures with clearly architectural
morphologies, such as the series of windows and paravents of the early-
to mid-1990s or the series of slender, clad columns succeeding them) the
radical breakdown of sculptural restraint, if not of sculptural control,
embodied by her suite of assemblages collectively titled *Empire/Vampire,
Who Kills Death,* begun in 2003, comes as something of a shock. The
antinomies economically alluded to and evoked in the earlier structures
now rupture the surface and wage full-blown war in the combat zone of
the pedestal. The dystopian, destructive, and negative clearly win the
day: Genzken gives free rein to the travesty, the comic-grotesque, the
diabolical act, and the hysterical outburst.

With *Empire/Vampire, Who Kills Death,* post-minimalist form
explodes into the myriad surfaces and shapes offered by consumer culture: action figures, denim jeans, straws, cheap glass goblets, sunflower
seeds, plastic flora, boots, and bread. Exuberantly spattered with glossy
paint (in blinding white or Day-Glo colors) and topped or wrapped in
sheets of mirror foil, these mad constructions defy all rules of compositional harmony, visual cohesion, or sculptural integrity. The architectural is hardly absent, but it has suffered grotesque and hilarious
disfigurement. Glass architecture is reduced to glass goblets and vases;
soaring arches are mimed (and maimed) by rubber tubing or by a sheet
of bent foil, held in place by liberal distribution of tape. (In her gratu-
itous use of tape, Genzken thumbs her nose at the architectural fetishization of the joint and seam.) The cheapness and tackiness of her materials,
too, is a reflection on the architectural context in Germany:

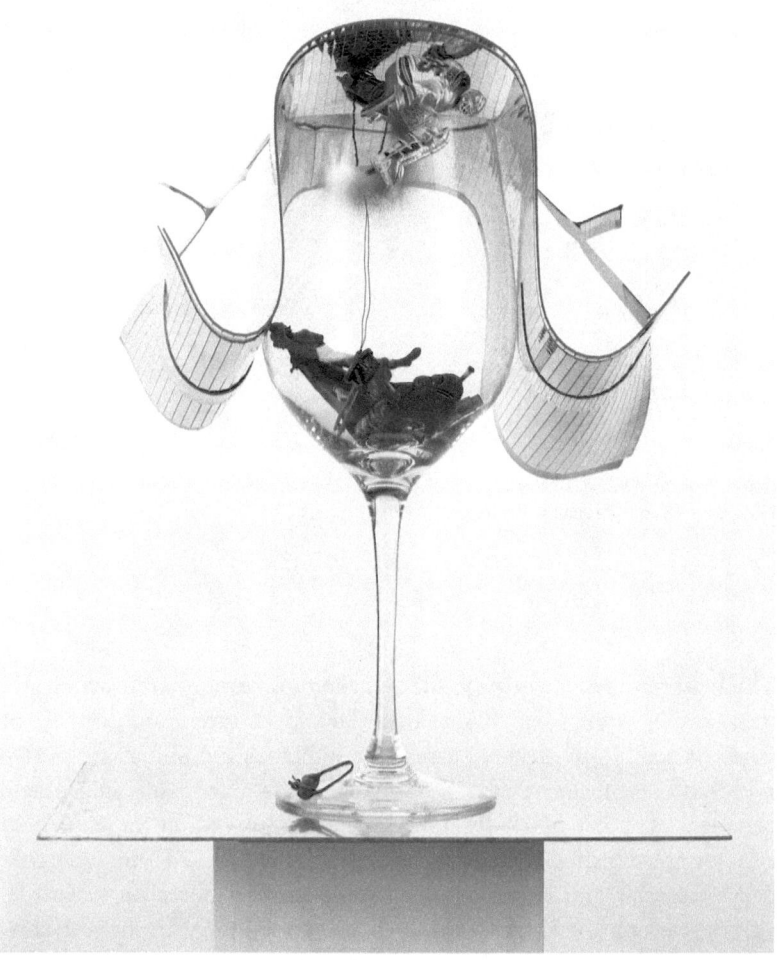

Empire/Vampire, Who Kills Death, 2002/2003 (detail). Mixed media, one of twenty-two parts.
208 × 60 × 50 cm; installation dimensions variable.

The awful thing about architecture here is that everything, almost everything, is done in the cheapest construction style, the cheapest. They don't make sure people use the best materials, they just use what's cheapest. Just look at Potsdamer Platz, it's like a piece of scenery![22]

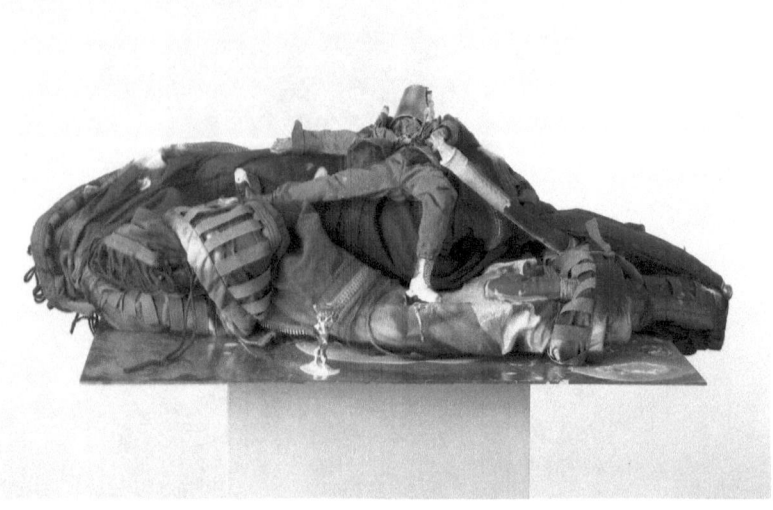

Empire/Vampire, Who Kills Death, 2002/2003 (detail). Mixed media, one of twenty-two parts. 172 × 87 × 49 cm; installation dimensions variable.

The new term here is *scenery*, for Genzken's sculptures are now clearly stagings. In scenes of destruction and deconstruction, armies of tchotchkes play out grisly warfare, both ludicrous and unnerving. A figurine of a goalie guards the mouth of a wine glass containing plastic prisoners. Another figure (friend or foe?) lies splayed on the battlefield of a crumpled brown jacket, spray-painted garish red and white. Discordances in scale and of genre (sleek sci-fi fighters, porcelain ballerinas, clumsy cartoon characters), heightened by seemingly haphazard construction, give the sense that a sadistic child has wreaked havoc on a world of unsuspecting playthings. The diabolical fervor and perverse humor of these works seem to be carried out under the aegis of the same sudden, irrational impulses that incite the idle dreamers of "The Bad Glazier" to action and that drive Baudelaire's narrator to torment the hapless glazier. He confesses, "More than once I have been victim of such attacks and outbursts, which justify our belief that some malicious Demons slip into us and, without us knowing it, make us carry out their most absurd wishes."[23] In his letter of June 26, 1860 to

Gustave Flaubert, Baudelaire writes, "…I realized that I've always been obsessed by the impossibility of understanding certain of man's sudden thoughts or deeds, unless we accept the hypothesis that an evil force, external to man, has intervened."[24] The diabolic, demonic, and evil as motivating forces in Baudelaire's work, particularly in *Les Fleurs du Mal* and *Paris Spleen,* have been dismissed by Fredric Jameson as the expressions of the "second-rate post-Romantic Baudelaire, the Baudelaire of diabolism and cheap *frisson,* the poet of blasphemy and of a creaking and musty religious machinery that was no more interesting in the mid-nineteenth century than it is today."[25] Jameson wants, instead, to home in on the postmodern Baudelaire, the one who speaks to his moment of late capitalism and image culture with an affectless euphoria. But if for Jameson, writing in 1985, the diabolic smacks of old wives' superstitions and symbolist gloom, there is a way in which our present moment, when postmodernism's endgame of simulacrum has dead-ended, might reach back to the diabolic—a pact with the devil to escape the end times—to find in it strategies for drastic action.

Benjamin seemed to understand the gambit of Baudelaire's invocation of the diabolic. "Spleen," he wrote, "is that feeling which corresponds to catastrophe in permanence."[26] That haunting phrase "catastrophe in permanence" would describe our inheritance from the twentieth century, heightened, renewed and compounded by the opening bars of the twenty-first century. Genzken has stated that *Empire/Vampire, Who Kills Death* responds to the attacks of September 11, 2001 (Genzken was in New York at the time), to America's political machinations in its aftermath, and to the threat of the Iraq War. Empire and vampire refer to American hegemony by metonymic proxies: the Empire State Building and its "vampiric" counterpart, the Chrysler Building. On the world stage the theater of war plays itself out in encore after encore (featuring frequent set, cast, and costume changes):

> The course of history as represented in the concept of catastrophe has no more claim on the attention of the thinking than the kaleidoscope in the hand of a child which, with each turn, collapses everything ordered into new order. The justness of this image is well-founded. The concepts of the rulers have always been the mirror by means of whose image an 'order' was established.—This kaleidoscope must be smashed.[27]

In a decisive gesture, Genzken slams the kaleidoscope against the sculptural pedestal on which she lets the pieces fall. The mesmerizing subterfuge of mirrors is diffused in the utter banality of mirror foil. In dropping the flowerpot-turned-missile, the narrator of "The Bad Glazier" does his part as well, irreparably shattering the myth of transparency. In "Some Motifs in Baudelaire" Benjamin describes the poet's artistic project as a "parrying of shocks" dealt by the city and by existence—one might add to this list those shocks dealt by catastrophe. Benjamin writes, "[Baudelaire's] shock defense is depicted graphically in an attitude of combat." Seized by a diabolic paroxysm, the Baudelairean figure takes aim.[28]

At her exhibition at the Vienna Secession in 2006, Genzken expanded on the sculptural idiom initiated in *Empire/Vampire, Who Kills Death*, and subsequently continued in *Wasserspeier and Angels* (Gargoyles and Angels) and *Der Amerikanische Raum* (The American Room), both from 2004. The untitled 2006 works, effectively installed as a motley group, are for me the culmination of a no-holds-barred, head-on strike against the sculptural form. In terms of shock value, these works offer the most devastating parry. For here—even more so than in *Empire/Vampire,* where the pedestal remained intact and the scenic aspect palpable—Genzken sabotages sculptural integrity, pushing it to its limits. If the earlier series addressed the catastrophe of architecture become theater, war turned deadly play, and world morphed into an aggregate of interchangeable commodities, these new works turn up the decibel of her commentary with strident effectiveness. Wheelchairs and walkers take the place of the base—how more succinctly could Genzken convey the crippled state of sculptural practice? Sculpture's body collapses into the wheelchairs as so many lengths of ribbon, unbuckled belts, and crumpled sheets of fabric and plastic sheeting; sculptural structure is deflated, flaccid, and formless. We are looking at the sorry degradation of sculpture's meticulous imitation of the fall of drapery. Long a means of implying an underlying form while transforming matter—marble into chiffon, wood into silk—drapery here is a formless heap of coarse ticking and polyester net. For all the seeming lack of restraint, however, these untitled works are remarkably economical sculptural puns: the walkers are armored vehicles that double as complex torture devices as well as rehabilitation aids for the war-wounded. Hi-tech crutches lean against the wall like rail-thin automatons or sci-fi firearms. The enlightened human comes in the form of a some-assembly-required torchiere lamp outfitted with stick-figure arms, legs, and head. Infant

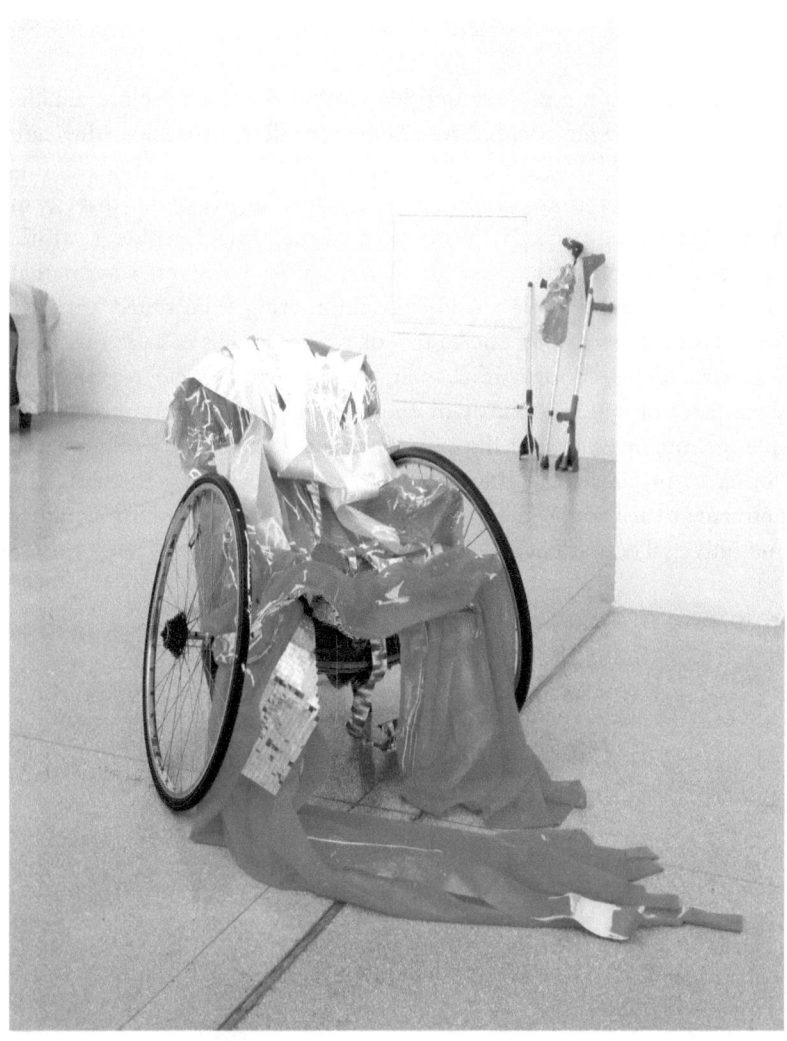

Untitled, 2006. Chair, wheels, mirror foil, fabric, ribbons, adhesive tape, and lacquer.
Approximately 92 × 77 × 142 cm.

dolls are shaded by slashed beach-umbrellas—like pint-size Buddhas, wise before their age. Two more dolls slouch over their plastic ponies, mockeries of the heroic genre of equestrian statues that are acute enough to elicit laughter. One of the two figures sports something on its head that looks like Napoleon's bicorn. They will never make it across the St. Bernard Pass.

Such a decoding of these untitled works belies their sculptural radicality; aggressive in address, trespassing on all conventions, they are decidedly in excess of comprehension or pithy summary. They distinguish themselves from similar contemporary aggregations that seem studied and caption-ready. Without mythologizing Genzken's artistic process as spontaneous release or id run amok, however, I assert that Genzken's works exhibit a deliberate unmooring from tested aesthetic formulas or conventions, the results of which read as ecstatic outburst. The structures—constructions built of destruction, held together by sheer force of will and exuberant energy—threaten at every moment to splinter into irretrievably disparate elements. These are works on the "brink of psychosis," as Buchloh usefully diagnoses. For Buchloh, the permanent catastrophe these works address is that of consumer culture and universal equivalence:

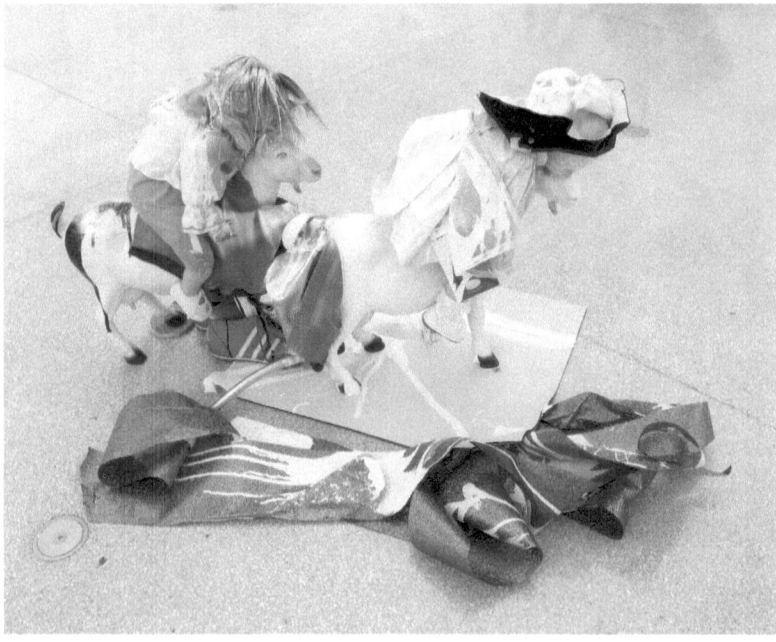

Untitled, 2006. Two plastic animals (goats), two dolls, pair of shoes, cap, plastic, foam, felt, fabric, metallic paper, adhesive tape, lacquer, and spray paint. 48 × 110 × 62 cm.

To have the self succumb to the totalitarian order of objects brings the sculptor to the brink of psychosis, and Genzken's new work seems to inhabit that position. However, since total submission to the terror of consumption is indeed the governing stratum of collective object relations, that psychotic state may well become the only position and practice the sculptor of the future can articulate.[29]

For both Buchloh's psychotic and Baudelaire's splenetic the spasm of inspiration—which physicians perceive as hysterical, the speaker of "The Bad Glazier" tells us—is a tenuously sustained refusal of total submission.[30] The "Baudelaire of diabolism and cheap *frisson*," or his proxy in "The Bad Glazier," would be Genzken's patron saint (or imp?), whose call to "Make life beautiful!" is accompanied by a convulsive, spontaneous action that results in shattered structures.

The flâneur, with his detachment and desire for incognito, is the figure whom we most often associate with Baudelaire. But taking a cue from Jameson, we should specify that while the flâneur may be exemplary for the Baudelaire of high-modernism, he is hardly so for the Baudelaire of diabolism. Instead, as Benjamin suggests, we have a figure in whom "composure has given way to manic behavior."[31] Hardly at home in the crowd, unable to quietly blend in, this figure calls attention to himself when suddenly seized by inspiration. He takes a combat stance against the world. With a reputation for being "a legendary fighting figure in the streets and bars of Manhattan," Genzken can productively be seen to inhabit such a persona.[32] In a 1996 conversation with Genzken, her friend Neil Logan recalls Genzken's destructive and aggressive attitude after her initial arrival in the city:

> What it seemed you were doing was putting yourself in the situation where you would be most vulnerable, and then lashing out at that situation. Like putting yourself on avenue A at five in the morning, and seeing what happens.... You told me that your favorite thing to do was to go somewhere and make a scene. You told me at one point that after five o'clock you liked to get aggressive.[33]

Without banking too much on art world gossip, cult of personality, or prurient fascination with self-destructive artists, in this context we ought to consider Genzken's obvious vulnerability, aggressiveness, and provocation to the world in relation to the "parrying of shocks" that returns blow for every blow dealt by experience and urban life. In this case the particular city would be New York, where Genzken came in the mid-1990s. Genzken made three collage books in 1995–96, which were published in facsimile a decade later as in *I Love New York, Crazy City*. Part diary, part archive, part uninhibited self-exhibition, the barrage of images and text coarsely attached with wide strips of colored packing tape embody an as-found rawness generated by the friction of pleasure and loathing. Takeout menus, hotel bills, ATM printouts showing dwindling funds, torn magazine pages, faxes to Germany asking for money, calendars of events (long since outdated), performance programs, business cards, and casual photographs of nothing in particular (the fluorescent pall of cheap eateries, skyscrapers viewed from the ground up, dimly lit interiors, construction sites): Genzken intended the collaged volumes to be a guidebook to New York. This seems ludicrous when one first encounters the dissociated, gritty contents. Scrapbook at most, it is certainly no guidebook. And yet, as with much of Genzken's work, its perverse logic makes itself felt in time. In fields of visual nonsequiturs, tangents, and fragments, Genzken takes pains to show phone numbers, addresses, menus, and maps. *I Love New York, Crazy City* travesties the guidebook genre's predication on vetted, scrubbed-down, and bite-sized versions of urban experience. Genzken's is a guidebook contra guidebooks, a walking tour for the walking wounded that enacts the shocks of urban reality across its ruptured pages. Driven by impulses, governed by no rules, Genzken models for us an attitude that subverts the tourism bureau's best intentions. Instead, she gives the city as good as she gets, parrying shocks, dealing blows, and showing us how to do the same.

The development of Genzken's work over the past twenty-odd years exemplifies a strategy of wholesale (even hyperbolic) embrace of an evacuated condition as precisely the only way *out* of that condition. It is a strategy found in Siegfried Kracauer's hotel lobby and in Walter Benjamin's notion of poverty. "We have become impoverished," Benjamin declares.

> We have given up one portion of the human heritage after another, and have often left it at the pawnbroker's for a hundredth of its true value, in exchange for the small change of "the contemporary."...

Holding on to things has become the monopoly of a few powerful people.... Everyone else has to adapt—beginning anew and with few resources. They rely on the men who have adopted the cause of the absolutely new and have founded it on insight and renunciation. In its buildings, pictures, and stories, mankind is preparing to outlive culture, if need be. And the main thing is that it does so with a laugh. This laughter may occasionally sound barbaric. Well and good.[34]

Barbaric—or diabolic, perhaps. Between spasms of convulsive laughter prompted by Genzken's constructions, we are commanded to "Make life beautiful!" even, or perhaps precisely, at our own risk.

Notes

1. See "Diedrich Diederichsen in Conversation with Isa Genzken," in Alex Farquharson et al., *Isa Genzken* (London: Phaidon, 2006), p. 15.

2. Robert Morris, "The Present Tense of Space," in *Continuous Project Altered Daily* (Cambridge, Mass.: MIT Press, 1993), p. 193.

3. Sigfried Giedion, *Building in France, Building in Iron, Building in Ferro-Concrete* (1928; Santa Monica, Calif.: Getty Research Institute, 1995), p. 150.

4. Paul Sigel, "The Future of the Slab," Goethe-Institut USA, July 2003, http://www.goethe.de/ins/us/lp/kue/arc/en51834.htm.

5. Benjamin H. D. Buchloh, "Isa Genzken: The Fragment as Model," in *Isa Genzken: Jeder braucht mindestens ein Fenster*, exh. cat. (Cologne: Walther König, 1992), p. 141.

6. Andreas Huyssen, "The Voids of Berlin," *Critical Inquiry* 24, no. 1 (Autumn 1997), p. 65.

7. Francesca Rogier, "Growing Pains: From the Opening of the Wall to the Wrapping of the Reichstag," *Assemblage* 29 (April 1996), p. 49.

8. Ibid., p. 48.

9. Ibid., pp. 55–57.

10. Ibid., p. 48.

11. Quoted in Caroline Tisdall, *Joseph Beuys*, exh. cat. (New York: Solomon R. Guggenheim Museum, 1979), p. 273.

12. All excerpts taken from Charles Baudelaire, "The Bad Glazier," in *The Parisian Prowler: Le Spleen de Paris, Petits Poèmes en prose*, trans. Edward K. Kaplan (Athens: University of Georgia Press, 1989), pp. 13–15. This is a different translation than the one published in the Phaidon catalog.

13. Sonya Stephens, *Baudelaire's Prose Poems: The Practice and Politics of Irony* (New York: Oxford University Press, 1999), p. 67, n. 80.

14. Paul Scheerbart, "Glass Architecture (excerpt)," in *Programs and Manifestoes on 20th-century Architecture*, ed. Ulrich Conrads (Cambridge, Mass.: MIT Press, 1971), p. 32.

15. Ibid.

16. Quoted in Reinhold Martin, "Atrocities. Or, Curtain Wall as Mass Medium," *Perspecta* 32 (2001), p. 68.

17. Dagmar Richter, "Spazieren in Berlin," *Assemblage* 29 (April 1996), p. 75.

18. Hal Foster, "The ABCs of Contemporary Design," *October* 100 (Spring 2002), p. 194.

19. Walter Benjamin, "Central Park," *New German Critique* 34 (Winter 1985), p. 39.

20. Baudelaire, "The Bad Glazier," p. 13.

21. Richard D. E. Burton, "Bonding and Breaking in Baudelaire's Petits poèmes en prose," *Modern Language Review* 22, no. 1 (January 1993), p. 72.

22. Isa Genzken, "Interview with Wolfgang Tillmans," in *Isa Genzken: 1992–2003, Ausstellungen, Arbeiten, Werkverzeichnis*, exh. cat. (Cologne: Walther König, 2003), p. 137.

23. Baudelaire, "The Bad Glazier," p. 14.

24. Rosemary Lloyd, ed. and trans., *Selected Letters of Charles Baudelaire: The Conquest of Solitude* (Chicago: University of Chicago Press, 1986), p. 155.

25. Fredric Jameson, "Baudelaire as Modernist and Postmodernist: The Dissolution of the Referent and the Artificial 'Sublime,'" in *Lyric Poetry: Beyond New Criticism*, ed. Chaviva Hosek and Patricia Parker (Ithaca: Cornell University Press, 1985), p. 247.

26. Benjamin, "Central Park," p. 34.

27. Ibid.

28. Walter Benjamin, "Some Motifs in Baudelaire," in *Illuminations: Essays and Reflections*, ed. Hannah Arendt, trans. Harry Zohn (New York: Schocken, 1968), p. 163.

29. Benjamin H. D. Buchloh, "All Things Being Equal," *Artforum International* 44, no. 3 (November 2005), p. 224.

30. "Notice, if you please, that the spirit of mystification which, among certain persons, does not result from effort or scheming, but from a chance inspiration, if only because of the desire's fervor, has much in common with that humor, hysterical according to physicians, satanic according to those who think a little more lucidly than physicians, which drives us irresistibly toward a multitude of dangerous or improper actions." Baudelaire, "The Bad Glazier," p. 14.

31. Benjamin, "Some Motifs in Baudelaire," p. 172.

32. Adrian Dannatt, "Dealers Gazette: Adrian Dannatt's Choice of New York Contemporary and Modern Galleries," *The Art Newspaper*, November 2000.

33. Isa Genzken, "Interview with Niel [sic] Logan held in New York, at a bar near the Brooklyn Bridge on Wednesday, July 9, 1996," in *I Love New York, Crazy City*, ed. Isa Genzken and Beatrix Ruf (Zurich: JRP Ringier, 2006), n.p.

34. Walter Benjamin, "Experience and Poverty," in *Selected Writings, Volume 2, 1927–1934*, ed. Michael Jennings et al., trans. Edmund Jephcott (Cambridge, Mass.: Harvard University Press, 1999), p. 735.

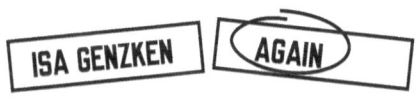

ISA GENZKEN | AGAIN

WHAT IF AGGRESSION IS NOT THE RESULT OF FEAR (VULNERABILITY)

BUT JUST AGGRESSION

THE CULTURE HAS A NEED TO HUMANIZE ALL VECTORS
(SUGAR COATING ON A BITTER PILL)

IN EFFECT

AN INTENT IS ATTRIBUTED

THIS INTENT IS IN CONTRAST

TO WHAT IS EXPLICITLY PRESENTED BY ISA GENZKEN

ANGRY WITH THE CONFIGURATION PRESENTED TO HER
& UTILIZING THE MATERIALS PRESENTED TO HER
BY THE SELF·SAME CULTURE
SHE BUILDS CAIRN AFTER CAIRN
TO PRESENT ANOTHER CONFIGURATION
BASED ON THE DIGINITY OF THE AGGRESSION

LAWRENCE WEINER
NEW YORK CITY · 2010

The Dialectic of Beauty: On the Work of Isa Genzken

Juliane Rebentisch

It is a commonplace today that art cannot be captured by the concept of the beautiful. The beautiful of art is, in modernity, no longer beautiful—it turns against the smoothness, the closure, the even calculation on the basis of which art so often in its history sold itself to ideology. Still, even the contemporary discourse on art seems incapable of entirely renouncing the category of the beautiful. Yet that this is so is not merely a sign of the helpless recourse to outdated concepts out of a lack of new ones; nor is it always a symptom of the reactionary longing for purity that, often with a fringe of nostalgia, is still directed at art today. Rather, the tenacity with which the category of the beautiful persists in aesthetic discourse contains also an indication that it cannot simply be subtracted from art. It is the memento of a constitutive aspect of art, one that explains its interest even though "beauty" is today no longer its immediately apposite designation. The category of beauty points to something essential to art, and yet it is in all its positive definitions inadequate to the latter. Aesthetic modernity has not attempted to dissolve this antinomy but rather has integrated it into the concept of the beautiful itself, setting the latter in dialectical motion. Similarly, the artistic movement against beauty's traditional form proceeds not in order to banish the beautiful from aesthetic practice altogether, but rather in order to save it. For even this gesture of negation testifies to an idea of the beautiful that neither modern art nor aesthetics can renounce because it constitutes their dynamic center: the modern idea of beauty lies precisely in its indeterminacy, in its defying any definition. Beauty is determined only by negation: by the wreckage of the attempts to pin it down. Hence its intolerance toward all formalization and convention.[1]

It is not least in this sense that Isa Genzken is a modern artist. An obsessive attention to the tensions within the concept of the beautiful itself pervades her work. It is perhaps also this obsession that holds the various phases of her oeuvre, frequently described by critics as markedly heterogeneous, together—indeed, even Genzken's courage to enter ever new uncharted territories, her affective aversion against the recognizable, seems driven by this obsession. It is similar to her sense for the historicity of art; little is as repugnant to her as the safety with which others accommodate themselves in the once successful—as though there were no history, as though what was once good could be preserved as such without having to submit, again and again, to renewed critical consideration. Yet Genzken's sensitivity to all pretence to transhistorical validity is more than an idiosyncrasy; her self-imposed obligation to the demands of the time is rooted, rather, in a deep insight into the incompatibility of convention and art. "Keep mixing things up!"[2] is an imperative incumbent upon Genzken's practice, directed against that which in artistic production has hardened into principle: an antiprinciple, erected in the name of art. For artistic success requires not only a dimension that can be generalized into the conception of an art, its idea—its principle, that is; but also a trait that points beyond this dimension and refuses such generalization. It is only by virtue of this second trait, with which the work resists summary inclusion under a principle, that it gains the quality of singularity that decides its aesthetic status: a beauty whose dignity arises out of its constitutive rejection of all attempts to objectify and thus to normalize it. Any idea of beauty conceived without this rejection, by contrast, would be tainted by the misery of "arts and crafts," or by fascism (or both).

To produce art, then, must mean, as Adorno puts it in a famous passage in his *Aesthetic Theory*, "to make things of which we do not know what they are."[3] This by no means entails (for either Adorno or Genzken) that artistic production ought to, or even could, do without the rational dimension of concept, idea, or principle. Someone who merely produces based on a gut feeling does not know what he is doing, but does not ipso facto make art. Art results not from the closed-minded celebration of the irrational but in a movement by which aesthetic rationality transcends itself, the reflective work with and on formal principles

immanently opening up to a dimension that no longer fits the calcula-
tions of such principles. Adorno calls this dimension "expression"—it is
the epitome of aesthetic beauty in modernity. Genzken's extraordinary
artistic capability is thus an expressive ability: she enacts the paradox—of
an act of making that turns against the logic of (technical) feasibility
itself—in her artistic production instead of covering this difficulty up
with false certainties, be they irrationalist or rationalist. Yet that Genzken has maintained this stance is evident not only in a perspective on the
ruptures in the history of her oeuvre, which have saved her and her
work from becoming categorized. Rather, such changes are only an
outward reflection of what, by force of the tension between the general
and the particular, urges toward expression in every one of her works. It
is also for this reason that even those groups of works that Genzken has
left behind—precisely as a means to remain true to them—continue to
stand up to critical consideration today. Because their forms resist closure, resist subsumption under a concept, an idea, or a principle, their
expression has been capable of continuous renewal; in the light of new
contexts of meaning (including those that emerge with her new works),
they present ever new and often surprising faces.

With the expressive quality of her work, Genzken also threw significant weight onto the scales of the debate over minimalism at the very
beginning of her career. From a position of sympathetic proximity, she
expressed strong reservations against an intellectual tendency within this
movement according to which art was to be reduced to the presumed
self-evidence, the "specificity" (Judd) of its form. For instance, while
formally participating in the minimalist sensibility, Genzken's elegant
Ellipsoids (1976–82) and Hyperbolos (1979–85), which hardly touch the
floor despite their elongated horizontal shapes, undermine, by virtue of
their semantic suggestiveness, the positivism of form that was programmatic for a part of minimalism. Genzken's works decidedly elude the
determination of formal facts; instead, they are set in motion again and
again by the associations they attract in the varying contexts in which
they are presented: for moments, they appear to resemble projectiles or
boats, husks or conches, to slash space or to measure it; now they look,
by virtue of their colors, like paintings, now like sculptures; their bodies
seem light or weighty, to be about to lift off or to land. Their expression
consists in this dynamization of form by a play of meanings entangled
with it.

The determination with which Genzken opposed, early on, the openness of expression to the literalist mentality in minimalism also manifests a skepticism, remarkably clear-sighted in today's perspective, toward the abstract antipsychologism of modernism. For the latter had one of its last peaks—for the time being—in minimalist positivism (another being the conceptualist reduction of art to its idea). There is no denying that the modern reservation against expression was to some degree justified by the critique of subjectivism. Yet when this reservation grows into a general enmity that denounces all expression as all too human, it enters into an alliance with the aversion against all ambivalence, incommensurability, openness; an aversion that is combative less against the ideology of subjectivism than against the possibility of subjective experience as such. Although Genzken shares the modernist reservation against the presumed immediacy of subjective expression, she has never been prevailed upon to exaggerate it into an enmity against expression. This stance was to the advantage not only of her own works, but also of those works of minimal art that had been produced under the sign of positivism; the latter were permitted, by virtue of the elective affinity that Genzken's early works sought with them, to appear in a different light as well. From the perspective of Genzken's double opposition—to the subjectivism of immediate expression on the one hand, and the antiexpressive positivism of sterile form on the other—a quality, to which subjectivism is as blind as positivism, becomes palpable: the abyssal semantic depth of the deceptively simple minimalist form, its expressive potential.

The sensory organ for the expression of the expressionless registers in minimalist objects a quasi-subjectivity that seems to stir precisely to the degree to which these objects pretend to have been purged of all subjectivity. In her works, Genzken has driven this effect further to the surface. Thus, she has shifted the engagement with the minimalist formal vocabulary into the vertical. The pertinent objects, a few Hyperbolos but, most important, the Columns from the late nineties, now confront the viewer standing upright. The latent anthropomorphism of these objects is underlined by the fact that their individual shapes interact with the names of the artistic and personal companions to whom she has dedicated the columns, such as *Andy* [Warhol] (1999), *Lawrence* [Weiner] (2000), *Kai* [Althoff] (2000), *Wolfgang* [Tillmans] (1998). To regard these abstract representatives as neutral objects is nearly as impossible as it is to tear the photograph of a beloved person to pieces as though it were only a sheet of paper. Despite their dissimilitude, the Columns function as portraits, if in the mode of withdrawal, of retraction. Again, militant enmity against expression has obviously been supplanted not by the simple affirmation of immediate expression but by an operation of critical melancholia. For the quite glamorous expression of these works, their stage presence, unfolds out of an experience of absence. Instead of attempting in vain to represent it, these works record subjectivity at the site of its absence—but precisely thus does this art succeed in developing a nonsubjective expressive quality that yet draws its force from deeply human sources: the logic of expectation, the not-yet of desire is mobilized, as is, in the dialectical countermove, the logic of remembrance, the no-longer of mourning.[4]

The experience of the expressivity of decidedly "object-like" works, however, corresponds with the renewed insight that expression is a quality that cannot be produced as such—as though it were about nothing more than another quality of form. Rather, expression accrues to the work when it is no longer reducible to the artistic subject's expressive intent or technical virtuosity or program but, to the contrary, emancipates itself from the latter. This may also be one of the reasons Genzken does not like to give interviews: less for personal than for substantive motives. Her art need not lean on the artist's intentions to hold its own: its expression is articulated autonomously. Indeed, the emancipation of the work, its liberation into autonomous expression, can be anticipated but never entirely recovered from the perspective of production. For its full development, the expressive quality of art requires the imaginative power of the viewer. It is only in the processes of aesthetic experience, in the chains of association that grow out of the specific work, that it is effected as a work, born into art. Hence, Genzken's works anticipate from the outset, if not rely on, the viewer. They share this with those strains of minimalism that were influenced by phenomenology. Genzken's intervention, however, makes it clear that the opening of the work toward the viewer does not break with but rather proceeds in consistent adherence to the modern idea of aesthetic autonomy. The commitment to this idea, however, is here framed as its critique; that is, as a critique of the modernist misunderstanding of which the autonomy of art consists in its independence of any viewer. For quite to the contrary, the expressive quality of art, its autonomy, is realized only, and ever anew, in the processes that take place between subject and object, between viewer and work.[5]

In these processes, the work does not rest in the presumed self-sufficiency and context-resistant impartiality that modernist aesthetics has associated with the notion of autonomy. Rather, it rises into expression by breaking down the barriers that separate its form from its literal spatial contexts, and its content from its social and cultural contexts. Yet this very movement of dis-limitation is not an objective property of the work under consideration. Instead, such dynamization occurs only in the processes of aesthetic experience, in the reflection upon the open question as to what the work includes, integrates, comprehends—in its content and its form. Genzken has made this aspect productive for many of her site-specific interventions, as in the case of the elaborate marriage, integrating the surrounding urban space with suspended cables, of a heavy flower sculpture with an old cast-iron streetlamp in front of the Munich Lenbachhaus (*Untitled*, 2004); or of the various windows made of concrete and epoxy resin, which seem to frame their respective environments. Precisely because the windows render the space around them visible only to the degree to which they also remove it can this space—both its formal and social dimensions, which would otherwise sink into the inconspicuous facticity of the familiar—enter consciousness.

Yet Genzken has reflected upon the dis-limiting dynamic of aesthetic experience with respect not only to works that enter into an interrelation with a concrete environment such that the latter will appear momentarily as a part of the work, if not its substantial and/or formal center. For instance, her small *Weltempfänger* (World Receivers) (1987–92) seem to be embodiments of the aesthetic object's potential, abyssal in this respect, of implicating the world. As works of meta-art, ironic and absolutely serious at once, these chunks of concrete extend their antennae-feelers toward us; those who are receptive will hear the world through them. Yet what they broadcast is not a universal language of art. Quite to the contrary, the world that seems to speak through them refers back to us, to the short-wave signals of our own projections, which these mute transistor radios receive and—in a peculiarly alienated form—send back toward us. This dimension, a quasi-psychoanalytical transference rather than a technical transmission between work and viewer, is present also in Genzken's photographs of female ears (1980): they seem to lend themselves to us, functioning as a sort of medium for

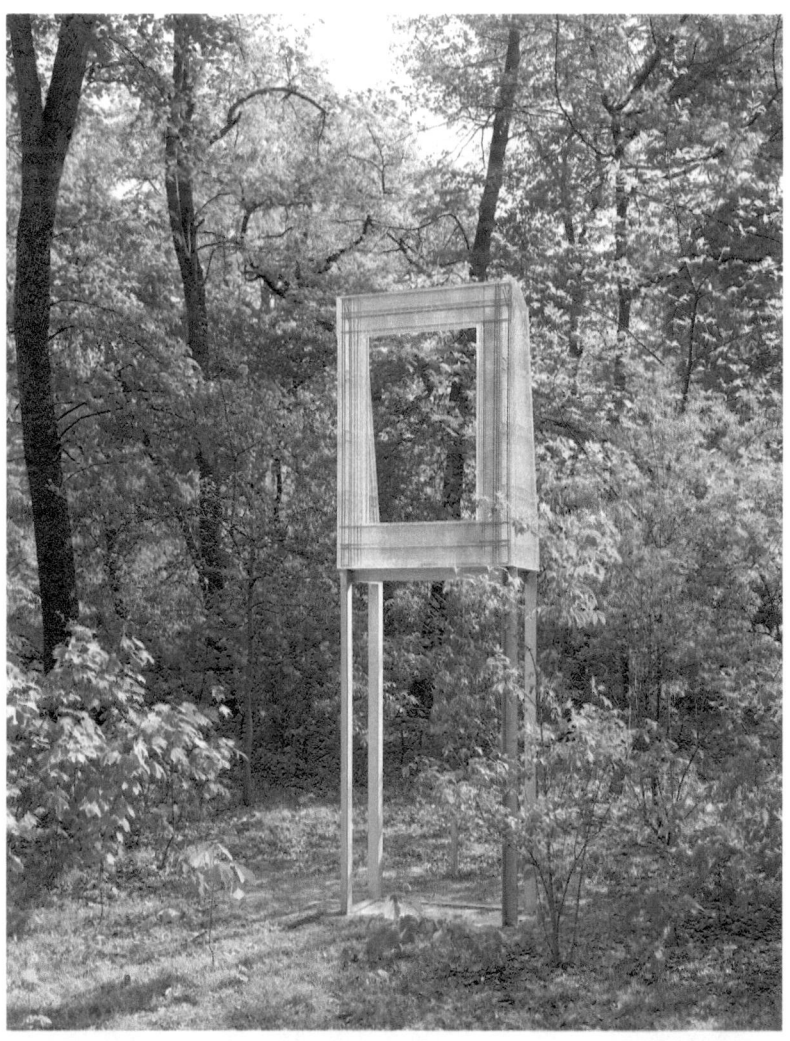

Zwei Fenster (Two Windows), 1993 (detail). Outdoor project in Antwerp, Middelheim, on the occasion of "Antwerp '93, European Cultural City." Epoxy resin and steel, in two parts. 282 × 89 × 51 cm; 395 × 119 × 61 cm.

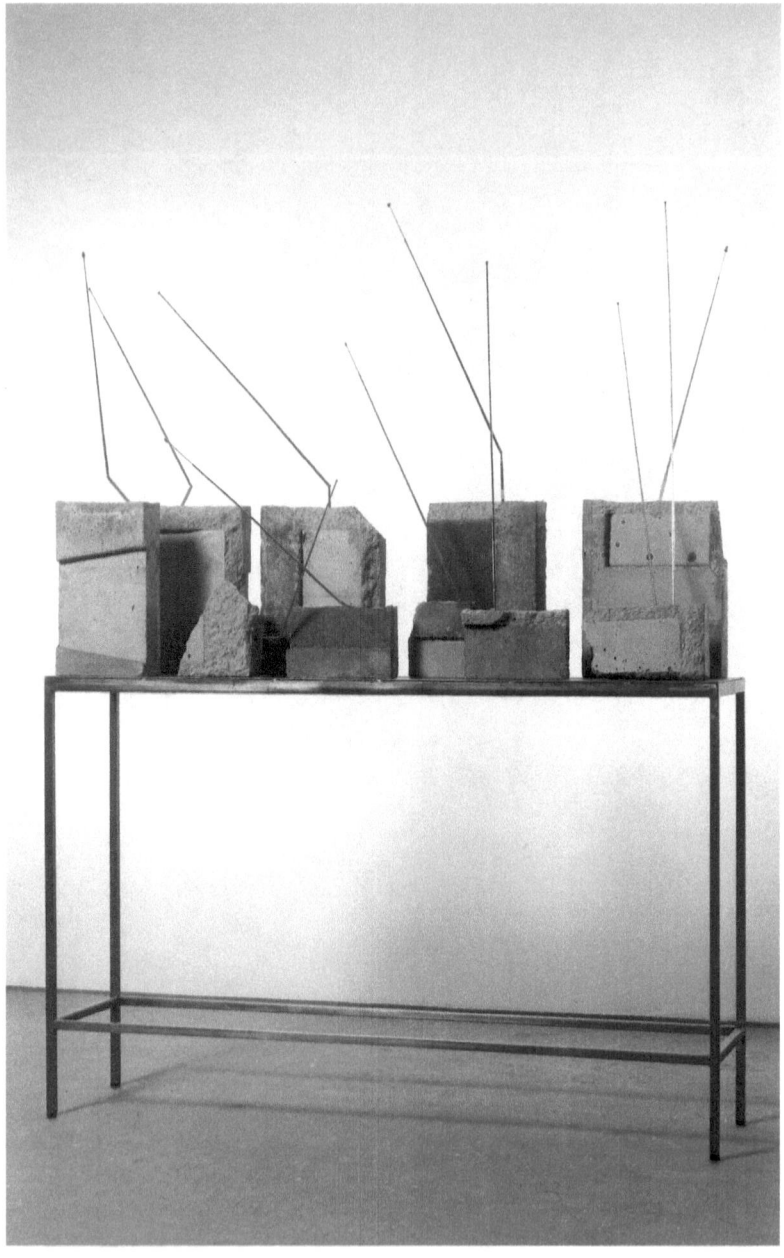

Weltempfänger (World Receivers), 1987–1988. Concrete, metal, and steel plinth. Installation dimensions variable.

the confrontation with our own projections and the prejudices that are at work in them. The photographs of the ears become such a medium, however, only insofar as they are never entirely reducible to our projections, remain noncommittal, time and again also closing us out and leaving us to ourselves and the meaning we have whispered into them—and thus becoming free to open toward us once more.

The viewer who is sustained in the resonant space of this art is obviously not the abstract viewer constructed by modernist aesthetics but in each case the concrete viewer. This turn against the universalist conception of aesthetic experience corresponds, on the side of art, to an infraction against the taboo that modernism had imposed upon the referentiality of art. For Genzken always insisted, against the modernist tendency to confuse the autonomy of art with its worldlessness, on the worldliness of her art. One might even say that her art is, in a certain sense, realist: not in the sense of a simple representation of empirical reality, nor even in the general sense in which any art is always itself part of reality. Genzken's art appropriates reality. It thus turns not only against Greenberg's prohibition of any representationality, but also against Adorno's attempt to commit art to a position as polemical against reality as it would be of another, utopian world. Genzken's works are too disarmingly concrete, and in this concreteness too complex, to be defined by any such generalized hypothesis (and the philosophy of history that undergirds it). What Genzken prizes in photography is the directness of the indexical relation to reality, and it is of great importance to her to produce something similar in her sculptural work.[6] The materials and elements of the latter, often taken from our daily lives, are decidedly ready-made: concrete, mirrors, toys, kitchen utensils, plastic flowers, apparel, books, pages from magazines, etc. By transposing fragments of empirical reality into her art, however, Genzken by no means aims to level the difference between art and reality. Things do not remain in her arrangements what they are outside, available to familiar perception: mere dull things. The aim is rather to help their use-worn form achieve its expression, and to unleash a beauty in it.

Still, Genzken does not attempt to subject objects of daily use to a state-of-the-art prettification in order to save them, before they are discarded, in the presumably safe domain of cultural value. She manifestly does not believe in such safety any more than she does in a beauty that would remain untouched by its opposite, decay. The beauty of Genzken's pertinent works emerges instead through a process of decay that is no longer covered up. For instance, her crannied concrete sculptures from the late 1980s sustain consideration not so much as immediate models for a future architecture; they acquire their explosive force for the latter rather from their state of advanced disintegration. These works appear as though fragments from the ruins of the very recent past.[7] Genzken shares this sense for a beauty that emerges out of decay with pop literature's fascination with the urban wasteland[8] and the 1980s Punk sensibility that arose from it: the burning concrete came from the demolition area. The dignified aura of Genzken's works in concrete is thus intimately linked to the impression of their dysfunction—the steel tables on which they are mounted at eye level emphasize both. Indeed, these sculptures appear almost as though Genzken had merely found them and exhibited them in order to make what has been left behind by the system of exploitation susceptible to redescription. That is the locus of their "realist" impulse. At the same time, by virtue of their segregation from all pragmatic relations, they retain an aspect of the alien that sustains extensive semanticization precisely because it radically eludes any specific description; hence their aura, which encompasses the realist impulse.

Now, the impression of dysfunctionality is here clearly of the artist's making. In contradistinction to Warhol or Duchamp, Genzken does not aim at an artistic decontextualization of what would otherwise be immersed in a context of use. Rather, and quite the reverse: she creates objects marked as art through and through that are reminiscent of a dysfunctionality already to be found elsewhere. Something similar obtains to more recent works. The assemblages of the 2003 series *Empire/Vampire, Who Kills Death*, for instance, not only remind one of surrealism by virtue of their daring compositions; they are also clearly marked as artistic works by being installed on pedestals. Furthermore, the extremely virtuosic play with proportions, compositions, explosive colors, and surprising choices of material documents the artist's expressive capability. Yet the expressivity would not be what it is if the artist's work were not again in this case transmuted into a site of apparent objectivity: what may at first sight appear to be the product of an anarchic eruption of individual creativity appears only a moment later like a catastrophic scenario that would seem to be only too realistic before the horizon of contemporary wars—like a world of injured things deserted by man. The object-world of empire presents itself here in a state abandoned by all purposiveness, telling individual and systemic stories of loss, disintegration, death, and madness.

Yet here, too, Genzken's art is pervaded by a sense for the beauty of what has been thus left behind by the systems of functionality. Beauty is here not constructed beyond the commodity fetish, as though that were possible, but rather, found—as expression—in the latter's decrepitude. The sensitive attention to the irreducible traces of humanity at the damaged spots of the discarded fetish corresponds, in Genzken, to a renewed posture and procedure of critical melancholia; here, she is camp. In Genzken's works, the flip sides of systems of exploitation, the rudiments of failure, the abandoned scenarios of history, promise—their morbidity notwithstanding—a different and better life. Still, the glamour of the ruinous, fraught with promise, could not, by virtue of its strict negativity, be further from the common (and commercial) ideas of beauty in our time. Against the brave new world of consumer capitalism, which ails from a sickness unto death in proportion to its desire to escape finitude, stands an art that has received the transience of things into itself because it sympathizes with the ephemeral in all that lives. Time, which tends to freeze beneath the smooth surfaces of reified relations, confronts in tattered things its own transitoriness. Genzken's art, by insisting on the flow of time, on history, opens up not a utopian vista but—and this is no small thing—the hope for change. This hope is represented, for instance, by the silver sparkle of the spray-paint in which Genzken frequently covers her scenes; the touching sight of a tacky flower garland; the flamboyancy of a neon yellow plastic boa; reflective sheeting from a discotheque, which seems to carry the energy of subcultural life; or the unlikeliness of the chance meeting of a beach shoe and a mounted boar's head on a pedestal. Yet hope is also articulated in the *New Buildings for Berlin* (2004), colorful glass sculptures that, in view of the architectural reality of Berlin, unleash an enormous power of negation not despite but because of their fragility; and it is hidden in the grace with which the steel rose, truly slender with its 25-foot stem, holds its own ground before the Leipzig trade fair center, where Genzken installed it (*Rose*, 1993/7).

Like the character who suddenly revolts against the ugliness of the false conditions in Baudelaire's prose poem on the bad glazier, so cherished by Genzken,[9] she also seems to believe that negation can revert, if not into the immediately positive, then at least into pleasure. In any

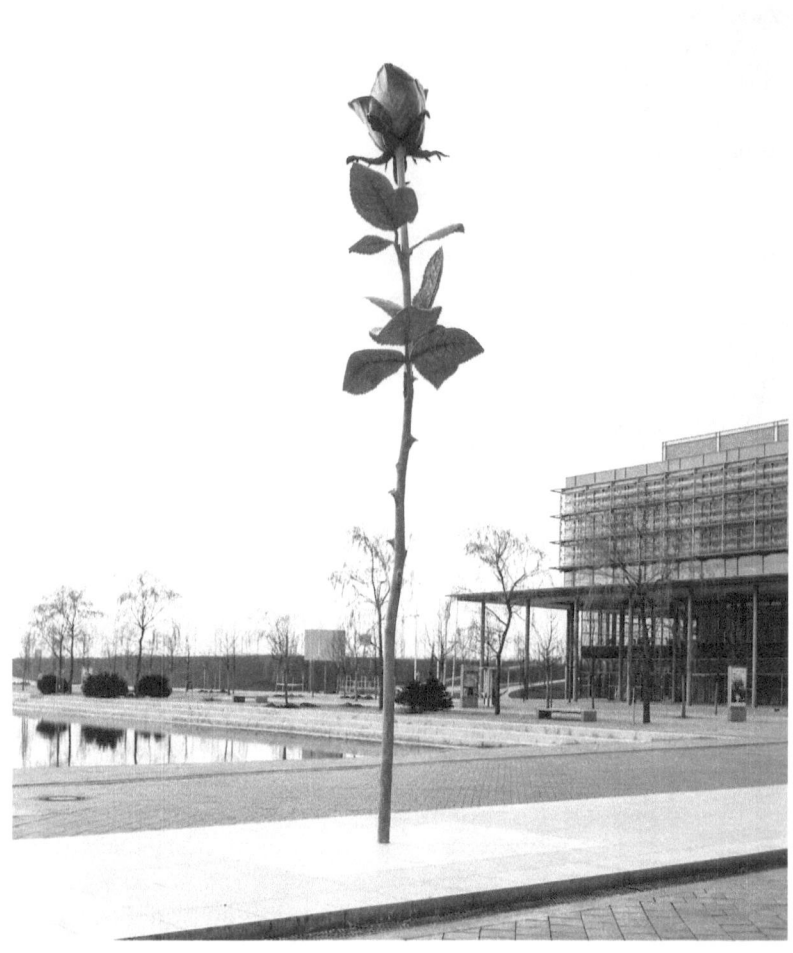

Rose, 1993/1997. Outdoor project in front of the Leipzig Trade Fair, on the occasion of "Realisation: Kunst in der Leipziger Messe," 1997. Stainless steel, aluminium, and lacquer. Height: 800 cm.

case, she, like this character, won't renounce the furtive delight in sometimes brutal and, on occasion, quite aristocratic gestures in the name of a life of beauty. Her chutzpah is our good fortune.

Notes

1. For a more detailed discussion see Theodor W. Adorno, *Aesthetic Theory*, trans. Robert Hullot-Kentor (Minneapolis: University of Minnesota, 1997), especially pp. 50–53.

2. Thus Isa Genzken on her productions, in "Who Do You Love? Isa Genzken in Conversation with Wolfgang Tillmans," *Artforum International* 44, no. 3 (November 2005), pp. 226–229.

3. Adorno, *Aesthetic Theory*, p. 114.

4. Regarding the dialectic of desire and mourning with respect to the anthropomorphic dimensions in minimal art, see also Georges Didi-Huberman, *Ce que nous voyons, ce qui nous regarde* (Paris: Editions de Minuit, 1992).

5. For a more detailed argument, see my *Ästhetik der Installation* (Frankfurt am Main: Suhrkamp, 2003); English translation published as *Aesthetics of Installation Art* (Berlin: Sternberg Press, 2012).

6. "[A] sculpture is really a photo," Genzken says in another conversation with Wolfgang Tillmans, "although it can be shifted, it must still always have an aspect that reality has, too." *Camera Austria* 81 (2003); reprinted in *Isa Genzken* (London and New York: Phaidon, 2006), pp. 129–137.

7. See Benjamin H. D. Buchloh, "Isa Genzken: From Model to Fragment," in *Isa Genzken: Jeder braucht mindestens ein Fenster*, exh. cat. (Cologne: Verlag der Buchhandlung Walther König, 1992), p. 134.

8. See Moritz Baßler, "'Totenpark mit Riesenrad.' Zum Verhältnis von Magischem Realismus und Pop," in *Abfälle. Stoff- und Materialpräsentation in der deutschen Pop-Literatur der 60er Jahre*, ed. Dirck Linck and Gert Mattenklott (Hannover: Wehrhahn, 2006), pp. 215–232.

9. For a book published by Phaidon, Genzken selected Baudelaire's "Le mauvais vitrier" from *Le Spleen de Paris* as her "Artist's Choice." See *Isa Genzken* (London and New York: Phaidon, 2006), pp. 116–20.

The Bum and the Architect

Yve-Alain Bois

"All objects which belong to a society have a meaning," notes Roland Barthes in a short essay written in 1966, at the height of the "semiological adventure." He adds:

> To find objects without meaning, we must imagine objects which are altogether improvised; now, to tell the truth, no such things can be found; a famous page of Lévi-Strauss's *The Savage Mind* tells us that *bricolage*, the invention of the object by a *bricoleur*, by an amateur, is itself the seeking-out and the imposition of a meaning upon the object; in order to find absolutely improvised objects, we should have to proceed to completely asocial states; we can imagine that a tramp, for example, improvising footwear out of newspaper, produces a perfectly "free" object; but even this is not so—very quickly, this newspaper will become precisely the *sign* of the bum.[1]

Several threads are intertwined in this compact passage, all of them having to do with various aspects of Isa Genzken's work, some more predominant than others in her recent production: the semantic *horror vacui* of objects (their incapacity to expunge meaning); the practice of bricolage, and, related to it, that of improvization; function and the asociality of its *détournement*.

There is something of Barthes's bum in Genzken. In some ways she is a bag lady, the 21st-century descendant of Charles Baudelaire's ragpicker, but in some ways only—that is, Baudelaire's description only

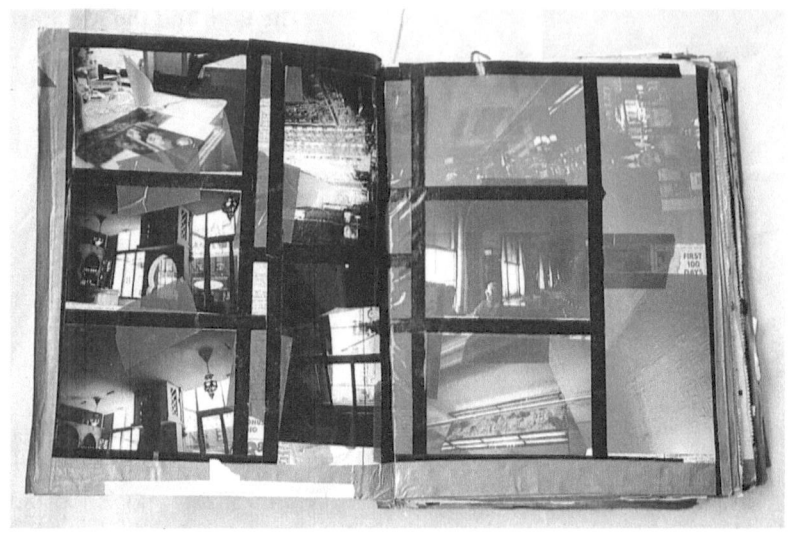

I Love New York, Crazy City, 1995/1996 (detail). Paper, gelatin silver and chromogenic color prints, and tape in three books. Each 45 × 30 × 10 cm.

partly applies.[2] In her mock tourist guidebook, *I Love New York, Crazy City*—the recently published facsimile of three scrap books obsessively composed in 1995–1996—she does "catalog and collect" refuse, but what she rummages through is mainly her own waste basket: pages of newspapers or magazines, receipts, menus, pieces of mail, advertisements, event programs, and above all snapshots that she took—of herself and some friends, of the city's architecture and street life (shot at pedestrian's level), but also of gloomy nondescript interiors—whose amateurish low standards are matter-of-fact, neither overplayed nor understated (just enough to signify that, even if they didn't, they *could* have come from her trash can). There are many superpositions, but a certain order is maintained—the dross is basically arranged in grid formation, the upright orientation is respected (no multidirectional Rauschenbergian flatbed). The connecting tissue, both as glue and framing device, is the colored tape (in all genres and widths—duct tape, packing tape, masking tape—and all hues). It is what imparts its grunge esthetic to the book, while providing much-needed visual accent to the undifferentiated profusion of rubbish. Could one say that, as Baudelaire's ragpicker, she "sorts things out" and that she "selects judiciously"? Only perhaps to signify non-choice—this is particularly evident in the last part of the book (presumably the third album) which is much more homogenous in its material (almost exclusively photographic): some double spreads are clearly focusing on certain "themes," on specific areas that Genzken traversed while she roamed through the city, on specific street events—but no effort is made to help identify them. For example, it is only if one has at least some knowledge in vexillology and cares to decipher the inscription on a banner brandished next to an Irish flag by one of the marchers ["ANCIENT ORDER OF HIBERNIANS"], that one can determine than the snapshots plastered over the spread are all devoted to a poorly attended St. Patrick's Day parade. True, the Gay Pride parade is much more easily identified, but even in this case one senses a reticence in Genzken's reportage: of an event that is all about a carnivalesque surfeit of signs, she squirrels away only a few emblems—rainbow colors of some flags, of an umbrella, of a dress; an obese drag queen. More shots are devoted to the onlookers behind the railings or to the surveying cops than to the extravaganza.

Baudelaire's ragpicker selects what he gathers with a purpose: he works for the 19th-century equivalent of a recycling plant. His stash of rags is to be sold to the goddess Industry who, in turn, will "remasticate" it and bring it back into circulation as goods of "use and delight." The recycling of trash into art ("delight") has a long tradition; it goes at least as far back as Schwitters, one of Genzken's heroes. But what of use? Lisa Lee stated it very well when she characterized *I Love New York, Crazy City* as a manual for survival: it

> travesties the guidebook genre's predication on vetted, scrubbed-down, and bite-sized versions of urban experience. Genzken's is a guidebook contra guidebooks, a walking tour for the walking wounded that enacts the shocks of urban reality across its ruptured pages. Driven by impulses, governed by no rules, Genzken models for us an attitude that subverts the tourism bureau's best intentions. Instead, she gives the city as good as she gets, parrying shocks, dealing blows, and showing us how to do the same.[3]

My only corrective would be that the tone of the book is not so dramatic. If anything one could speak of deflation as the overall flavor of the album: do not set your hopes and expectations too high; despite all the hype about the city-that-never-sleeps, nothing much ever happens. Yet do not despair either: life is life as usual there too, with its daily flow of insignificance.

But if I have some hesitation in casting Genzken wholly in the role of the ragpicker, it is not so much with regard to *I Love New York, Crazy City* than to the rest of her production, particularly that of the recent years—at least since *Empire/Vampire, Who Kills Death*, of 2003, up to *Oil*, her installation at the Venice Biennale in 2007. A good point of comparison would be the work of Bruce Conner, who so identified with the figure of the ragpicker that he gradually stopped making his classic murky assemblages wrapped in nylon stocking when he moved to Mexico, for the simple reason that he had too many competitors in the poor population of scavengers surrounding him and could no longer find enough appropriate detritus in the trash bins of their richer neighbors.[4] Even a rapid look at Genzken's aggregates of objects of the past five years is enough to make one realize not only that she does not suffer from such rarefaction of raw material but on the contrary that she courts (and comments upon) a situation of overabundance. If she is a bag lady, she is one that has the means to purchase the goods (often made of plastic) that, aggressively stripping them of their use, she will vandalize and smear in her assemblages. She is a voracious consumer, but one who is at war with the merchandise: all she buys—even the most expensive design objects— she immediately declares as trash. There is a lot of rage in Genzken's recent treatment of objects—something which Lisa Lee convincingly associated with Baudelaire's satanic drive and his celebration of *spleen* (in the words of Walter Benjamin) as "that feeling which corresponds to catastrophe in permanence."[5] And in this fury Genzken looms dangerously close to madness, as Benjamin H. D. Buchloh has pointed out.[6]

The fact that toys (a lot of dismembered figurines) bear the brunt of Genzken's wrath allows me to invoke yet another Baudelairian figure: that of the child who, in what the poet praises as the first manifestation of a metaphysic impulse, cannot resist to open up—and thus destroy—his toy in order to see its soul. "But where is the soul?" the child asks in vain once the carcass lays cracked. "It is then," states Baudelaire, "that hebetude and sadness kick in."[7] Yet despair does not follow after Genzken's bouts of anger—perhaps because she is not a flâneur indolently window shopping, she has no time for that; she does not empathize with the merchandise, knowing full well it has no soul, even if it has invaded ours.[8]

Spleen is "a bulwark against pessimism," notes Walter Benjamin, who adds: "Baudelaire is no pessimist. This is because, with Baudelaire, a taboo is placed on the future."[9] No utopia is allowed for those who expect "catastrophe in permanence." Nor for those consumed by rage—a dystopian feeling if ever there was one. However it seems that in one aspect of her work, at least, Genzken is willing to lift the ban on the future. Not unequivocally, not without a good dose of sarcasm, but still with a glimmer of hope. I am alluding here to all that part of her production that addresses architecture, particularly the numerous models she has constructed over the years. Most might be intended as critique, as we shall see, and almost none would be buildable—but still, even as mere concept an architectural model always belongs to the sphere of projection: one has only to think of Constant's all-consuming preoccupation with his dream city of the *New Babylon* for almost twenty years to know that conditions unfavorable to realization never prevent architects from thinking ahead (it might in fact be the reverse).[10]

A good place to start, perhaps, would be the set of seven sculptures, each resting on a plinth made of plywood on wheels, forming the set collectively titled *Ground Zero*, exhibited in London in 2008, if only because they are clearly a response to catastrophe (both to a past, historically situated catastrophe, and to that feeling of a potential "catastrophe in permanence" particularly unshakable for anyone who was a witness to 9/11, as Genzken was). Each individual piece has its own title, which clearly designates it as the makeshift model of a specific type of building (with a specific function) commonly found in urban centers: *Memorial Tower, Church, Osama Fashion Store, Hospital, Car Park, Disco "Soon,"* and *Light* (this last one not referring to a building per se but to an item nevertheless belonging to the sphere of architecture, requisite as it is in any cityscape: the lamp post). And, to further emphasize that these disparate objects mimic architectural models, Genzken had a team of architects concoct a sequence of photomontages (reproduced in the exhibition catalog[11]) in which their photographs in color and to scale have been pasted onto black-and-white shots of their putative urban context. The contrast between the grim pictures of the site (mostly gray, often blurry, and with signs of the historic devastation here and there) and those, in sharp focus, of the perky and colorful intrusions imagined by Genzken, belongs to the codes of architectural practice (especially favored when the fate of projected corporate buildings are at stake): such photomontages are today's equivalent of the (perspectival) presentation drawings architects used to submit for a competition or show a potential client at an early stage of the design process.[12] In one of them we see four of Genzken's models massed behind, and towering above, a sea of much smaller buildings (the view seems to have been shot a good twenty blocks north of the real Ground Zero empty lot); in all the others the beholder is positioned at the site itself and only one or two of these colored interventions per image is offered for our appreciation.

Two of the models stand out—the least and the most colorful ones. Unlike the others, they are both adorned with electric lights (small light bulbs at the end of twisted tentacles in the case of *Light*; ropes of light beads in that of *Disco "Soon"*); but more importantly they evoke violent destruction. *Light*, the only work of this series to be deprived of vivid color (it is metallic gray, with different degrees of sheen, from burnished steel to chrome), is a conglomerate of various objects, including several stanchions adorned at one or two extremities with a ridiculous ornamental fleur-de-lys, four of which step out of the trapezoidal plinth-on-wheels on which the assemblage stands and nosedive to the ground, this

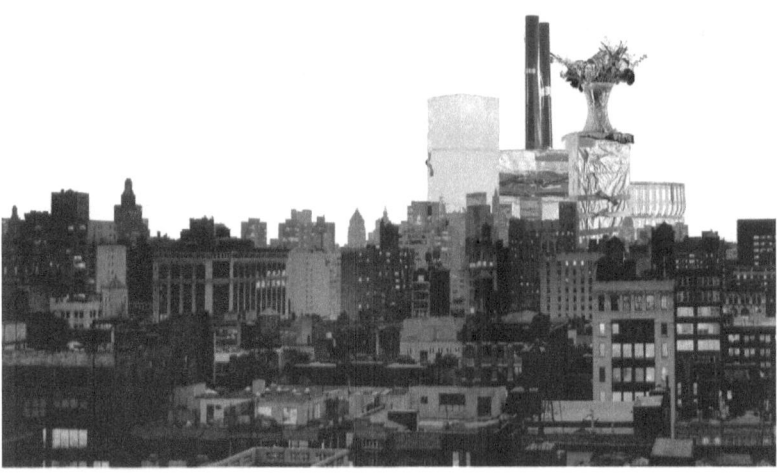

Ground Zero, 2008. Photomontage using images reproduced from Joel Meyerowitz, *Aftermath: World Trade Center Archive* (© Phaidon Press Limited). Copyright: Isa Genzken, Stefan Zappe, Zappe Architekten, Berlin. Courtesy Galerie Buchholz, Berlin/Cologne.

multiplication of supporting props increasing rather than assuaging a general feeling of instability. *Disco "Soon"* comprises two main elements: the first, resting on wooden blocks, is a cardboard box covered either with mirror foil or sheets of colored plastic, soiled with paint (some are folded over its top edges and fall inside), with a slanted mirror leaning on one of its sides and bearing the eponymous ad oddly printed on a French flag sticker: "Discothek/SOON/N.Y./24h Open"; connected to it by several ropes of beads and other forms of plastic vermicular tubing, the second element consists in several tall free-standing frames (perhaps rescued from a discarded folding screen) from which a cascade of colored strings fall, lit or not, and precariously crowned (high above the beholder's head) by a thin metallic plate partially covered with a modular grid of shiny golden tiles—alluding, no doubt is allowed, to the superficial glitz of night club decoration.

Both these sculptures, I just noted, evoke violent destruction—the crumpled rods of metal emerging from the ruins of a bombed-out building, the color-coded wiring systems suddenly revealed as panes of drywall collapsed. One thinks of the famous anecdote according to which Picasso, asked by a Nazi officer looking at *Guernica* if he had done it, responded: "No, *you* did!" Curiously, however, there is nothing particularly morbid about these two works; rather, the tone is more ironic and ludic than tragic. Because it looks so much like a piece of bombastic public sculpture—of the kind that has invaded our urban squares for a good half-century—*Light* can be seen as a comic indictment of art-as-ornament[13]; and because the chaos of its flashy beads stumbling to the floor is more festive than the regimented decor of the usual discotheque, *Disco "Soon"* might be read as staging a revenge of the material against robotized entertainment, the innards of architecture suddenly spilling over.

However, the ludic is not necessarily antithetical to the lugubrious, as two pieces of the *Ground Zero* ensemble attest, *Church* and *Hospital* (both of them, it should be noted, have two sets of wheels—one belonging to the object positioned at the bottom of the pile they each form, and one to the plinth on which each of these piles rest, a strange redundancy which signals unsteadiness rather than mobility). In the first, Genzken-the-bag-lady pilfers even the possessions of Barthes's bum: she takes the shopping cart, that is an object belonging far more to the panoply of the homeless than to that of the supermarket customer, who has only a fleeting relationship to it, and transforms it into ersatz building material (two carts are interlocked, in fact, one standing up, its sides covered with sheets of green translucent plastic kept in place by silver duct tape, the other supine, over which a sheet of yellow plastic, splashed with paint, has been draped).[14] A cross affixed to the "roof" (the fragile yellow membrane) is adorned with a golden (plastic) skull sprayed with red and green paint: the church is the supermarket of death, its only redemptive function is the soup kitchens it eventually sets up. *Hospital* is no less sinister, despite (or perhaps because of) the bouquet of artificial flowers that caps it. It is the most anthropomorphic of the *Ground Zero* pieces, the vase at the top reading as the neck of an interminably long body swathed in several layers of wallpaper, mirror foil, and (hospital green) synthetic fabric held tight by checkered bandages of various colors; the drink trolley, replete with a row of nine shot glasses, register- ing as pelvis and skinny legs improbably carrying all the weight of what's stacked up above (the main body of the sculpture is made of a hollow cardboard, but its mummified mass nevertheless conveys a sense of heaviness). For whom are the shot glasses? For the seven dwarfs of Snow White and two extras, perhaps? But which event would they dare cele- brate in the presence of such a lofty sentinel? In any case, there is neither bottle nor carafe on the tray.

It is in the three last items of the *Ground Zero* series that the particu- lar brand of Genzken's playfulness best reveals itself, one that clearly connects the activity of the model maker to that of the bricoleur and, in doing so, opens the sculptural practice to the scale of toys. The purest example, perhaps, is that of *Car Park*, for there Genzken's intervention was at its most economical. It was enough for her to stack up eight simi- lar round plastic fruit bowls (only differing in color and degree of opac- ity) stuffed with miniature models of cars (in plastic, of course), to interrupt this vertical stack midway with a layer of upturned cereal bowls (also of plastic), and to rest the whole on three circular mirrors, in order to produce the perfectly plausible (if a bit overpowering and much too lavish) prototype of a high-rise parking garage flanked by reflecting pools. Of course, the tiny toy cars are particularly important in immedi- ately attributing a function to the projected building, and for providing a scale ratio to its model—but even without them it would not take long for anyone to see in *Car Park* a strident criticism of current architectural practice. Architects, particularly of corporate buildings, often attempt to escape the contradictions of their trade and regain their autonomy from

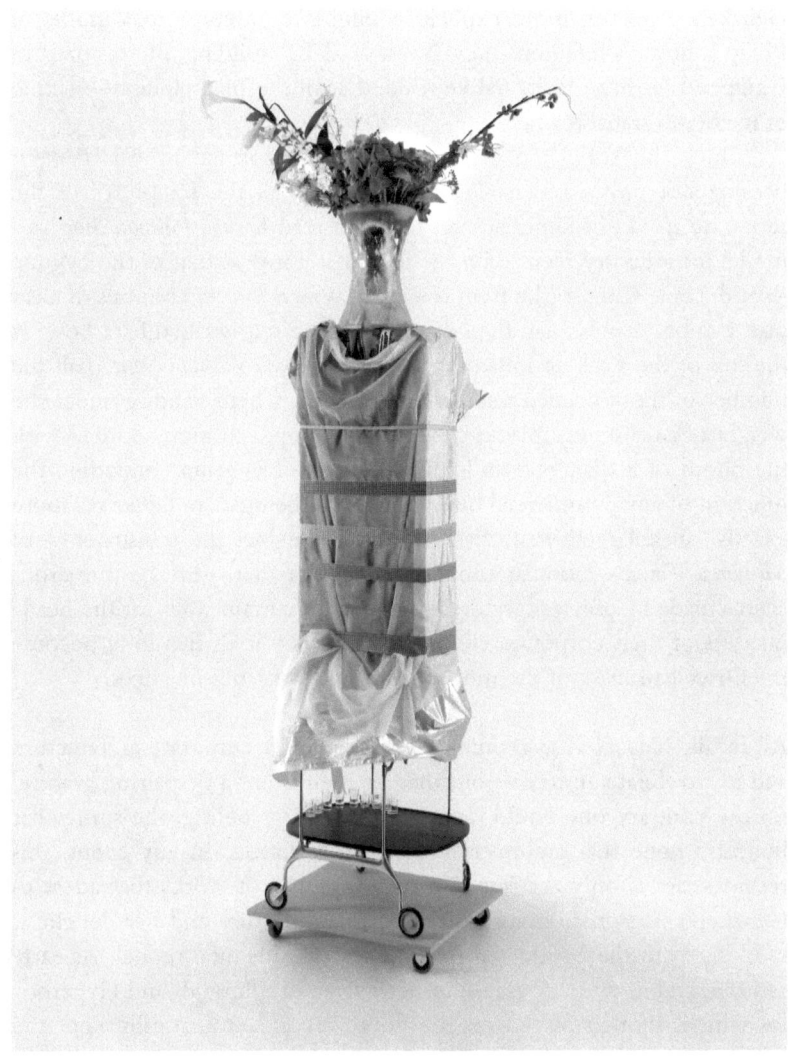

Hospital (Ground Zero), 2008. Artificial flowers, side cart, fabric, plastic, metal, glass, acrylic, spray paint, mirror foil, fiberboard, and casters. 312 × 63 × 76 cm.

their über-capitalist clients by playing at being sculptors: it shows, responds the artist, for they are rarely attentive to the scale at which their designs will be executed and the finished products more often than not look like blown up bibelots. (For her *Deutsche Bank Proposal* of 2000,

Genzken was even more explicit: adding two antennas to a model of Philip Johnson's infamous New York ex-ATT building, she restored its Chippendale shape to its native scale, that of the mantelpiece—making of it a bogus transistor radio).

Once this scale conversion had been performed in *Car Park*, it became not only irreversible but applied to all the sculptures of the series; no need of Lilliputian cars for us to read *Osama Fashion Store* as a model for a luxury retail shop, or *Memorial Tower* as that of the bygone World Trade Center (the twin towers of which its two columns of clear plastic cubes depict). On the contrary, the arbitrarily tilted fruit bowl at the top of the stack of four that make up *Osama Fashion Store* (half the number of those needed for *Car Park*), as if it where slanting under the weight of its contents (plastic shopping bag, rope, cushion adorned with the photo of a tiger cub and smeared with silver paint) underline the function of any commercial building: that of being a container or, more exactly, an enlarged waste basket. And what does the transparency of *Memorial Tower*'s modular units reveal, if not that, *pace* the numerous claims made by postwar architects in favor of curtain walls for the head-quarters of their corporate clients, transparency itself had long become the Orwellian mask of the most opaque and nefarious practices?

All in all, *Ground Zero* mounts a charge against corporate architecture and its inveterate amnesia—but that, in itself is not a despairing gesture; on the contrary one could detect, behind the scolding, the somewhat hubristic hope that architects might pay attention. In any event, this recent series is only the last of a large number of works that attest to Genzken's passionate involvement with architecture and her delight at working with the contracted space of the architectural model. As early as 1984, and in direct response to her oversized Ellipsoids and Hyperbo-los which, though placed on the floor, almost automatically kept the beholder at a distance, she realized several formless small concretions whose dominant material was plaster and whose titles often referred to architecture (*Haus* [House] *I* and *II*, for example), not to speak of the occasional inclusion of doll house furniture (as in a work called *Data*). These were followed a year later by a whole series of plaster casts look-ing like crude architectural models (the material used for the mold was rugged planks of wood, whose grain is often imprinted on the plaster), and given titles that corroborated such a reading: *Bahnhof* (Train

Station); *Kleine Kapelle* (Small Chapel); *Kirche* (Church); *Bank*; *Fassade* (Facade), but also, betraying a precocious fascination with New York's World Trade Center, *Yamasaki*. All these plaster sculptures, for the most part of vertical configuration, are set on a high pedestal, to be viewed at eye level, which "forces the viewer to look up as if s/he were standing at the base of a building" and bestows on them a monumental air underscored here and there (but perhaps also ridiculed) by the presence of human figurines that specify their scale.[15] Let us note as well, in this series, two works in concrete, of a more squat format, each entitled *Model für eine Gartenskulptur* (Model for a Garden Sculpture), and looking like miniature ruins: the fact that nothing indicates that these two works were ever meant to be built—no more than any other works in plaster—suggests that Genzken was very much at ease, early on, in working at the conceptual scale of fantasy.

As is well known, however, there is something of a hiatus in her production, in that the following works, notably all her concrete sculptures that immediately follow these fictional models (1986–1990), purport to be at a 1:1 scale. High on soldered steel bases (thus seen mostly from below), they read as fragments, not as models, of wrecked buildings—even though they are often shaped liked bunkers. A meticulous attention has been paid to the joints between layers of concrete (their irregularity was hard won) and to the corrugated surfaces. A similar 1:1 scale characterizes the next batch of works (1990–1994), for the most part dedicated to building parts (windows, doors), realized not only in concrete but also in the slightly repulsive material of translucent epoxy (also used for several gloomy floor lamps). Some of these sculptures actually exceed the 1:1 scale—they are enlargements (notably the *Fenster* [Window] shown at Kassel in 1992, the hinged frame of a gigantic three-story bow-window whose upper part, improbably in concrete, is piled up on the top of two similar sections, albeit in epoxy). In general, however, Genzken's infrequent oversizing during this ten-year period is an attribute of her public sculpture, and one must assume that in such rare cases, given the urban context and engineering issues stemming from the large scale (I am thinking of *Two Lines* of 1991, which consists of two wires connecting three high-rise buildings, or the 30-meter high *Spiegel* (Mirror) of 1992, or the threatening *Rose* of 1993), models must have been provided to the sponsoring institutions—but if they have existed, they all seem to have disappeared. Obviously Genzken does not

have an instrumental conception of the model: whenever they happen
to be necessary (to plan a large-scale outdoor sculpture), she does not
seem to consider them as works in themselves (the same is true for her
drawings). In other words, she is not interested in the actual translation
of the miniature to the scale of our daily world, only in its imaginary
conversion. And her quasi-exclusive return to the diminutive scale after
the 1990s might not be due to the scarcity of commissions for public
sculpture, but to her intuitive agreement with Gaston Bachelard for
whom "imagination does not work in both ways with the same conviction"—that is, "a sprig of moss can be a pine tree, a pine tree will never
become a sprig of moss."[16]

It is with the slick Columns of 1998–2000, followed by the funky
beach cabins of 2000, and the exhibition *Fuck the Bauhaus* of the same
year that Genzken re-entered the realm of the architectural model
proper, the most faithful to the codes of the professional practice being
the series called *New Buildings for Berlin* (2001–2004), elaborated in the
context of Berlin's construction boom after the fall of the Wall and con-
juring up memories of 1920s *Glasarchitektur*. What all these works have
in common is the use of polychromy, something rare in the production
of architectural models, and in deliberate contrast with Genzken's plaster
and concrete works of the 1980s. But this shared characteristic is not
enough to conceal that they do not all relate to their referent (modern
architecture) in the same manner.

The Columns are, actually, of a transitional nature as far as scale is
concerned: they are taller than a human being (often higher than 3
meters), and rest directly on the ground (no pedestal). Once again
Yamasaki's World Trade Center comes to mind (though she produced a
number of Columns after 9/11, it should be noted however that the first
batch of the series predates the calamity): in a photograph issued during
the planning process of the Center one sees its architect mounted on a
step ladder between his two towers reduced at a scale of 1:16—not at all
a common ratio for the model of a tall building.[17] Given the sheer opposition between their austere shapes (high pillar of rectangular or square
base) and the vast array of materials and colors of their skins, Genzken's
columns are an obvious put-down of corporate architecture, but not
only that. They are covered with stuff whose thinness is emphasized—
mirrors, photographs, perforated sheets of metal, gridded foil, veneer,
colored tape: high-rise buildings are all glitz, all surface, they seem to

say. At the same time, and perhaps because they refer as well to minimalist sculpture, notably by the dull simplicity of their volume and the way they occupy the galleries in which they stand, especially when exhibited in groups, and to the reputed hollowness of this category of work, they also remind us that color has long been—and in many ways still remains—prohibited in modernist architectural and sculptural practices, a prohibition that painters have often dreamt of overturning. Given the dreaded banality of corporate architecture, why not add some cacophonous pizzazz? Not that it would altogether absolve such architecture of all its sins, far from it, but it could lessen the boredom. The *Soziale Fassade* (Social Facade) series of 2002, belongs to the realm of painting or at the very least to that of collage (colored tape and sheets of various reflective material pasted on wood), and its gaudy material pokes fun at the tradition of geometric abstraction—obviously, for Genzken this route is no longer passable, except as sheer decor. But even though the target of Genzken's causticity is painting in this series, the *Soziale Fassaden* are a direct offshoot of the Columns, and could be seen as a fall-back gesture (painting as the practice one addresses when architects don't care to listen). Read urbanistically, they have the acidity of Jonathan Swift's 1729 "A Modest Proposal" (suggesting that the famished Irish eat their own children), and are just as unlikely to be ever acted upon given that, except for small areas designated for tourism, such as Times Square, the real estate establishment that shapes our cities is not yet ready to admit that the economy of the spectacle reigns supreme.

A similar impulse (half critique, half bailing out) is at work in the *New Buildings for Berlin* series, all made from narrow sheets of variously colored and textured glass of the same height, leaning on each other like the rusty steel plates of a monumental vertical sculpture by Richard Serra that would be demoted to the status of an art object. The eye-level pedestal has been reinstated, and though the size of these models is modest (they are all 80 cm high), they loom over the beholder. What is perhaps most striking is their serial nature: they are variations on a theme, trumpeting, under the spotlights that make them glisten, the interchangeability of their color scheme (unlike all the models that Genzken made in the last ten years, these consist of only one material, which further underscores the condition of seriality). "If you are going to endlessly give us high-rise buildings with curtain walls," goes the harangue uttered by these standardized objects to the architectural profession, "at least give us that!" In both the Columns and the Berlin models Genzken proposes a travesty of corporate architecture—but the masquerade is also the promise of redemption via humor.[18]

None of this willingness to compromise (nor desire to travesty) can be detected in the *Strandhäuser zum Umziehen* models or in those of the *Fuck the Bauhaus* series. The first totally ignore the corporate mold, the second constitute such a violent assault against it (but also against the slickness of even the buildings that are programmatically erected against the ascetic language of modernism) that no reconciliation seems possible between Genzken's poetic bricolage and the current activity of professional architects. Paradoxically, I would venture, it is these quasi-primitivist constructions that are poised to have the strongest effect on the profession.

Though the ten *Strandhäuser* have often been exhibited in a serial manner (as the *New Buildings for Berlin* models would be soon after), aligned on a row of white pedestals of the same height, and all of the same relatively modest scale, each of them is strongly individualized. What they all share is a contradiction between the deliberate clumsiness of their assembly, the deliberate poverty of their materials, and the lushness of their colors. Sometimes resting on sand, and with a roof that wind could easily blow away (no visible attachment: gravity is the sole cement), they evoke the flexibility and necessary lightness of nomadic dwelling—tents or cheap bungalows, erected on the move with whatever is at hand and wherever one feels the desire to bivouac, never forgetting some bright piece of fabric or other ornamental item to declare the temporary pad home.[19] They celebrate the insouciance of leisure (one of these, in the tradition of the *architecture parlante* of the French revolutionary architects of the 18th century, is designated as a "pleasure cabin": on two of its sides, behind films of yellow and pink plastic, one can see photos of young men having sex). For the first time perhaps in Genzken's production, plastic is not connoted as the nasty non-biodegradable dreck that the postwar economy has forced upon us, the flotsam and jetsam that pollutes our beaches, but celebrated for its... plasticity, especially its capacity to take on any color. To be sure, we are still in the land of a ragpicker, but now it is a ragpicker with a lyrical mind. One thinks of *Architecture without Architects,* Bernard Rudofsky's poignant photographic compilation of "nonpedigreed architecture," as this quintessential nomad called the object of his life-long quest around

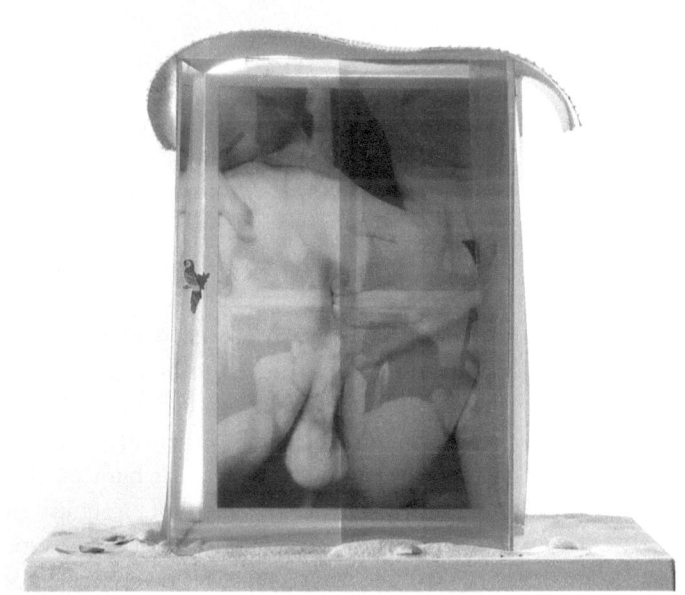

Strandhäuser zum Umziehen (Beach Houses for Changing), 2000 (detail). Mixed media; one of ten parts. Dimensions variable. Collection FRAC Nord-Pas de Calais, Dunkerque.

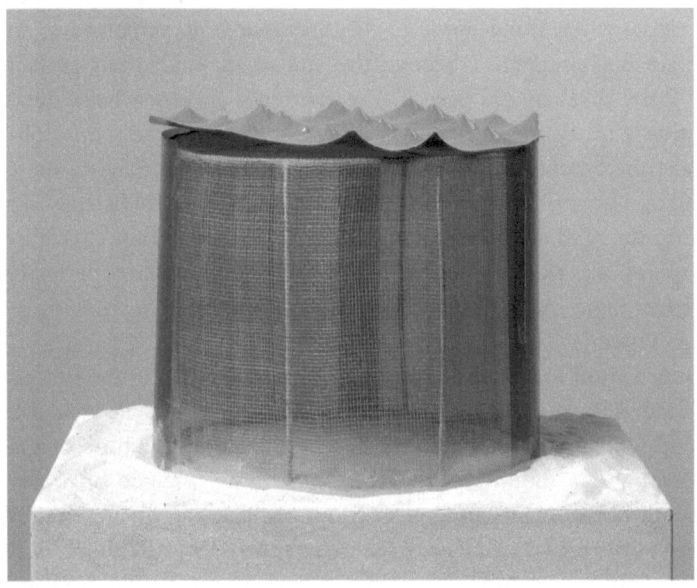

Strandhäuser zum Umziehen (Beach Houses for Changing), 2000 (detail). Mixed media; one of ten parts. Dimensions variable. Collection FRAC Nord-Pas de Calais, Dunkerque.

the globe, but also of the architecture of Rio's favelas.[20] Indeed, it is to
Hélio Oiticica's *Bolides,* small manipulable sculptures directly inspired by
his direct experience of Morro da Magueira, one of Rio's most popu-
lous favelas, that Genzken's *Strandhäuser* best compare formally, as well
as to the *Penetrables* that Oiticica realized in the late 1960s (such as *Eden,*
at the Whitechapel Gallery in London) and the many models he made
for others that were never built.[21] Yes, there is something paradisiac in
this architectural robinsonade (the word is rare, I know, but it is perfectly legitimate: it refers to all fantasies having to do with Robinson
Crusoe's adventure and it applies here in particular to both the "desert
island" connotation of the beach cabins, and to his improvisatory
genius): everything can become building material, particularly in a state
of penury. And just as the newspaper shoe of Barthes's bum quickly
becomes the sign of the bum, the capacity to see a piece of mosquito net
as a potential wall or one of those protective molded sheets of plastic
(formerly in papier maché) that line fruit crates as a potential roof
becomes the sign of the architect as visionary, as capable, like all bricoleurs, of metaphorical thinking.

But why is it that Genzken's stacking of fruit bowls for her imaginary *Car Park* was deemed an indictment of corporate architecture, and
that her reuse of discarded items in the *Strandhäuser* is perceived as so
euphoric, so encouraging? I believe this has to do with their perfect
pitch in scale: in these models all the materials she uses have been
brought down to, or chosen because they conform to, the same doll-
house scale: the bamboo sticks that stand for the open framework (per-
gola like) of one of the roofs are thin twigs; the sea shells that are
scattered on the sand are tiny; the plastic roof I just mentioned, with its
reticular spikes, is perfectly plausible in this Lilliputian universe, perfectly
adapted to its logic. As for the occasional wall photographs, they fit in
once read as murals.

A confirmation that scale constancy is the major factor in the success
of these models is provided by the *Fuck the Bauhaus* series, where it also
applies, and which is as high-spirited despite the aggressive tone of the
title. The rough and hollow pedestals of low-quality plywood partially
covered with plastic sheets and colored tape are not without reminders
of the *laissez-faire* mood of *I Love New York, Crazy City*: architecture is
crap, these plinths seem to say, it does not deserve any formal dressing.
Yet the rage is no longer there. Metallic disks from some motor, orange

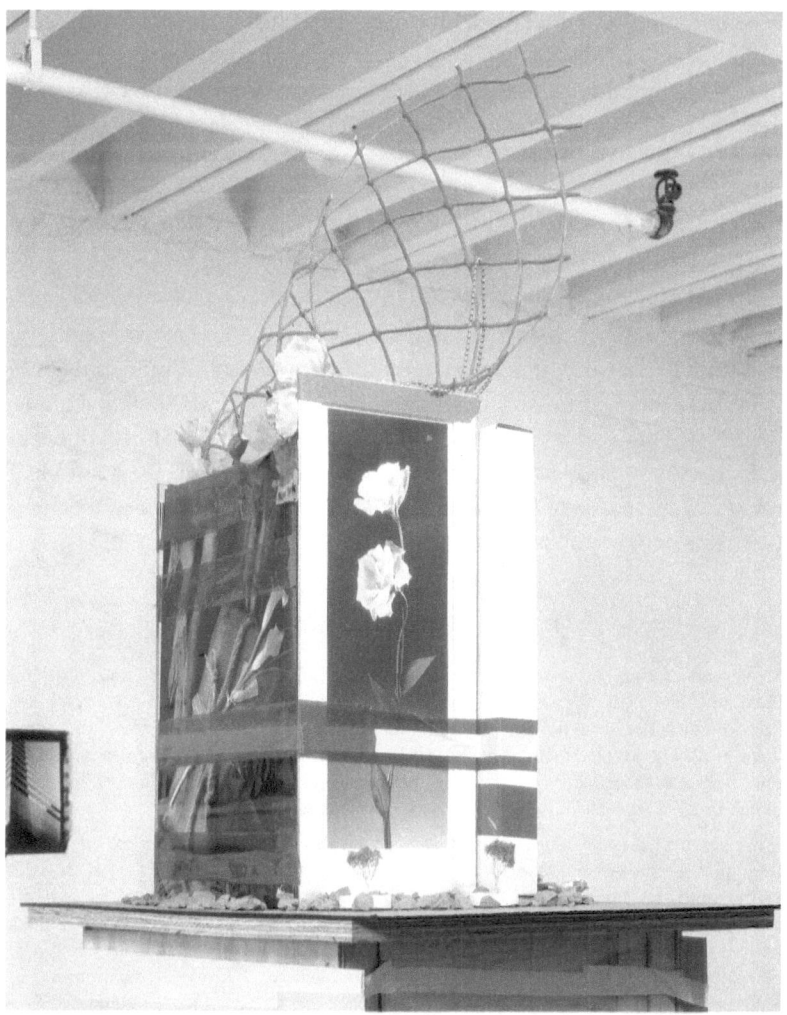

Fuck the Bauhaus #2, 2000. Plywood, plastic, metal, paper, cardboard pizza box, plastic flowers, stones, tape, model trees, and toy car. 210 × 70 × 51 cm.

wire netting used on construction sites, distended yellow and pink coil, lampshade—none of these objects are brought in to be wrecked but instead to function as elements of flamboyant structures whose scale is determined by tiny fake bonsai trees. The zaniness and panache, the elegance and energy are far superior to anything architects have been able to produce in the past decade with all their huge technical means. What Genzken is telling them is to forget their computers and return to the sandbox.

There is a pedagogical impetus in Genzken's gesture—which is why I claim that in such works she bets on the future. The interesting thing to be noted here is that the maligned Bauhaus produced models that are very much akin to those fragile assemblages—not in the design studios, but in the famous *Vorkurs*, the preliminary course (that of Josef Albers in particular). Obviously the architects who graduated from the school had forgotten the basics of their formation: it's time for their successors, says Genzken with a wink, to return to them.

Notes

1. Roland Barthes, "Semantics of the Object," in *The Semiotic Challenge*, trans. Richard Howard (New York: Farrar, Straus and Giroux, 1988), pp. 182–3. The Lévi-Strauss passage to which Barthes refers is to be found in "The Science of the Concrete," the introduction of *The Savage Mind* (Chicago and London: University of Chicago Press, 1966), pp. 16 ff. It is immediately followed by a discussion of the "small-scale model," directly linked in Lévi-Strauss's mind to the activity of the bricoleur.

2. "Here we have a man whose job it is to gather the day's refuse in the capital. Everything that the big city has thrown away, everything it has lost, everything it has scorned, everything it has broken he catalogs and collects. He collates the archives of intemperance, the capharnaum of waste. He sorts things out, selects judiciously; he collects, like a miser guarding a treasure, refuse which once remasticated by the goddess Industry, will become objects of use or of delight." Charles Baudelaire, "Du vin et du hachish," in *Oeuvres Complètes,* volume I (Paris: Gallimard, Bibliothèque de la Pléiade, 2006), p. 381.

3. Lisa Lee, "Make Life Beautiful!: The Diabolic in the Work of Isa Genzken (A Tour through Berlin, Paris, and New York," in *October*, no. 122 (Fall 2007), p. 68.

4. As Conner recalls: "Things that were in the street were picked up by people who made their living selling what they found in the street…anything that was in a street—a piece of metal, paper, wood, whatever—was immediately taken and used." Quoted by Peter Boswell, "Bruce Conner: Theater of Light and Shadow," in *2000 BC: The Bruce Conner Story Part II*, exh. cat. (Minneapolis: Walker Art Center, 2000), p. 44.

5. Lee, "Make Life Beautiful!," p. 64. The quotation is from Walter Benjamin's essay, "Central Park."

6. "To have the self succumb to the totalitarian order of objects brings the sculptor to the brink of psychosis, and Genzken's new work seems to inhabit that position. However, since total submission to the terror of consumption is indeed the governing stratum of collective objects relations, that psychotic state may well become the only position and practice the sculptor of the future can articulate." Benjamin H. D. Buchloh, "All Things Being Equal," in *Artforum International*, vol. 44, no. 3 (November 2005), p. 224.

7. Charles Baudelaire,"Morale du joujou," *Oeuvres Complètes, vol. 1,* op. cit., p. 587.

8. "If there were such a thing as a commodity-soul (a notion that Marx occasionally mentions in jest), it would be the most empathetic ever encountered in the realm of souls, for it would be bound to see every individual as a buyer in whose hands and house it wants to nestle. Empathy is the nature of the intoxication to which the flâneur abandons himself in the crowd." Walter Benjamin, "The Paris of the Second Empire in Baudelaire," in *Selected Writings,* vol 4, eds. Howard Eiland and Michael W. Jennings (Cambridge, Mass., and London: Harvard University Press, 2003), p. 31.

9. Walter Benjamin, "Central Park," idem, p. 162.

10. Great periods of architectural inventions often coincide with pure stagnation in the realm of construction (the ideal example is that of early constructivist architecture in Russia, say the work of Ivan Leonidov); by contrast, when economic conditions are favorable and architectural projects in high demand, overbooked architects tend to repeat themselves (for lack of time) and their work tends to become rote—at least this is what we have been witnessing in the past decade. It will be interesting to see how the current economic downturn will transform this state of affairs.

On Constant's utopian model, see Mark Wigley, *Constant's* New Babylon*: The Hyper-Architecture of Desire* (Rotterdam: 010 Publishers, 1998).

11. See *Isa Genzken: Ground Zero,* exh. cat. (Göttingen: Steidl 2008), pp. 2–9.

12. In this context, it should be noted that the catalog, designed to Genzken's specification, is a parody of a lavish fashion magazine (think *Vogue*), minus the advertisements, of course.

13. In "All Things Being Equal," Benjamin H. D. Buchloh recalls that Joseph Beuys once called this type of sculpture, "inimitably and untranslatably, the *Stahl-und-Eisbein Skulptur* (steel-and-pig's-knuckle sculpture)." Op. cit., p. 223.

14. It should be noted that the carts in question are not the ones usually found in food supermarkets but rather in hardware stores patronized by building contractors (they have only two sides, so as to allow the loading of long planks or pipes).

15. Dieter Schwarz, "World Band Receiver," in *Isa Genzken,* exh. cat. (Munich: Verlag Silke Schreiber, 1988), p. 87.

16. Gaston Bachelard, *La poétique de l'espace,* chapter "The Miniature" (Paris: Presses Universitaire de France, 1957 [reprint 1983]), p. 152.

17. The photograph, dating from circa 1969, is reproduced in Karen Moon, *Modeling Messages: The Architect and the Model* (New York: Monacelli Press, 2005), p. 53. This photo, or others similar to it, were widely disseminated during the 1970s.

18. On Genzken's work and travesty, see Lee, op. cit., pp. 58 ff. After having noted, like other commentators, the similarity of Genzken's Berlin models with Serra's sculpture, Lee constructs her analysis of these pieces, as well as of most of the "architectural" corpus in Genzken's production, on the text chosen by the artist to accompany their reproduc-

tion in the Phaidon monograph dedicated to her work in 2006. In this text dating from 1869, "The Bad Glazier," Baudelaire recalls how the absence of any colored glass in the stock of an ambulatory glazier he had summoned to his apartment lead him to destroy all the poor man's cargo in a fit of rage, shouting at him "Make life beautiful! Make life beautiful!"

19. In this context it is interesting to contrast the nomadism gently advocated by Genzken in her *Strandhäuser* to that dogmatically proposed by Constant, both of which are grounded in a conception of man as *homo ludens*. Here is Constant, in "New Babylon: Outline of a Culture" (1974): "As a way of life Homo Ludens will demand, firstly, that he responds to his need *for playing, for adventure, for mobility,* as well as all the conditions that facilitate the free creation of his own life. Until then, the principle activity of man had been the exploration of his historical surroundings. Homo Ludens himself will seek to transform, to recreate, those surroundings, that world, according to his new needs.... Thus we will be present at an *uninterrupted process of creation and re-creation,* sustained by a generalized creativity which is manifested in all domains of activity" (reprinted in Wigley, op. cit., p. 160). See also "On Traveling" (1969): "Sedentary man is dying out; we are becoming nomads once more, wandering over the earth, not looking for rest but for dynamic motion" (idem, p. 201). The contradiction between Constant's utopian dream and the megalomaniac model of his *New Babylon,* an authoritarian megastructure that could only have dwarfed subjectivity is all the more striking when compared to Genzken's lightness of touch.

20. Rudofsky's *Architecture without Architects* functioned as the catalog of the exhibition he curated for the Museum of Modern Art in New York in 1964 and which toured many countries over the following 11 years (it had 88 venues!). It consisted in a vast photographic reportage of anonymous buildings and vernacular forms from all around the world (with an emphasis on what was then called the Third World) and classified according to a taxonomy that was variably formal, technical, or functional. Its huge impact on the architectural thought of the 1960s is discussed in the various essays contained in the collective volume *Lessons from Bernard Rudofsky: Life as a Voyage,* published under the aegis of the Getty Research Institute (Basel: Birkhäuser Verlag, 2007).

21. Hélio Oiticica's *Bolides* and *Penetrables* are discussed by Guy Brett in, among several essays, "The Experimental Exercise of Liberty," in *Hélio Oiticica,* exh. cat. (Rotterdam: Witte de With Center for Contemporary Art, 1992), pp. 222–239. See also the exhibition catalog *Hélio Oiticica: The Body of Color* (Houston: The Museum of Fine Arts, 2007) for its excellent color reproductions of the *Bolides.* The *Box Bolides* are wooden boxes of various shapes, with drawers and enclosures one can open at will (some of them containing pure pigment), and painted in warm hues such as yellow and orange. Of orthogonal configuration when closed, they immediately evoke architecture. The *Glass Bolides* are more varied in material as well as in color, and their heterogeneity makes them even more closely resemble Genzken's *Strandhäuser.* A good example is the *Glass Bolide no. 5, 'Homage to Mondrian',* made of a carafe containing a yellow liquid from the neck of which sprout crumpled pieces of coarse fabric (hemp, cheese cloth) soaked in blue, gray, or red.

Isa Genzken: Sculpture as Narrative Urbanism

Josef Strau

Like almost no other European artist, Isa Genzken constantly refers to New York in her projects, and like scarcely anyone else's, her references reveal an ability to assimilate without prejudice this city that is never the same, but is permanently in a state of change. Not only is her working method free from the traditional (or at any rate typical and most frequently formulated) European prejudices, but here too she demonstrates an extraordinary ability to define herself as a medium in the process between the perception of external circumstances and their transformation by means of productive appropriation. This text is a tentative attempt to describe Genzken's ability to act as a medium not only in relation to New York, but also to a varied range of other urban environments, and on occasion to drastic changes in urban paradigms.

My first visit to Isa Genzken's studio at the end of the eighties was also my first encounter with an artistic production that was very much shaped by architectural discourse. Only now is it clear to me that her concrete and metal sculptures in those days looked like anticipatory models for the theoretical field of the "deconstruction of architecture" in the nineties. Like the average consumer of international art and of developments in international art and art theory, perhaps, I knew supremely little about this field. In artistic circles in the eighties, to relate art to architecture was generally considered suspect. Now, ten years later, their relationship has become unavoidable as a leitmotif in most exhibitions. During and after my visit to her studio I slowly and very gradually had to discard my prejudice, which had conformed to the

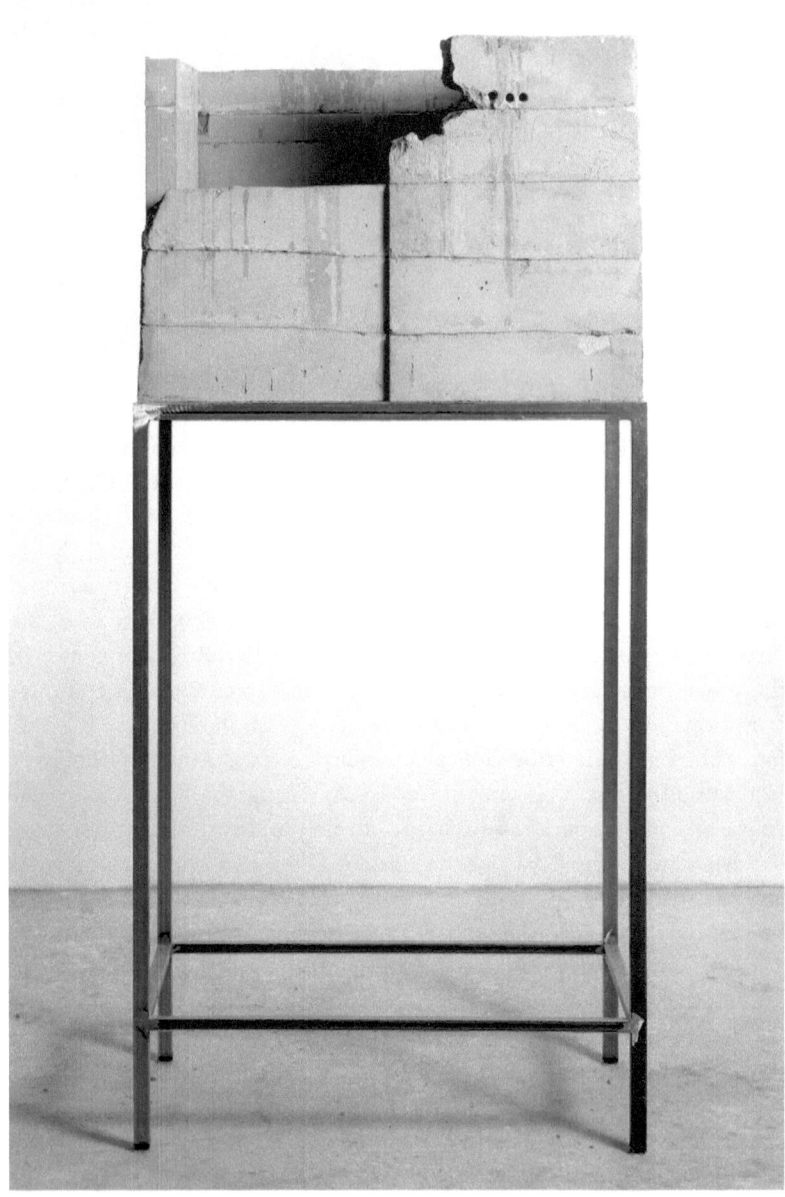

Halle (Hall), 1987. Concrete, spray paint, and steel. 204 × 97 × 62 cm.

mood of the times. As is so often the case, the attraction of the decade's prevalent fashions was just approaching its end in those years. The studio visit had given me food for thought, but only from today's perspective can I see it as the beginning of a long-term engagement with Genzken's work. Genzken, with her ability to anticipate and to superimpose supplementary parallel narratives on a particular field of discourse, clearly could not simply be relegated to the category of an architecture artist, although as a frame of reference architecture had to determine the first impression of her.

My questions today are: How did it come about that not only Genzken, as the producer of these sculptures, but I too, as a passive, unprepared viewer and consumer of them, was able to slowly anticipate a later theory? How did it come about that her work facilitated my access to that theory, and made it easier for me to liberate myself from the prejudices of that time against architectural theory?

By the mid-eighties the days of modernist engagement with architecture, or, in banal terms, of an engagement solely in terms of visual or purely structural formal relations, were quite rightly outdated and at an end. In order to use architecture again as an intellectual framework, narrative relationships had to be introduced into architectural forms, or architecture had to be rediscovered as a narrative form. On the one hand, precisely this function could be attained theoretically by using so-called deconstruction. On the other hand it could be achieved in a certain sense by the works of Genzken that were architecture-related but nevertheless also overlaid by parallel narratives.

The works of two deconstruction theorists, Mark Wigley and Anthony Vidler, hardly addressed architecture in the traditional sense, but they collected reflections on the literary functions of architecture, using mainly psychoanalytical, philosophical, or poetic narration for this purpose. My first experiences with a discursive engagement with architecture that was new at that time came about not as a consequence of theoretical studies but, as I have said, during the visit to Genzken's studio, which suddenly opened up to me, amid the ignorance of architecture and abstraction that was so typical of the eighties, the possibility of viewing architectural forms as artistic narrative practice. At that time I was still unable to imagine the consequences of this step. Only later in the nineties, as a result of this step—namely of connecting architecture with the most varied narrative structures, and not understanding and

analyzing architecture solely as building forms—was it possible to identify the new possibilities of extending this perspective to urban theory
and urban development as the central theme of social and aesthetic narratives. In this way it became possible not only to view the sculptures in
Genzken's studio as forms of architectural narrative enhanced by psychoanalytical references, but also to see them in relation to the city in
which they were produced.

Terms like "the uncanny" and "the subconscious" play a central
role in the deconstruction of architecture, which has its literary and
philosophical foundations in works from Schelling to Freud where the
uncanny in space means not only romantic haunted houses, but also, in
archeological terms, the burial and return of narrative. Archaeology is
evaluated as a leitmotif in Freudian psychoanalysis, extending to special
fears such as being buried alive and the like, while the psychoanalytical
narrative is used to describe aesthetic experiences such as the unsettling
side of modern culture, or the modernist existential dilemma of
not-feeling-at-home-with-yourself.

Deconstruction theory is also interested in forms that dismantle the
privilege of the classical body, disassemble and break up classical form,
and, psychologically speaking, produce the dismemberment of the body.
It also dissolves the ruling order of design, replacing it with an act similar
to automatic writing; in this way it practices architecture as the reacti-
vated unconscious. Regardless of how modernist existence may have felt,
the interesting thing about the so-called deconstruction of architecture in
the nineties was the allegorization of architectural forms and the ability to
use them for narrative purposes, without regard in the first instance to
whether societal, social, or psychological narratives were meant.

The spaces that Genzken builds into her more recent sculptures are,
certainly, when compared to the concrete sculptures, distinctly more
fragmentary. As with most of her works, they are not only constructive
spatializations of her narratives. They may also be understood, in terms
of deconstruction, as an archeology of the specific urban situation, a
description of a particular historical point in time, and at the same time a
parallel archeology of psychoanalytical narratives. As distinct from the
concrete sculptures, they abandon the enclosed modernist space. Yet, in
discursive terms, they can continue to be read as narrative spatializations.
It would undoubtedly be too banal, too casual a way of verbalizing her
extreme visualization of narrative complexity to describe these new

works of Genzken's as surreal. However, if one understands classical surrealism as a counter-activity to social or urban de-historization, as a subtext to the tendency to constantly delete the memory of the immediate past, Genzken's new work could in certain circumstances be located in a historical artistic context—not as a way of finding an immanent concept, but as a way of narrating her immanent subconscious, so to speak. In the typical urban changes in the last twenty years a process of eliminating nonsynchronic elements could be observed, as if the aim behind the construction of the city of the future was a city without memory. Despite this, the official voice has said the exact opposite, speaking of reconstruction and places of remembrance. To that extent that Genzken's sculptures are a recollection of surrealism as the activity of attempting to stroll through the uncontemporaneous aspects of the past into the present, into the so-called subconscious of the city, they are comparable in their way to psychoanalytical dreamwork. So it might be possible after all to find a productive back entrance that would make it possible to declare Genzken's productions, with their tendency to constantly reconstruct themselves, to be "surrealism" conceived in urban terms. The changes made in Berlin in the recent decades are actually not the rather dull new buildings that the city officially showcases, nor the official places of remembrance, but the nonsimultaneousness of various spaces that have been wiped out by urban renewal, the fragments of everyday life that have been removed, or the ruins, the eliminated indeterminateness of no man's land. Without weeping tears of cultural pessimism for the destroyed past, what is striking by contrast in New York are the permanent nonsimultaneities of social life, the variety of spaces for everyday life and individual behavior.

In her productions Genzken often pursues paradigmatic architectural forms that are also to be understood as concrete suggestions (as for example in a project like *Ground Zero*), but she very rarely attempts to illustrate the general, rather indeterminate lines of urban enquiry indicated above. One could nevertheless use her work in a wider urban narrative about the deconstructive modes of the "the subconscious" or the "the uncanny" in the city, and use it in a distinctly biographical mode as a description of various types of urban self-definition. In this narrative her work could be used as an aesthetic roadmap in order to give precise information about both innovations and losses at a particular time in a particular urban environment. In the course of this metaphorical projection of biographical

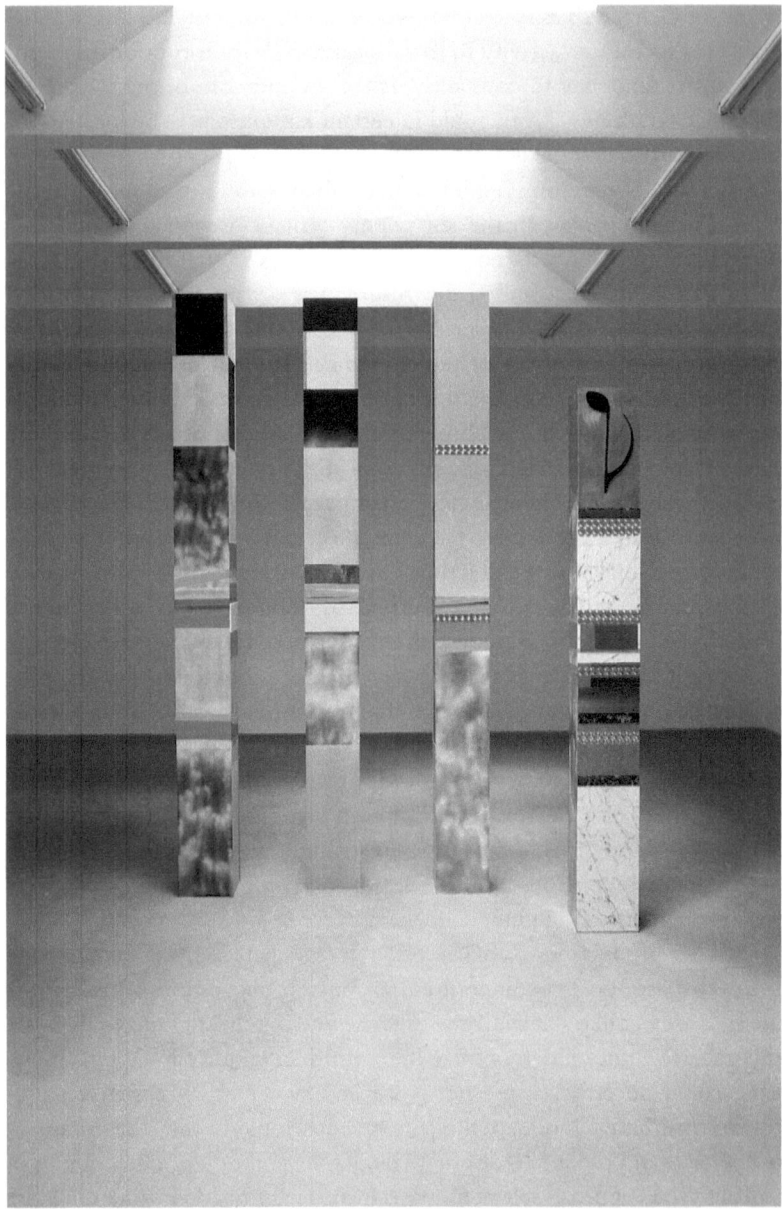

A, B, C, D, 2002/2003. Wood, adhesive tape, spray paint, mirrored glass, aluminum, and marble boards in four parts. 320 × 30 × 27 cm; 320 × 30 × 30 cm; 320 × 30 × 30 cm; 260 × 29 × 30 cm.

narratives onto the urban space, one might also find information about how specific artistic personas establish themselves at a specific point in time as a reaction to the urban historical structure, and, so to speak, reconstruct the exemplary allegorical meta-figure of city development.

Genzken's biographical model designates a mode of production whose first reaction is always temporary, but which then works on this temporariness in itself, and in this way constantly renews itself. This text is intended only as an attempt to describe her very specific relationship to urban time and historicity, and to formulate, however roughly, her deconstructive act of bringing narrative and natural architectural space production together in a complex combination.

Fantastic Destruction

Hal Foster

The Isa Genzken retrospective seen in the United States in 2013–14 revealed both the range and the ambition of this influential artist—an important outcome in a country where her work is still not well known.[1] Yet, in this light, responses to the exhibition proved more problematic than usual: though often positive in tone, many reviewers positioned Genzken in relation to the art-worldly men in her life, both older (Benjamin H. D. Buchloh, her onetime partner, and Gerhard Richter, her former husband) and younger (her close friends Wolfgang Tillmans and Kai Althoff), and some dwelt on the fact that her paternal grandfather (whom Genzken barely knew) was a prominent Nazi. It is not likely that a male artist of her stature would be treated in this fashion; certainly he would not be subject so often to the epithet "crazy." Although this is a term Genzken has also used (as in her 1995–96 collage ode *I Love New York, Crazy City*) in the course of a life that could hardly be called trouble-free, there is a great deal of method in her performance of the madness of everyday existence under advanced capitalism. Her work not only possesses historical sweep—from reconstruction Germany to the "War on Terror"—but also articulates a grimly dialectical view of that history. In this sense, Genzken has picked up in art where Rainer Werner Fassbinder left off in film, at once following her vision and tracking her times mercilessly.

From the start Genzken has engaged modernist art and architecture in ways that are both idiosyncratic and astute. Like Blinky Palermo (whom she met at the Düsseldorf Academy of Fine Arts in the early

1970s), she took postwar American abstraction as her point of departure: for example, the lacquered wood strips of *Untitled* (1974) resemble Barnett Newman zips pulled from his paintings and propped against the wall, and her long and sleek Ellipsoids (1976–82) and Hyperbolos (1979–83), also in lacquered wood, lie and stand on the floor with an engineered precision that outperforms any minimalist object. Yet in this turn to American sources Genzken did not simply evade German associations, as is sometimes claimed: her nonobjective *Basic Research* (1988–91) and *More Light Research* paintings (1992) are in direct dialogue with the oddly null abstractions of Richter as well as the faux-kitsch patterns of Sigmar Polke; and in the gimcrack models of her *Fuck the Bauhaus (New Buildings for New York)* (2000) and *New Buildings for Berlin* (2001–04), Genzken alludes, brutally enough, to key Germanic modernists such as Herbert Bayer and Mies van der Rohe. These are all aesthetic connections, not personal ones, and she is the agent that binds them.

Genzken is also keenly involved with modern media, technology, and commodity culture: for instance, the recent retrospective began with *Weltempfänger* (World Receiver) (1982), her presentation of a multiband radio as an immaculate readymade, and followed with her appropriations from the late 1970s of magazine advertisements for high-end stereo equipment by high-tech corporations (represented here are the languages of four powerhouses of the postwar period: the United States, West Germany, Japan, and France). With these enthusiasms—Genzken once said of her radio that "sculpture must be at least as modern"—she shows her affinities with Pop art too (the technophilic designs of Richard Hamilton come to mind). Yet once again things took a turn for the worse, and by the time Genzken got to her caustic proposals of the 2000s—for mock memorials to the afflicted powers that brought us the wanton wars in Afghanistan and Iraq (*Empire/Vampire, Who Kills Death*, 2003–2004) as well as for mock institutions to be sited at Ground Zero in New York (e.g., *Osama Fashion Store*, 2008)—she had soured on our contemporary version of modernity almost completely. As there is a lot of burlesque in this art, none of these concerns is straightforward, yet a through-line does emerge. It is a dialectic that almost revels in the dystopian underside of utopian dreams, whether proposed in prewar modernism or in postwar consumerism, but it is also one that glimpses a weird vitality in the midst of these ruins—that reveals not merely the failure of utopia (which is easy enough to do today) but also the energy in disaster.

In the world according to Genzken, this dialectic has penetrated into the very nature of things. For example, only two years separate her high-tech radio from her near-*informe* plaster sculpture *Müllberg* (Pile of Rubbish) (1984), and in her hands a single substance like concrete or epoxy can appear both perfect and corrupt. As Genzken stacked her concrete blocks roughly or bore through them excessively in the 1980s, this key material of twentieth-century architecture returned to us as failed, not much distinct from rubble, as if any reconstruction—whether after the catastrophe of World War II, after the fall of the Wall, or after the collapse of the Twin Towers—could only end up as another form of destruction. Despite titles that allude to rooms, pavilions, and galleries, her structures in concrete and in epoxy are either too closed or too open to offer any shelter; Genzken reveals structure to be no less degraded than material. In another instance, even as her *New Buildings for Berlin* allude to the visionary skyscrapers that Mies proposed for the German capital after World War I, they also underscore how distant the modernist vision of glass architecture now appears. These colored planes, some in glass, others in silicone, prop each other up with adhesive tape in a way that has no tectonic integrity: like the modernist value of truth to materials, the modernist faith in rationality of structure dies a definitive death here.

In related works, Genzken highlights how reflective glitz has triumphed over modernist transparency in the capitalist environment at large; her *Soziale Fassaden* (Social Facades) (2002), made of strips of reflective metal, mosaic foil, and plastic, come across as a riposte to the floating world produced by spectacle architecture in recent decades. At the same time, such pieces express a delight in immersive effects, a delight that extends to the gritty ambience of Berlin club interiors and graffitied city walls evoked in other projects. Genzken has also produced columns in metal, wood, and mirror named after her friends; there is one (from 2000) called *Isa* too, so she seems to identify with these tacky surfaces as well. Obviously, then, her models are not proper studies for actual buildings; even less are they models in the sense of ideal structures—just the opposite, in fact. At the same time, only a true believer could still be disappointed enough by the shortcomings of the Bauhaus to tell it to fuck off, and, though her absurdist proposals for Ground

Zero are scathing in their send-up of urbanist business as usual, they
remain committed to the enterprise of metropolitan life.[2]

This grim dialectic governs her view of technology and media too,
as Genzken moves from her early enthusiasm for radio and stereo equipment to later work such as *Da Vinci*, 2003, which consists of four pairs
of airliner windows, the last one splattered with paint in a way that suggests an exploded body: here the dream of flying machines in Leonardo
collapses into the nightmare of weaponized jets on 9/11. The same
ambivalence is active in her relation to the modernist idea of art as
experiment. Her *Basic Research* paintings, in which Genzken squeegeed
oil paint across canvas placed flat on her studio floor, evoke demonstra-
tions of indexical mark-making from Surrealist *frottage* to process art; and
her *More Light Research* paintings, in which she stenciled images of
designer lamps and other abstract forms with spray paint or lacquer on
canvas or fiberboard, allude to the experiments with light by László
Moholy-Nagy and his Bauhaus colleagues. Yet her versions of these
practices seem intentionally flat, almost rote, without the access to the
unconscious sought by the Surrealists or the faith in technology sustained by the Bauhauslers; in short, they parody the idea of art as experiment even as they perform it. At the same time—and here again a
dialectical twist comes into play—Genzken remains resourceful, not to
mention unpredictable, in her use of materials and techniques alike.

Modernist art and architecture are not the only ruins in Genzken;
the contemporary capitalist subject is also in deep trouble. Her own
image appears often in her shows and in her catalogs, sometimes via
photographs by Tillmans, and, though Genzken worked as a fashion
model in her art school days, this staging is the opposite of vain: instead
she documents the ways in which time can not only age the body but
also ravage the soul. *Self-Portrait* (1983), now destroyed, was a misshapen
head in clay that imagined the artist as Elephant Man, and *Mein Gehirn*
(My Brain) (1984) is another near-*informe* mound of plaster with a wispy
wire on top like a dead antenna. The *X-Rays* (1989–91) in which Genzken exposed her own skull as she laughed and drank, fall into this same
line of black humor: here again she inverts the techno-optimism of
Moholy even as she also invokes any number of German death-heads
from Dürer to Dada and beyond. These stark images are followed by
Haube I (Frau) and Haube II (Mann) (Bonnet I [Woman] and Bonnet II
[Man]) (1994), produced the year of her divorce from Richter. Made of

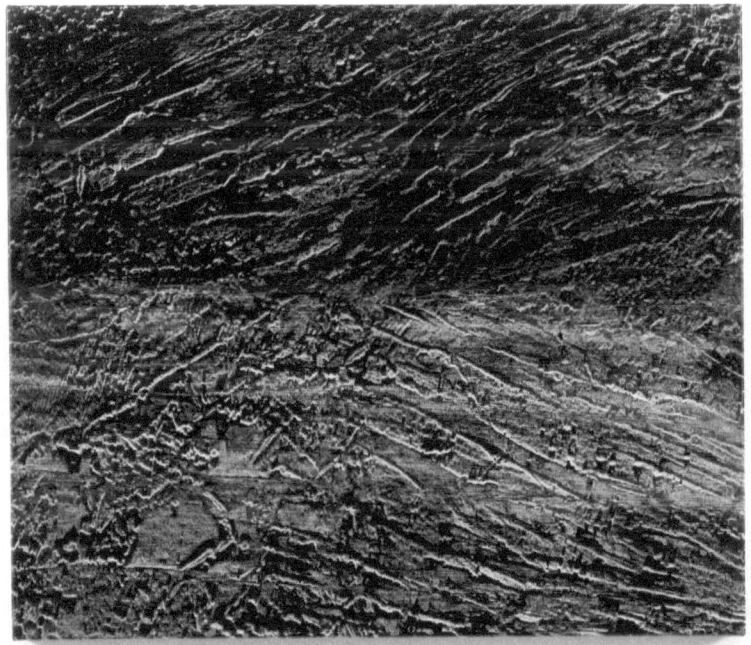

Basic Research, 1989. Oil on canvas. 75 × 90 cm.

fabric hardened with epoxy, these lurid helmets, which appear almost viscous, are stuck, like chopped-off heads, atop steel poles, and they rotate slowly toward and away from each other: a portrait of husband and wife (*Mann* and *Frau* mean this too) as coupled Medusas whose gazes bring mutual petrification. After a typical performance at the Cabaret Voltaire, one that likely featured primitivist masks by Marcel Janco, Hugo Ball wrote in his diary of Zürich Dada, "The Gorgon's head of a boundless terror smiles out of the fantastic destruction."[3] So it is with these bonnets.

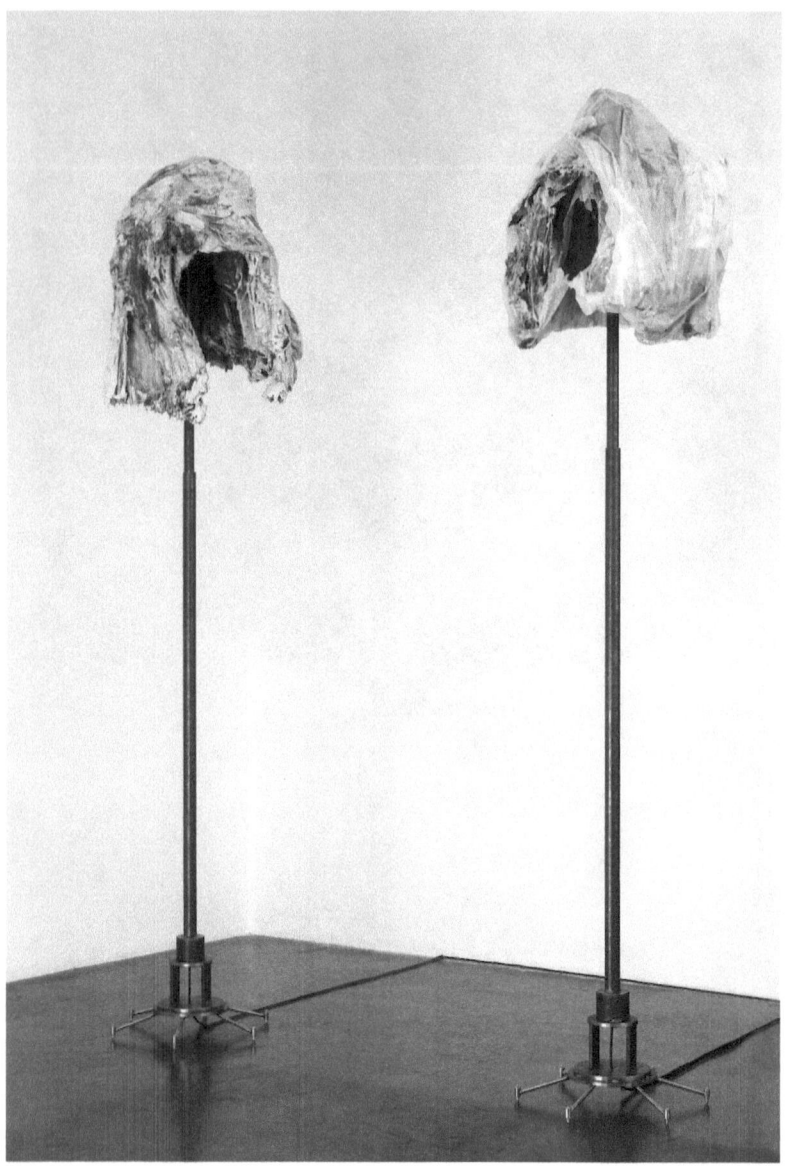

Haube I (Frau) and *Haube II (Mann)* (Bonnet I [Woman] and Bonnet II [Man]), 1994. Varnish on epoxy resin and fabric, steel, and motors. 266 × 54 × 54 cm; 272 × 60 × 60 cm.

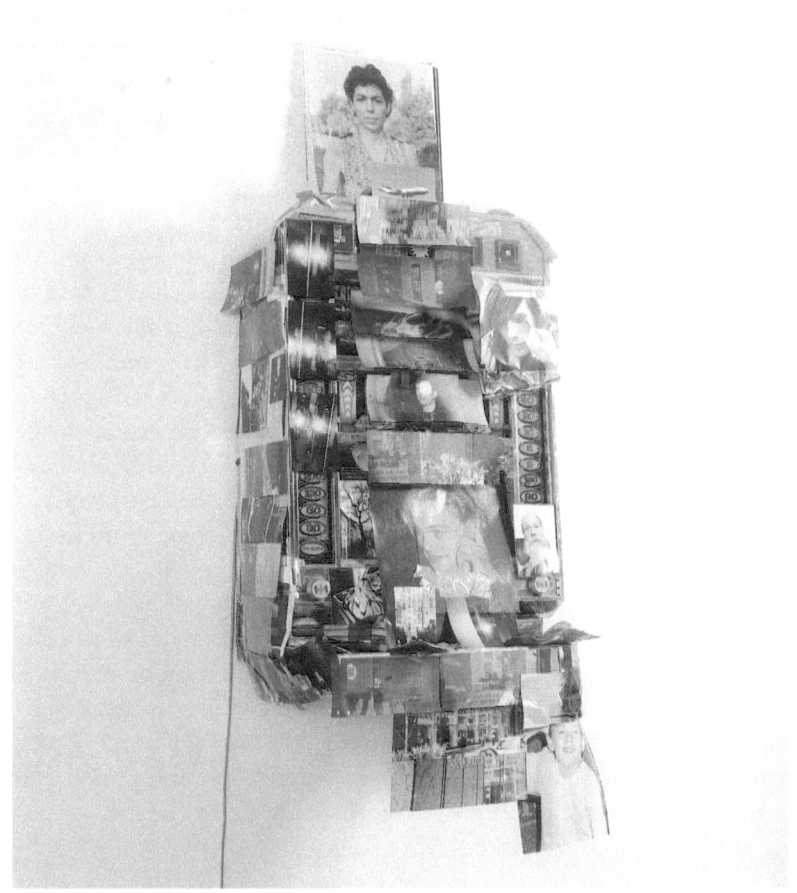

Spielautomat (Slot Machine), 1999/2000. Slot machine, paper, photographs, plastic foil, and adhesive tape. 160 × 65 × 50 cm.

The pièce de résistance in this portraiture of the ruined self is *Spiel-automat* (Slot Machine) (1999–2000), an actual slot machine covered with photographs of Genzken, friends, strangers, and celebrities mixed with urban scenes of streets and facades. Ever since Walter Benjamin speculated on the herky-jerky behavior of Charles Baudelaire, we have understood the modern subject to be one that must parry the shocks of the world in order to survive, but the trope of the self as a slot machine, in which all play appears scripted (including aesthetic *Spiel*) and all chance automated (beyond anything Duchamp foresaw), is still hard to take, even as today we must come to terms with the algorithmized sub-ject as well.[4] In this piece Genzken places her friend Lawrence Weiner next to the celebrity Leonardo DiCaprio as though they were separated at birth: totally effaced here is any boundary between private and public or inside and outside, the very distinction once thought to be the pre-condition of a self. According to Freud, the ego is, in the first instance, a body image, a figure that Lacan developed in architectural terms (in his "Mirror Stage" paper, he refers to the "I" as "a fortress or a stadium"); with Genzken, however, this ego architecture is broken down.[5] Yet once more she provides a dialectical fillip, for in the end her work valo-rizes a fragmented ego over a fortified one, which can turn aggressive (as Lacan knew) in its very armoring. In this way, Genzken suggests a cri-tique of the subject that is different from "the death of author" per-formed by poststructuralist theorists and postmodernist artists, even as it is akin to the dismantling of the self sometimes staged by her contempo-raries Martin Kippenberger and Mike Kelley.

By the time of her *Fuck the Bauhaus* models, in which commodity junkspace overwhelms all design schemes, Genzken came to rely on the readymade, so Duchamp would appear to be a primary resource; yet, especially in her work of the last decade, the commodity and the ready-made are ruined too. (As with Rachel Harrison, with whom Genzken is sometimes associated, this assault seems to take in the product lines of Jeff Koons, Takashi Murakami, and other corporate studios as well.) The *Merz* collages of Schwitters come next to mind, and with its associations of commerce, *Schmerz* (pain), and *merde*, the neologism *Merz* does suit the later Genzken well; postwar bricoleurs of trash, both American and German, such as Robert Rauschenberg, Ed Kienholz, Joseph Beuys, and Dieter Roth, are also recalled. In the end, however, the artistic lin-eage that Genzken reanimates is that of Berlin and Zürich Dada, for she, too, practices a mimetic exacerbation of the emergency conditions around her: if those Dadaists exaggerated the subjective effects of both military collapse and political crisis, both mechanization and commodification, Genzken pushes the distracted-compulsive behavior of the contemporary city-dweller of consumerist empire to the edge of breakdown. "The Dadaist suffers . . . from the dissonances [of the age] to the point of self-disintegration," Ball wrote in his diary, and Genzken embraces this sacrificial kind of artistic passion too.[6] In this way her work stands as an effective diagnosis of our times, the beer belly of post-1989 Germany and post-9/11 America cut and probed with her distinctive kitchen knife.

Notes

1. "Isa Genzken: Retrospective," organized by Sabine Breitwieser, Laura Hoptman. Michael Darling, and Jeffrey Grove, appeared at the Museum of Modern Art in New York, the Museum of Contemporary Art Chicago, and Dallas Museum of Art from late 2013 through 2014.

2. Even in her acerbic mock models for Ground Zero structures, a glimmer of the modernist faith in social transformation through new materials and ideal forms sometimes shines through—but this glint of utopia only makes the pieces all the more infernal.

3. Hugo Ball, *Flight Out of Time: A Dada Diary* (1927), trans. Ann Raimes (New York: Viking Press, 1974), p. 56 (the entry is dated March 11, 1916).

4. See Walter Benjamin, "On Some Motifs in Baudelaire" (1939), in *Selected Writings, Volume 4, 1938–1940*, ed. Howard Eiland and Michael W. Jennings (Cambridge, MA: Harvard University Press, 2003), pp. 313–55.

5. See Jacques Lacan, "The Mirror Stage" (1949), in *Écrits: A Selection*, trans. Alan Sheridan (New York: W.W. Norton, 1977), p. 5.

6. Ball, *Flight Out of Time*, p. 66 (the entry is dated June 12, 1916). For more on this strategy of mimetic exacerbation, see my "Dada Mime," *October* 105 (Summer 2003). Genzken dedicates her retrospective catalog to Jasper Johns, an artist who pioneered a posture of sufferance, but she seems closer in this respect to Andy Warhol (after whom she names one of her columns). Mimetic exacerbation is a tricky business, and for all her hits there are a few misses. For example, with its toy eagles and Uncle Scrooge CEO, *American Room*, 2004, is trivial is in its presentation of corporate power, and her recent tableaus of deranged mannikins strain after their punk effects.